Contributions to International Relations

This book series offers an outlet for cutting-edge research on all areas of international relations. *Contributions to International Relations* (CIR) welcomes theoretically sound and empirically robust monographs, edited volumes and handbooks from various disciplines and approaches on topics such as IR-theory, international security studies, foreign policy, diplomacy, peace and conflict studies, international organization, global governance, international political economy, the history of international relations, International law and related fields.

All titles in this series are peer-reviewed. This book series is indexed in Scopus.

Fatima Roumate
Editor

AI, Information, and Global Dynamics

Shaping the Future of Geopolitical Landscape

Springer

IISR

GNAI&IS

Editor
Fatima Roumate
Global Network on AI and International
Society (GNAI&IS), and Mohammed V
University, FSJES Agdal,
Rabat, Morocco

ISSN 2731-5061 ISSN 2731-507X (electronic)
Contributions to International Relations
ISBN 978-3-032-13527-8 ISBN 978-3-032-13528-5 (eBook)
https://doi.org/10.1007/978-3-032-13528-5

This Springer imprint is published by the registered company Springer Nature Switzerland AG.
The registered company address is: Gewerbestrasse 11, 6330 Cham, Switzerland

Introduction

In the era of AI-driven information, the intersection of AI and information is a key component of geopolitical dynamics. This intersection widely influences the transition to a multipolar world order based on a new balance of power, ranging between geostrategic interests and the race for technological sovereignty. From education to the military, AI-driven information is transforming all sectors and deeply influencing the interaction between humans and AI. Trends related to AI and information will certainly increase new types of power, particularly the combination of AI and information power. AI-driven information is revolutionizing all dimensions of international relations, from economic interactions based on information and data to AI diplomacy, where information is considered the new oil. The military is also revolutionized considering the weaponization of both AI and information in a global landscape characterized by new wars and new weapons. Furthermore, given the significant role of information in hard, soft, and smart power, this revolution increases the diffusion of power, which is not limited to great states. Small states and non-state actors are also competing for power in international society. This competition imposes serious risks, particularly from non-state actors, especially transnational ones, who possess AI technologies and information. This raises the race for technological sovereignty first between states, and second, between states and transnational corporations.

From the Middle East to Europe, and from the wars in Syria and Gaza to the war in Ukraine, AI and information have been used as a new "weapon" that significantly contributed to the new balance of power and the geostrategic changes in these regions. From map wars to ocean and international crossing wars, the weaponization of AI and information is influencing geopolitical dynamics and changing both geographic borders and the balance of power. The weaponization of AI and information is altering the meaning of power and other notions like geopolitics, with the emergence of new types of power such as information power and AI power. The weaponization of AI and information is a key element for understanding and predicting the future of the economic conflict between the US and China, which could escalate to war after the end of the war in Ukraine. In this conflict, AI and information serve as both a "weapon" and a goal, as the conflict is based on the race for technological sovereignty, which depends on the ability of the US or China to become the global leader in AI, innovation, and science—all of which are grounded in information and knowledge.

The weaponization of AI and information is facilitating the shift from a unipolar to a multipolar world. A complex and controversial characteristic of the new world order arises from the augmented role of AI-driven information. Understanding the tangible and intangible impacts of these technologies in terms of geopolitical dynamics represents a significant challenge for researchers, diplomats, and policy-makers. Therefore, this book, titled "AI, Information, and Global Dynamics—Shaping the Future of Geopolitical Landscape," aims to provide a scientific contribution to the global debate on the interactions among the three elements of AI, information, and geopolitical dynamics. In it, the editor and the contributing authors examine how the powers of AI and information are reshaping geopolitical dynamics now and, in the future, within the context of the transition from unipolarity to multipolarity. Fundamental new notions, such as the geopolitics of AI and information, as well as the power of information, the weaponization of AI, and information warfare, will be discussed in this volume through the lens of several theories, ranging from information and computational science to geopolitics, international relations, and international law.

This volume aims to achieve the following five core objectives:

1. The first goal is to provide tools and methods to understand the intersection between AI and information, and how this intersection has emerged as a critical strategic asset, fundamentally reshaping the geopolitical landscape and global power dynamics. It will explore the intersection of the powers of AI and information to provide a comprehensive understanding of the global landscape.
2. The second objective is to explore the weaponization of AI and information, examining its role as a transformative tool that redefines the nature of modern conflict and military strategies. This includes a close look at AI's malicious use in disinformation campaigns, psychological warfare, and intelligence gathering.
3. The third goal is to analyze the risks and threats posed by AI-driven information, including through social media, to international psychological security and geopolitical dynamics. The book will investigate how the emerging frontiers between AI and information can be leveraged to manipulate public opinion and create internal instability within nations to achieve geostrategic interests.
4. The fourth goal is to investigate the economic transformation driven by AI and information and assess how this shift is leading to a new balance of global economic power and a new world economic order. It will examine the rise of information-based economies as a new step toward multilateralism, with closed borders and an open society regarding data.
5. The final objective is to analyze the complex challenge of balancing control and security, including maritime security, in the era of AI-driven information. This volume will identify an AI governance framework based on ethics, regulation, and policy actions adopted by international and regional institutions and by

states in the global North and South. The book will explore the geopolitics of AI ethics and regulation concerning technological sovereignty.

Methods

Given the complexity and interconnectedness of AI, information, and geopolitics, no single method would be sufficient. A multidisciplinary view and a multi-methodological approach are crucial to achieving the book's goals.

To that end, we employ an interpretive and comparative framework that systematically combines legal, doctrinal, political, economic, technological, transnational, and prospective approaches. The analysis is built upon a four-dimensional analytical framework. First, it explores the conceptual evolution of AI and information warfare, establishing a clear and coherent theoretical foundation. This step is crucial for framing the book and ensuring it avoids merely reiterating existing literature.

Second, the book examines the geopolitical and strategic implications of AI-driven information by state and non-state actors from both the global North and South. This comparative approach highlights the different national doctrines and strategic priorities currently in play. This comparative approach is complemented by the political analysis to measure the impact of AI-driven information on geopolitical dynamics.

Next, a doctrinal approach is adopted to review the existing laws, regulations, and scholarly literature in the field of AI, as well as the challenges related to international law. The transnational approach is applied to measure how AI-driven information influences non-state actors and individuals during information and psychological warfare, in AI diplomacy, during economic and trade warfare, or even as targets of AI autonomous weapons during war. A technological approach is employed to understand how AI and its evolution influence technical information. Institutional analysis is the most adequate method for understanding the management of AI's implications on information in cases like China, considering the interconnection between the local and global. The prospective approach is used to analyze the challenges related to trends in AI-driven information.

A multidisciplinary approach is evidenced by the points of view presented in this book by authors from various fields of research, such as information sciences, international relations, international economic law, international maritime law, public law, journalism, and communication. In this book, we present viewpoints from both globally recognized experts and young researchers, from practitioners and the academic world.

Additionally, a case study serves to evaluate how the use of AI-driven information influences global debates on AI, information, geopolitical dynamics, and the future of the global landscape. The qualitative case studies are drawn from distinct geopolitical contexts, particularly from the global North and South, with a focus on powerful states like the US, China, the EU, Russia, Japan, and India. The aim is to show the trends and challenges of contemporary AI approaches linked to media (communication and journalism) and their implications for international security from various theoretical perspectives and paradigms.

The combination of these diverse approaches facilitates the transition from theoretical analysis to practical application, offering a comprehensive and well-supported argument on each of the core objectives.

Chapter 1 provides a foundation for the analysis presented in the following chapters. It is dedicated to the conceptual framework and the intersection between AI, information, and geopolitical dynamics. It demonstrates that AI is not only a tool but also a transformative paradigm in how great powers compete for global leadership in this new multipolar world order, particularly through the weaponization of information and AI.

This first chapter represents a comprehensive analysis of the complex interactions between artificial intelligence, information, and geopolitical dynamics. As AI and information influence other key topics related to the title of this volume, the following chapters will cover essential elements for understanding their implications and developing appropriate responses. The framework presented here provides a foundation for such analysis while acknowledging the inherent uncertainties and complexities involved in predicting future developments in this rapidly changing field.

Viktor V. Zinchenko, Mykhailo I. Boichenko and Iryna I. Drach explain that understanding the intersection between AI-driven information and geopolitical dynamics should consider the mutual influence of AI and humans, observed at three levels:

1. The micro level, referring to interactions between AI and individuals (Chap. 2).
2. The intermediate level, encompassing corporations, regions, and national societies (Chap. 2).
3. The global macro level, considering that "the global dynamics of power is largely determined today not so much by competition between the world's states or global transnational corporations, including those that produce AI, but by competition between democratic and authoritarian styles in introducing AI into social processes—production, policy, cultural projects, etc." (Chap. 2).

The authors of Chap. 3, Carlos Enrique Fernández García and Ciencias Humanas, explain how AI and information represent a new battlefield for technological superpowers, considering the role of media in the context of information warfare. Both traditional and digital media are seen as platforms for strategies and tactics to achieve geopolitical interests (Chap. 3).

Sergey Davydov and Anna Kartasheva, authors of Chap. 5, explain how the combination of AI and information in both media and social media "makes information warfare more powerful," considering AI's implications for the promotion and dissemination of ideology and propaganda. They also note that these advanced technologies create new risks, such as automation bias and other vulnerabilities specific to AI-driven processes (Chap. 4).

Marta N. Lukacovic and Deborah D. Sellnow-Richmond discuss the implications of social media on the global power landscape, examining how generative AI and algorithms are increasing the role of social media not only in decision-making but also in their implications for the psychological security of individuals, communities, and especially international psychological security (Chap. 5).

This leads us to the growing importance of AI in offensive and defensive information operations, as argued by Hajji Said in Chap. 6. He explains how AI-driven information is reshaping "the logic, speed, and scope of influence operations, eroding the boundaries between 'times of war' and 'times of peace,' between physical and digital space, and between fact and manipulation" (Chap. 6).

In this context, Pavel Sharikov argues that "AI is no longer a supplementary tool but a pivotal driver of military innovation, influencing not only tactics and capabilities but also the very principles of strategy formulation" (Chap. 7). This chapter is dedicated to explaining how AI and information have become pivotal powers in modern military strategy. It highlights how the intersection between AI and information is reshaping hard power—not only as a notion but also as tools, strategy, goals, and the legal framework, which should be updated to address current and future challenges related to AI-driven information and the military.

From the military to the economy, a key feature of the era of AI is the shift to a new economic world order. This shift is illustrated, according to Viktor V. Zinchenko and Mykhailo I. Boichenko, authors of Chap. 8, by the "economic value which is created not through traditional factors—labor, capital, or natural resources—but through the capacity to collect, store, analyze, and monetize data" (Chap. 8). This leads us to another key actor in Industry 6.0: transnational corporations.

According to Rossana Soriano, "AI is capable of learning to identify patterns, turning information into strategic intelligence, and some industries are turning information into strategic assets." To illustrate this idea, Rossana Soriano selected several case studies from multiple sectors—encompassing media, finance, e-commerce, and healthcare (Chap. 9). This leads us to maritime security, considering that "more than 90% of global trade is transported by sea," as stated by the author of Chap. 10, who discusses AI's transformation of maritime security and its implications for global trade. According to Zaeem Mehmood, AI and information management could "secure critical maritime infrastructure amidst trade wars, cyber threats, and escalating great power competition" (Chap. 10).

International security, including psychological, information, and maritime security, depends on international instruments on AI ethics, as well as regional and national regulations and strategies. AI ethics and regulations are discussed transversally in all chapters of this volume, as well as in Chap. 11, which is dedicated to the global landscape of diverse approaches related to AI ethics, regulation, and strategies concerning the ethics of AI, information, and geopolitics. The chapter first discusses international instruments on AI ethics, including the recommendations on AI ethics adopted by UNESCO in 2021, and the resolution adopted by the United Nations General Assembly on AI and sustainable development in 2024. Next, the chapter covers regional instruments, particularly the European AI Act, the Continental AI Strategy adopted by the African Union in 2024, and the BRICS AI strategy. Finally, the chapter discusses diverse approaches adopted by several countries from the global North, focusing on the major technological powers, and the global South, emphasizing that the race for AI ethics and regulation is not only a legal response to AI challenges but also a vital component of geopolitical power.

The last chapter of this volume is dedicated to the future of geopolitical strategies, which will be based on the power of AI and information. According to Marius Vaccarelu, the author of this chapter, soon only national political leaders who are "capable of passing the 'data quantity test' will be able to remain in the 'laboratories where geopolitical strategies are conceived" (Chap. 12).

In conclusion, AI combined with information will revolutionize geopolitical dynamics, starting with how AI and information transform the balance of power at the micro, intermediate, and global macro levels, and how the intersections of these three parameters included in the title of this volume are changing regulations, strategies, policies, actors, and the tools used for peace or war.

Ultimately, the transformation of geopolitical dynamics by AI and information technologies represents both an opportunity and a challenge for the international community. Harnessing these technologies for beneficial purposes while managing their risks will be one of the defining challenges of the twenty-first century. Success in this endeavor will require new forms of thinking, cooperation, and governance that can adapt to the realities of an AI-driven world while preserving the values and institutions that have underpinned international stability and prosperity.

The stakes of this transformation are high. The nations and international institutions that successfully navigate these challenges will be well-positioned to shape the future of international relations and global governance. Those that fail to adapt may find themselves increasingly marginalized in an international system where AI and information power determine the future of geopolitical dynamics. The choices made today about how to develop, deploy, and govern AI, and the way states use information power to achieve their national interests, will have profound implications for the future of international relations and the new world order.

Fatima Roumate
Founding Member of the Global Network on
AI and International Society (GNAI&IS)
Professor at Mohammed V University,
FSJES Agdal, Rabat, Morocco

Contents

List of Contributors

Mir Faraj Abasov Department of Marketing and Management, University of Tourism and Management, Baku, Azerbaijan

Mykhailo I. Boichenko Department of Theoretical and Practical Philosophy, Taras Shevchenko National University of Kyiv, Kyiv, Ukraine

Sergey Davydov HSE University, Moscow, Russia

Iryna I. Drach Department of the Research Activities of Universities, Institute of Higher Education, National Academy of Educational Sciences of Ukraine, Kyiv, Ukraine

Carlos Enrique Fernandez-Garcia Universidad Nacional Mayor de San Marcos, Lima, Peru

Luciana Fernandez-Valdivieso Universidad Nacional Mayor de San Marcos, Lima, Peru

Samantha Gómez Gamboa Universidad Nacional Mayor de San Marcos, Lima, Peru

Anna Kartasheva HSE University, Moscow, Russia

Marta N. Lukacovic Department of Communication and Mass Media, Angelo State University, San Angelo, Texas, USA

Zaeem Hassan Mehmood Department of Social Sciences and Humanities, Greenwich University, Karachi, Pakistan

Fatima Roumate Global Network on AI and International Society (GNAI&IS), and Mohammed V University, FSJES Agdal, Rabat, Morocco

Hajji Said Mohammed V University, Rabat, Morocco

Deborah D. Sellnow-Richmond Department of Applied Communication Studies, Southern Illinois University, Edwardsville, Illinois, USA

Pavel Sharikov Institute of Europe, Russian Academy of Sciences, Moscow, Russia

Rossana Soriano Vergara Universidad Femenina del Sagrado Corazón, Lima, Peru

Marius Vacarelu Faculty of Public Administration, National School of Political and Administrative Studies, Bucharest, Romania

Viktor V. Zinchenko Department of Social and Institutional Transformations in Higher Education, Institute of Higher Education, National Academy of Educational Sciences of Ukraine, Kyiv, Ukraine

Understanding the Intersection of AI, Information, and the Geopolitical Dynamics

Fatima Roumate

1 Introduction

The intersection of AI, information, and geopolitics is one of the most important characteristics of international relations today. This intersection has intensified since 2020, with the beginning of the COVID-19 pandemic marking a new phase of multilateralism, characterized by a blend of open-source data and AI surveillance. The pandemic accelerated the adoption of AI and its implications across various fields, including the geopolitical changes associated with the growing importance of information in this emerging "new culture" of sharing, liking, and commenting. This chapter serves as a preliminary overview, aiming to clarify the relationship between the implications of AI on information and the geopolitical changes occurring in the global landscape. Understanding this intersection will help us realize that AI and information are not merely changing geopolitical tools but are fundamentally altering the diffusion of power between states and non-state actors in a new multipolar world order.

2 Methodology

This chapter aims to explore and gain a comprehensive understanding of the intersection between the three parameters: AI, information, and geopolitical dynamics. Our research is guided by the following questions:

F. Roumate (✉)
Global Network on AI and International Society (GNAI&IS), and Mohammed V University, FSJES Agdal, Rabat, Morocco
e-mail: iirs.institute@gmail.com

F. Roumate (ed.), *AI, Information, and Global Dynamics*, Contributions to International Relations,
https://doi.org/10.1007/978-3-032-13528-5_1

- What is the convergence between AI and information?
- How is AI influencing information?
- What is the intersection between AI's implications on information and geopolitical dynamics?

To address these questions, we employ several approaches necessary for understanding the intersection of AI, information, and geopolitical dynamics. The starting point is a qualitative research approach, focusing on comprehending concepts and notions, interpreting information, and deriving insights rather than relying solely on numerical calculations. Our primary tool is an in-depth literature review and detailed conceptual analysis to explain the complex intersection between AI and information, as well as the implications of AI transformation in information and geopolitics. Additionally, we maintain a critical geopolitical perspective using diverse approaches.

First, a political approach is necessary to measure the impact of AI and information on geopolitical dynamics. The second approach is doctrinal, involving a review of existing scholarly literature in the field of AI and its challenges related to information and geopolitics. The third approach is technological, considering the interaction between AI and information.

3 AI, Data, and Information: Connecting Points and Diversity

The AI revolution relies heavily on information—data that has been processed and structured for meaning (Actian Corporation, 2023). While "data" and "information" are often used interchangeably, they refer to different stages in a continuum, especially in computing and information science (Actian Corporation, 2023). As Unstop notes, "data" comes from the Latin "datum," meaning "something given"; "datum" is rarely used as the singular form (UNstop, 2025). A datum is "an abstraction of a real-world entity (person, object, or event)" (Kelleher & Tierney, 2018, cited in MacDowell, 2021, p. 1226). Data are "symbols that represent," collected from an environment as "products of observation" (Ackoff, 1989; Rowley, 2007, cited in MacDowell, 2021, p. 1226).

Data refers to raw, unprocessed facts and figures that lack context or interpretation on their own (Knowmax, 2025). It can include numbers, images, characters, symbols, and observations of certain events or entities (Actian Corporation, 2023). Without additional processing, raw data can be difficult to understand or apply (Knowmax, 2025). This means it has no logical meaning and is difficult for an observer to interpret or use meaningfully unless it is processed (UNSTOP, 2025).

All types of data are acceptable for collection, such as text or multimedia, including pictures, audio, and videos, which are used for decision-making in several sectors, including geopolitics, diplomacy, governance, and warfare (Knowmax, 2025). Processing is a significant step that makes the difference between data and information. In information science, information is data that has been processed, organized, or structured to convey meaning and significance. Information also means "things fed into a computer" (Ma, 2012, cited in MacDowell, 2021, p. 1226). Thus, information is data after its transformation process, which involves four steps to ensure that data is comprehensible and usable in various sectors, scientific fields, or even for decision-making. Transforming data into information involves first collecting data from various sources, second, cleaning the data to ensure accuracy and consistency, third, analyzing the data using statistical methods and computational algorithms to identify patterns and trends, and fourth, interpreting the data to make sense of the analyzed information by providing context and explaining what it signifies. The final step is data presentation, which involves organizing the data in a coherent and visually appealing manner, such as charts, graphs, or reports, to effectively communicate the information (Knowmax, 2025).

The massive use of AI since COVID-19 explains the emergence of new types of power in international society, which conditions the ability of states to achieve their geopolitical interests. These "new" types of power include the power of data, the power of information, and the power of knowledge. These three types are central to all geopolitical changes related to the new balance of power, which ranges between the race for technological sovereignty and geopolitical interests (Roumate, 2024, pp.). This leads us to the DIKW model, which is often "used implicitly in definitions of data" (Rowley, 2007, cited in MacDowell, 2021, p. 1226). DIKW "has also been called the information hierarchy, the knowledge hierarchy, or the wisdom hierarchy" (MacDowell, 2021, p. 1226).

According to Calzati, recent studies in information science and knowledge management contest the DIKW pyramid by examining the role of "implicit knowledge" (Day, 2005, cited in Calzati, 2025, p. 3763), tracing the emergence of "information literacy" (Lloyd, 2009, cited in Calzati, 2025, p. 3763), addressing the epistemological foundations of "understanding" (Gorichanaz, 2017, cited in Calzati, 2025, p. 3764), and exploring the information-processing capabilities of various living species (Solhjoo et al., 2024, cited in Calzati, 2025, p. 3764). Nevertheless, these studies do not constitute a cohesive framework for the ideas of information, data, and knowledge (Calzati, 2025, p. 3764).

In the era of AI, the DIKW process remains unchanged, even with AI's influence on each level and how the interaction between humans and AI affects the process between data and knowledge (Calzati, 2025, p. 3763). Understanding the impact of this interaction is important. Both human intelligence and artificial intelligence influence the process from data creation and collection to the dissemination of information and knowledge. Both humans and AI create data and information, and both use processed data to create and disseminate knowledge. In fact, the interaction between humans and AI increases the production of information and its dissemination within the growing "culture" of "share, like, and comment." This massive use of AI offers new opportunities to enhance language production; however, it also imposes challenges related to the malicious use of AI, particularly when it comes to using this technology in creating information or content that could be used for decision-making in geopolitics.

Understanding the interaction between humans and AI, as well as its influence on information, requires a clear comprehension of the intersection between AI and information. We begin by acknowledging that AI thrives on data. AI uses both data and information, including textual, numerical, video, audio, structured, and unstructured data, to train itself. The interaction between AI and data, including structured and meaningful data (information), starts from acquisition to processing, considering ethical implications before it is used by AI or humans for decision-making. Data acquisition methods involve processes ranging from web scraping to sensor data acquisition.

The massive use of AI since COVID-19 has increased the interaction between humans and machines, and between machines and their environments. AI is not only a tool for content creation; it is also used to transform data into information. AI impacts the process between data and information, influencing the entire transformation process—from data collection to data interpretation. AI provides new tools for content creation (audio and visual analyses), which means that it creates new opportunities to influence the process between information and users. This influence can be positive or negative and may be executed by governments as a means of controlling content or by other state or non-state actors (Roumate, 2024, p. 112). AI systems used by various actors and sectors, including media and social media, amplify these implications. These implications are heightened by the interaction between humans and AI, as well as between AI and the environment.

Information lies at the heart of the intersection among humans, AI, and the environment. Both humans and AI utilize information to create knowledge and enhance intelligence, as well as to drive geopolitical changes. This intersection is based on a new "oil," which is information. This leads us to a deeper consideration of the new dimension that encompasses AI, information, and geopolitics. The goal of this intersection is the race for the power of data, the power of information, and the power of knowledge. These three types of power serve as the pillars of soft, hard, and smart power.

The intersection between AI and humans has sparked discussions regarding ethical considerations to ensure transparency, accountability, and equity. Data privacy is a primary concern and is the focal point of all international and regional instruments on AI ethics. Data privacy protects the personal data used in the development of AI by employing techniques such as federated learning, differential privacy, and anonymization. Equally important is bias mitigation, which involves identifying and correcting inherent biases in data that can result in discriminatory or unfair AI outcomes. These biases often arise from skewed sampling or historical prejudices and can be addressed using techniques such as data rebalancing and fairness-aware machine learning. Data security is paramount for protecting information from unauthorized access or disclosure, requiring robust measures such as encryption, access controls, and regular security audits to uphold confidentiality and integrity. Finally, data provenance and transparency demand comprehensive records of data sources, preprocessing, and model development, enabling thorough auditing, debugging, and a clear understanding of the AI system's limitations and potential biases.

The global debate around ethical considerations is intensified by the increasing human-AI intersection from the perspective of AI, which involves using data to simulate human behavior. AI "simulates human intelligence by analyzing data, recognizing patterns, and understanding natural language. Knowledge matching and explaining data through cognitive computing is the central part of AI functioning" (Rashid & Kausik, 2024, p. 2). From a human perspective, intersections are illustrated by the pervasive use of AI in all aspects of life, considering that "AI is expected to power 95% of customer interactions by 2025" (Rashid & Kausik, 2024, p. 2). This percentage should be critically examined in light of global investments in AI, as this 95% is one of the outputs of the global race for AI. This leads us to the geopolitics of AI and the geopolitics of information. Both are key bases for understanding the three key concepts composing the title of this chapter and this book: AI, information, and geopolitics. After explaining the intersection between AI and information, we will place this intersection within the context of geopolitics.

4 AI and the Geopolitics of Information

AI serves as a geopolitical tool, much like information, especially considering the intersection between the two, as explained in the earlier section. AI is based on the new oil—information, or structured and meaningful data—and information depends on AI for dissemination and utilization across various fields, including geopolitical interests. Traditionally, the notion of geopolitics has been linked to politics and economics. However, in the era of AI, we observe an increasing importance placed on the role of information as a geopolitical power, which conditions both economic and political power. The nature of power itself has evolved through AI, enhancing the influence of information.

Most researchers who have studied the balance of power, geopolitics, and the position of the Global South in the geopolitical landscape typically restrict their analyses to the political and economic aspects of power. They aim to explain the global dominance of major states and the dependency of the Global South on the Global North. However, this research often neglects the influence of the geopolitics of information, which reveals that this dependency can be attributed to the monopolization of information power by the Global North, particularly the West. The AI revolution enhances the role of information in international relations, especially in this new phase of multilateralism that emphasizes an open society and open data, even amidst the closed borders witnessed during COVID-19. "AI is leading an information revolution that portends to hold global-level impact" (Bowen, S. A. 2024).

According to Eric Rosenbach and Katherine Mansted, this AI revolution "has revolutionized each of the four key facets of information power: to influence the political and economic environment of other actors; to create economic growth and wealth; to enable a decision-making edge over competitors; and to communicate quickly and securely" (Rosenbach & Mansted, 2019, p. 2). In the era of Industry 6.0, information power is transforming hard, soft, and smart power, with these three types being fundamentally based on information power. The influence of information power on global affairs and international relations is not new. "In 1928, Edward Bernays, the father of public relations, explained that the 'astonishing success' of World War I's mass broadcast propaganda opened his eyes to the immense commercial and political possibilities of 'regimenting the public mind'" (Rosenbach & Mansted, 2019, p. 2). The AI revolution only increases the influence of information and propaganda on international relations during both peace and war. In the era of AI, information warfare has emerged as the most impactful military front (Bowen & Erzikova, 2024).

To understand the geopolitics of information, we must first identify who holds the power of information. This notion refers to "the strategic ability of a state to acquire, control, and leverage information to advance its interests. It involves not only creating and possessing information but also skillfully employing it to drive innovation, shape beliefs, build narratives, and influence and outmaneuver other states and non-state actors" (Edwards, 2024). Information power encompasses a wide range of tools, from espionage and hacking to more subtle skills like public diplomacy and media influence. In the age of AI, countries that successfully harness information power must learn to use technology to acquire, utilize, preserve, and share information intelligently (Edwards, 2024).

In this new world order, characterized by the widespread use of AI in international relations, information power serves as a potent force relying on technological power and a deep understanding of human-AI interactions, particularly concerning the psychological dimension (Edwards, 2024). Information and technological power are both key elements for comprehending the complex issues surrounding international relations today and in the future. These factors explain the substantial investments made by information-powerful states in both information and information technology. Several indicators are employed to identify the leading nations in information technology, particularly their leadership in technological capability, the quality of their advanced infrastructure, and their significant contributions to the global IT market.

The United States is recognized for its leadership in innovation and research and development (R&D), hosting major global tech companies and boasting the most data centers worldwide, indicating a vast digital infrastructure (Statista, 2024). Additionally, the U.S. leads in producing top AI models and private AI investment (Maslej et al., 2025).

China is a rapidly ascending force, heavily investing in digital transformation, AI adoption, and data center development. It has the highest number of internet users globally and is a major player in emerging technologies (Data Reportal, 2024; Huawei, 2024). China is also expected to hold a significant share of the world's AI patents (Maslej et al., 2025).

South Korea is highly regarded for its advanced e-governance and smart city initiatives, driven by a strong focus on digital innovation and cutting-edge technologies. It excels in advanced IT infrastructure and areas like smartphones, high-speed internet connectivity, and the widespread adoption of AI and generative AI (Bright Nation, 2024). According to the Global Innovation Index 2024, South Korea ranks 6th among 133 economies (WIPO, 2024).

Bright Nation (2024) emphasizes that Japan consistently excels in advanced technology sectors such as robotics, electronics, and automotive engineering, significantly contributing to global innovation while maintaining a strong emphasis on research and development (Bright Nation, 2024; WIPO, 2024).

Germany is renowned for its engineering prowess and technological excellence. Its focus on precision, quality, and industrial innovation has led to remarkable advancements in IT fields, including industrial automation, software development, and sustainable technology solutions (Bright Nation, 2024). Germany also has a high number of data centers in Europe (Statista, 2024).

Other notable countries frequently cited for their strong IT contributions and innovation include the United Kingdom, recognized for its advancements in AI and cloud computing; Singapore, acclaimed as a top "smart city" for its digital transformation and competitiveness; Switzerland, highly innovative in precision technology and R&D (WIPO, 2024); and Sweden, consistently ranking high for innovation and digitalization (WIPO, 2024). These countries collectively shape the global information power landscape through their continuous investments in digital infrastructure, R&D, and the adoption of advanced technologies.

Assessing information power is a complex endeavor. To evaluate informational power, one must assess a state's capabilities in several key areas: innovation, digital infrastructure, technological leadership, data centers, and cyber power. The potency of information is primarily determined by a state's capacity for innovation and research and development, which includes investment in research, the number of patents, and the quality of scientific publications.

The quality of digital infrastructure—including the quantity of data centers, internet penetration rates, and broadband accessibility—is the second indicator for evaluating informational power. This leads us to the third indicator, which focuses on data control and flow, referring to the state's ability to acquire, process, and utilize extensive datasets. The fourth prerequisite is technological leadership, which encompasses the state's ability to innovate future technologies.

The final indicator relates to cyber capabilities, including the robustness of cybersecurity and cyber warfare. Additionally, it involves the state's capacity to utilize all preceding conditions to exert influence over global standards, including its role in the global governance of artificial intelligence and its impact on the development of international instruments related to AI ethics.

China also leads in scientific publications, particularly with journal articles totaling 485,085 and open-access articles at 245,476, followed by the United States with 352,549 journal articles and 168,012 open-access articles. The U.S. leads in preprints with 51,587, followed by China with 41,005 (Scilit, 2025). According to the AI Index Report 2025 published by Stanford University, "In 2024, U.S.-based institutions produced 40 notable AI models, compared to China's 15 and Europe's three. While the U.S. maintains its lead in quantity, Chinese models have rapidly closed the quality gap: performance differences on major benchmarks such as MMLU and

Human Eval shrank from double digits in 2023 to near parity in 2024" (Gil & Perrault, 2025). The landscape of this dual power, composed of information and advanced technologies, is constantly evolving, with new players emerging and existing powers adapting to rapid technological advancements.

Information power is wielded by states at both national and international levels to shape the dynamics of societal interaction within their borders and the global landscape beyond. This leads us to the implementation of the "DIME framework—Diplomatic, Informational, Military, and Economic" for understanding how states employ power in international society to defend and ensure their national interests (Edwards, 2024).

In diplomacy, information power facilitates negotiation and consensus-building, making it easier to identify common ground. States leverage their economic power in diplomacy, particularly in economic diplomacy. Economic power is also utilized by states in military contexts, where possessing information power becomes increasingly vital for military operations, as military outcomes influence geopolitics by transforming military capabilities. Information power strengthens the other three pillars of the DIME framework through diplomatic and economic influence and information warfare (Edwards, 2024).

The intersection of artificial intelligence and information systems has emerged as one of the most significant and paradigm-shifting geopolitical landscapes, considering its tangible and intangible implications for international relations (Farrell & Newman, 2019; Deibert, 2019). Information and emerging technologies, particularly AI and generative AI, are transforming every aspect of statecraft, from diplomacy and strategic communications to citizen diplomacy and public opinion, and from intelligence gathering to economic competition (Buchanan, 2020; Konaev, 2019) during both peace and war. The use of AI and information as weapons represents a crucial sign of this new era, marked by a more advanced form of multilateralism and a shift toward a new Westphalian system.

5 AI and Information: A New Balance of Power in Geopolitics

The new balance of power, which ranges between geostrategic interests and the race for technological sovereignty, can explain the AI transformation in geopolitics. Competition in this era is not limited to states; major technological companies are also significant players in the geopolitical sphere, influenced by Industry 6.0. The AI transformation in geopolitics is changing the balance of power at both global and regional levels. These changes are leading to diverse types of warfare, such as cyberwarfare and digital map warfare, which rely on technologies like drone strikes, missile targeting, and high-resolution satellite imagery. AI and cyber capabilities are key elements for manipulating or jamming map data during both information warfare and military conflicts, which heavily rely on geospatial intelligence and geographic information systems.

The Westphalian system of international relations, built on concepts of territorial sovereignty and state-to-state interaction, is being challenged by AI-enabled information flows that transcend borders, creating new spheres for cooperation and conflict, as well as new types of power. This transformation necessitates a fundamental reexamination of how we understand international relations, security, and the nature of conflict in this new phase of multilateralism, characterized by closed borders—like during COVID-19—and an open society with open data (Rid, 2020). The AI transformation in information leads us to consider its geopolitical implications.

COVID-19 marks a significant turning point in the history of international relations, signaling the end of the Westphalian system established in 1648, which developed through various historical periods until the creation of the United Nations in 1945 (Roumate, 2021). This period was characterized by information warfare dominated by major powers with significant resources and sophisticated intelligence services. COVID-19 also heralds the beginning of a new Westphalian system influenced by AI's impact on the balance of power, contributing to the "democratization" of many capabilities, allowing smaller nations, non-state actors, and even individuals to conduct sophisticated influence operations (Roumate, 2021). This democratization presents both significant opportunities and challenges for international peace and security.

The information revolution is changing the nature of conflicts due to its implications on the rise of "multiorganizational networks" and the migration of power to non-state actors (Arquilla & Ronfeldt, 2001, p. 1). The AI-driven information revolution empowers small states and enhances their capabilities in conducting information warfare, making it accessible to a broader range of actors. Small states can now leverage AI and information to achieve their national interests by incorporating these dual powers into the DIME framework. However, small countries face two challenges: the gap between great and small states, and the increasing difficulty of engaging in information warfare, particularly with semi-states and the growing competition between states and companies, including mercenary firms (Egloff, 2022, p. 127). These challenges complicate small states' contributions to this dynamic global landscape, particularly amid the increasing weaponization of AI and information.

AI superpowers, like the USA, China, and Russia, are transforming conflict through strategic communication and information warfare orchestrated and controlled by AI (Bowen, 2025). AI has transformed information from a mere tool of influence into a weapon of warfare (Singer & Brooking, 2018). The ability to generate and disseminate false information at scale, combined with the precision targeting capabilities of modern platforms, allows states to achieve strategic objectives through information operations alone. This weaponization serves as a tool for the three types of power: hard, soft, and smart power. This leads us to the diverse dimensions of the weaponization of AI and information.

The first dimension is economic warfare, where information manipulation can target various markets and economic indicators, particularly concerning "potential threats to financial stability created or facilitated by algorithmic trading" (Kirilenko & Lo, 2013).

Given the AI transformation in industry and the massive use of AI across different sectors, the economy is increasingly based on information rather than solely on knowledge. AI-driven analyses of market sentiment and automated trading systems can be exploited to create artificial market movements or exacerbate existing economic instabilities. Moreover, mind privacy targeted by AI for marketing purposes, with its ability to predict consumer behavior and guide choices toward certain products over others, could also be used as a "weapon" in economic warfare.

The second dimension is psychological warfare, which, through AI-enabled disinformation, can create political changes and influence elections and democratic processes (Roumate, 2020). The power of fake news is determined by the virality of the lie it propagates, the speed of its dissemination without timely contradiction, and the extent to which people receive and believe the falsehood (Persily, 2017, p. 70). New AI systems dramatically increase the use of disinformation and fake news, considering their capability to generate content and ensure sophisticated coordination across multiple platforms simultaneously. Bradshaw and Howard (2019) found evidence of organized social media manipulation campaigns in 70 countries, up from 48 countries in 2018 and 28 countries in 2017. This growth partly stems from new entrants experimenting with the tools and techniques of computational propaganda during elections or as new tools for information control (Bradshaw & Howard, 2019, p. 2). By 2050, numerous societies globally may possess advanced information and AI literacy; however, disinformation efforts may persist (Lukacovic & Sellnow-Richmond, 2024).

The third dimension is social warfare, where AI-amplified content can exacerbate existing social divisions and create conflicts within countries between groups with diverse ideologies and ethnicities. AI provides new opportunities to identify and exploit social fractures through data analysis, combined with the capacity to generate emotionally charged content. This could be used to instigate social movements or revolutions that create political changes serving the geopolitical interests of certain parties (Roumate, 2021).

These dimensions lead us to the rise of "techno-nationalism," driven by the strategic importance of AI capabilities. Techno-nationalism is a renewed form of national interest fused with scientific and technological advancement. It redefines sovereignty, security, and economic competitiveness by promoting scientific progress (Akhtar, 2025). This trend explains the global race for technological sovereignty and sovereign AI, which manifests in various ways across the geopolitical landscape (Roumate, 2021).

These diverse dimensions of AI and information's implications on the geopolitical landscape are also highlighted by the race for AI surveillance to protect state interests, considering the previous dimension of the weaponization of AI and information (Roumate, 2021). In this context, states are focusing on reinforcing their ability to create new technologies, particularly digital technologies, as these are crucial for politics, security, and economic growth. This competition is exemplified by the U.S.-China relationship, marked by close commercial cooperation yet deep governmental distrust (Lewis, 2018). The competition over semiconductors between great powers, particularly between the United States and China, serves as a prominent example of this trend (Lewis, 2018).

The trend of weaponizing AI and information has far-reaching consequences across various fields, including international economic law and international investment law. In this context, rethinking international economic law is an obligation rather than a choice, given the urgent need for new regulations to ensure coexistence between states and transnational technological corporations (Kissinger et al., 2021).

The race for sovereign AI is accompanied by various levels of competition, including the race for national AI strategies and regulations, which serve not only to maximize benefits from AI and address its challenges but also symbolize geopolitical power. Garcia, C.E.F., Gamboa, S.G., and Castillo, P.G. (Garcia et al., 2025) argue that the contributions of technology corporations have become a key pillar in the new global balance, owing to the implications of these transnational corporations on technological sovereignty and geopolitical dynamics (Garcia et al., 2025, p. 37).

Neurosymbolic Artificial Intelligence is transforming geopolitical dynamics as it is applied in strategic sectors like defense, homeland security, and government automation (Garcia et al., 2025, p. 38). These advanced technologies present several risks to another strategic sector: media diplomacy (Hajji, 2025), especially regarding the proliferation of malicious uses of AI (Hajji, 2025). In this regard, Lukacovic and Sellnow-Richmond (2025) advocate for information literacy combined with social responsibility to combat the malicious use of AI-driven information. This approach emphasizes the crucial role of communication in enhancing social responsibility and improving social inclusion in AI regulation, as well as in the identification, implementation, and evaluation of policy actions related to AI-driven information (Lukacovic & Sellnow-Richmond, 2025, p. 32).

Trends related to the weaponization of AI and information lead us to potential geopolitical scenarios that could result in the emergence of new spheres of power, increasing extraterritorial relations, and escalating challenges related to cyberwarfare. These trends heighten international tensions and the potential for conflicts to escalate rapidly to nuclear warfare.

6 Conclusion

The intersection of artificial intelligence, information, and geopolitical dynamics represents one of the most significant transformations in the international system since the end of the Cold War. This transformation encompasses not merely advanced technologies, including AI and generative AI, but also fundamental changes in geopolitical dynamics. It raises questions about how the combination of AI and information influences the exercise of power, conflicts, negotiations, the economy, and military interactions, as well as how states engage with each other and other actors in international society.

The analysis presented in this chapter demonstrates that AI-driven information is reshaping traditional notions of geopolitics, giving rise to several types or levels of geopolitics, such as the geopolitics of AI, the geopolitics of information, and the geopolitics of information technologies. AI-driven information is also transforming power structures, increasing the importance of various types of power—not only hard, soft, and smart power but also information power and technological power. Concepts of technological and data sovereignty are increasingly conditioned by sovereign AI and information power.

This leads us to the geopolitics of AI ethics and regulation. In this context, the global race for national AI strategies, regulations, and ethical frameworks reflects differing visions and approaches regarding how AI-driven information should be developed and deployed. These differences have significant implications for global AI governance, international security, and the emerging global order. Ultimately, these varying approaches will reshape the future of the global landscape and geopolitical dynamics.

References

Ackoff, R. L. (1989). From data to wisdom. *Journal of Applied Systems Analysis*, *16*(1), 3–9. https://doi.org/citeulike-article-id:6930744

Actian Corporation. (2023). *Understanding the difference between data and information*. https://www.actian.com/blog/data-intelligence/understanding-the-difference-between-data-and-information/

Akhtar, N. (2025). *Techno-nationalism: Redefining power*. https://policyeast.com/techno-nationalism-redefining-power/

Arquilla, J., & Ronfeldt, D. (2001). *Networks and netwars: The future of terror, crime, and militancy*. https://books.google.co.ma/books?id=cL_3CsUvxMMC

Bowen, S. A. (2025). Artificial intelligence, warfare, and the surveillance/information state. In *Artificial intelligence, media and international security*. Springer. https://doi.org/10.1007/978-3-031-95757-4_1

Bowen, S. A., & Erzikova, E.(2024). Devolving ethical standards of 2050: International and disciplinary failure. *Public relations and strategic communication in 2050*. 1st Routledge. https://www.taylorfrancis.com/chapters/edit/10.4324/9781003426653-6/devolving-ethical-standards-2050-shannon-bowen-elina-erzikova?context=ubx&refId=e6acf8a0-6619-46a7-8af2-0f18bd2c85c6

Bradshaw, S., & Howard, P. N. (2019). The global disinformation order: 2019 global inventory of organised social media manipulation. https://demtech.oii.ox.ac.uk/wp-content/uploads/sites/12/2019/09/CyberTroop-Report19.pdf

Bright Nation. (2024). *Top 20 global leaders countries in digital public services in 2024*. Bright Nation Creative Studio. Retrieved from: https://brightnation.studio/blog/top-20-global-leaders-countries-in-digital-public-services-in-2024

Buchanan, B. (2020). *The hacker and the state: Cyber attacks and the new normal of geopolitics*. https://www.hup.harvard.edu/books/9780674987555

Calzati, S. (2025). An ecosystemic view on information, data, and knowledge: Insights on agential AI and relational ethics. *AI Ethics*, *5*, 3763–3776. https://doi.org/10.1007/s43681-025-00665-0

DataReportal. (2024). *Internet use in 2024*. https://datareportal.com/reports/digital-2024-deep-dive-the-state-of-internet-adoption

Day, R. E. (2005). Clearing up "implicit knowledge": Implications for knowledge management, information science, psychology, and social epistemology. *Journal of the American Society for Information Science and Technology*, *56*(6), 630–635.

Deibert, R. J. (2019). The road to digital unfreedom: Three painful truths about social media. *Journal of Democracy*, *30*(1), 25–39. https://www.journalofdemocracy.org/articles/the-road-to-digital-2unfreedom-three-painful-truths-about-social-media/

Edwards, A. (2024). *Geopolitics, DIME, and information power*. https://www.ipia.au/theory-page-1

Egloff, F. J. (2022). *Semi-state actors in cybersecurity*. Oxford University Press, https://www.google.co.ma/books/edition/Semi_State_Actors_in_Cybersecurity/U_hQEAAAQBAJ?hl=fr&gbpv=1&dq=Egloff,+F.+J.+(2022).%E2%80%AFSemi-state+actors+in+cybersecurity&printsec=frontcover

Farrell, H., & Newman, A. L. (2019). weaponized interdependence: How global economic networks shape state coercion. *International Security*, *44*(1), 42–79. https://doi.org/10.1162/ISEC_a_00351

Garcia, C. E. F., Gamboa, S. G., & Castillo, P. G. (2025). Digital imperialism: Neurosymbolic artificial intelligence, international security, information flows, and social media in the Twenty-First century. In F. Roumate & A. La Rosa (Eds), *Artificial intelligence, media and international security. Contributions to security and defence studies*. Springer. https://doi.org/10.1007/978-3-031-95757-4_4

Gil, Y., & Perrault, R. (2025). *The AI Index Report 2025*. https://hai-production.s3.amazonaws.com/files/hai_ai_index_report_2025.pdf

Gorichanaz, T. (2017). Applied epistemology and understanding in information studies. *Information Research: International Electronic Journal*, *22*(4), n4.

Hajji, S. (2025). Media diplomacy in the age of AI: Transformative potential and ethical challenges. In: F. Roumate, & A. La Rosa, (Eds), *Artificial intelligence, media and international security*. Contributions to security and defence studies. Springer, Cham. https://doi.org/10.1007/978-3-031-95757-4_6

Huawei. (2024). *Global Digitalization Index (GDI) 2024*. https://www.huawei.com/en/gdi

Kelleher, J. D., & Tierney, B. (2018). *Data science*. MIT Press Direct. https://doi.org/10.7551/mitpress/11140.001.0001

Kirilenko, A. A., & Lo, A. W. (2013). Moore's law versus Murphy's law: Algorithmic trading and its discontents. *Journal of Economic Perspectives*, *27*(2), 51–72. https://doi.org/10.1257/jep.27.2.51

Kissinger, H., Schmidt, E., & Huttenlocher, D. P. (2021). *The age of AI: And our human future*. Little Brown & Company. http://103.203.175.90:81/fdScript/RootOfEBooks/E%20Book%20collection%20-%202024%20-%20G/CSE%20%20IT%20AIDS%20ML/The%20Age%20of%20AI_%20And%20Our%20Human%20Future.pdf

KNOWMAX. (2025, June 30). *Data vs information vs knowledge: Understand the difference*. https://knowmax.ai/blog/data-vs-information-vs-knowledge/

Konaev, M. (2019). With AI, we'll see everything: US military intelligence and the promise of artificial intelligence. *War on the rocks*. https://warontherocks.com/2019/11/with-ai-well-see-everything-us-military-intelligence-and-the-promise-of-artificial-intelligence/

Lewis, J. A. (2018). *Technological competition and China*. https://www.csis.org/analysis/technological-competition-and-china

Lloyd, A. (2009). Informing practice: Information experiences of ambulance officers in training and on-road practice. *Journal of Documentation*, *65*(3), 396–419.

Lukacovic, M. N., & Sellnow-Richmond, D. D. (2024). The growth of malicious AI: Countering disinformation and deepfakes amid mega-crises. *Public relations and strategic communication in 2050*. 1st Routledge.https://www.taylorfrancis.com/chapters/edit/10.4324/9781003426653-4/growth-malicious-ai-marta-lukacovic-deborah-sellnow-richmond?context=ubx&refId=7b7c4918-0011-463b-90e0-2a40ca743555

Lukacovic, M. N., & Sellnow-Richmond, D. D. (2025). Communication dimensions in mitigating the global security threats of malicious AI/artificial intelligence. In: F. Roumate, & A. La Rosa, (Eds), *Artificial intelligence, media and international security*. Contributions to security and defence studies. Springer, Cham. https://doi.org/10.1007/978-3-031-95757-4_3

Ma, L. (2012). Meanings of information: The assumptions and research consequences of three foundational LIS theories. *Journal of the American Society for Information Science and Technology*, *63*(4), 716–723.

MacDowell, K. (2021). Storytelling wisdom: Story, information, and DIKW. *Journal of the Association for Information Science and Technology*, *72*, 1223–1233. https://doi.org/10.1002/asi.24466

Maslej, N., et al. (2025). *The AI Index Report 2025*.

Persily, N. (2017). The 2016 US election: Can democracy survive the internet? *Journal of Democracy*, *28*(2), 63–76. https://www.journalofdemocracy.org/wp-content/uploads/2017/04/07_28.2_Persily-web.pdf

Rashid, A. B., & Kausik, M. A. K. (2024). AI revolutionizing industries worldwide: A comprehensive overview of its diverse applications. *Hybrid Advances*, *7*, 100277. https://doi.org/10.1016/j.hybadv.2024.100277

Rid, T. (2020). *Active measures: The secret history of disinformation and political warfare*. https://academic.oup.com/ia/article-abstract/97/1/244/6041478

Rosenbach, E., & Mansted, K. (2019). *Geopolitics of information*. https://www.belfercenter.org/publication/geopolitics-information

Roumate, F. (2020). Mechanisms of advanced international psychological security in the age of artificial intelligence. *Communications. Media. Design*, *5*(1), https://owl.purdue.edu/owl/general_writing/grammar/using_articles.html

Roumate, F. (2021). Ethics on AI and technological sovereignty. *Communication. Media. Design*, *6*(4), 139–151. https://cmd-journal.hse.ru/article/view/13766

Roumate, F. (2024). *Artificial intelligence and the new world order: New weapons, new wars and a new balance of power*. Springer. https://link.springer.com/book/10.1007/978-3-031-50312-2#accessibility-information

Rowley, J. (2007). The wisdom hierarchy: Representations of the DIKW hierarchy. *Journal of Information Science*, *33*(2), 163–180. https://doi.org/10.1177/0165551506070706

Scilit. (2025). *Countries Ranking*. https://www.scilit.com/rankings/countries

Singer, P. W., & Brooking, E. T. (2018). *Like war: The weaponization of social media*.

Solhjoo, N., Krtalić, M., & Goulding, A. (2024). The in-between: Information experience within human-companion animal living environments. *Journal of Documentation*. https://doi.org/10.1108/JD-08-2023-0160

Statista. (2024). *Chart: Which countries have the most data centers?* https://www.statista.com/chart/24149/data-centers-per-country/

UNstop. (2025). *5 Important difference between data and information explained!* https://unstop.com/blog/difference-between-data-and-information

WIPO. (2024). *Global Innovation Index*. https://www.wipo.int/gii-ranking/en/rank/

AI, Information, and Global Power Dynamics: Shifting Centers of Global Influence and the Threat of Totalitarian Digitalization Policies (Case of the People's Republic of China)

Viktor V. Zinchenko, Mykhailo I. Boichenko, and Iryna I. Drach

1 Introduction

Attempts by the modern Chinese government to use social networks and AI to establish total control over segments of society demonstrate both the threat of new digital totalitarianism and the potential for the expanded influence of AI technology on politics, ethics, and human nature. Modern researchers understand this situation when "digital networks allow for a granularity and pervasiveness of surveillance by government and corporate entities" as such a threat that "creates power asymmetries where each citizen's daily 'data exhaust' can be used for manipulative and controlling ends by powerful institutional actors" (Filimowicz, 2022). As for the threats, it is already obvious that certain tendencies of authoritarianism are growing, limiting the use of citizens' freedom, and generally narrowing the scope of liberal values. This appears not only as a result of the spread of totalitarian ideology, as in classical totalitarian societies, but also as a result of total surveillance, which makes certain freedoms impossible not only at the ideological level, but at the technological and even biological level (Fasman, 2021). The US Department of Homeland Security gives following

V. V. Zinchenko (✉)
Department of Social and Institutional Transformations in Higher Education, Institute of Higher Education, National Academy of Educational Sciences of Ukraine, Kyiv, Ukraine
e-mail: vvzinchenko@ukr.net

M. I. Boichenko
Department of Theoretical and Practical Philosophy, Taras Shevchenko National University of Kyiv, Kyiv, Ukraine

I. I. Drach
Department of the Research Activities of Universities, Institute of Higher Education, National Academy of Educational Sciences of Ukraine, Kyiv, Ukraine

F. Roumate (ed.), *AI, Information, and Global Dynamics*, Contributions to International Relations,
https://doi.org/10.1007/978-3-032-13528-5_2

understanding of biosurveillance: "Biosurveillance primarily focuses on developing effective surveillance, prevention and operational capabilities for detecting and countering biological threats" (US Department of Homeland Security, 2025).

Changes in politics, ethics, and economics are inevitable: AI simplifies the solution of many problems, makes a significant number of abuses impossible, and, in general, not only narrows the old spaces of freedom but also creates new, previously unknown dimensions of human freedom. This manifests itself in changes in human nature. The control over any actions is increasing, as databases of human biological characteristics make it possible to detect any participation of a specific person in any social action or any social communication. On the other hand, identifying the potential of each person at the biological level creates prospects for a more rational use of these potentials and new challenges to human freedom. In addition, there is the ethical question of not allowing a person to neglect his own potential, even if this would bring both benefit and risk to society.

AI opens up new, previously unseen opportunities to influence social processes—primarily at the global level. Previously, one of the restraining factors for the deepening of globalization was the difficulty of processing the huge amounts of information that appeared with the growth of international communication—economic, political, cultural, etc. Without properly processing this information, it was difficult not only for governments and companies, but also for citizens to make sufficiently well-founded and pragmatically successful decisions—because global factors increasingly influenced even those local processes that were previously (or at least pragmatically appeared) completely self-sufficient in their course. Ultimately, perhaps it was the awareness of the determining influence of global factors at the local level that became the decisive argument in the widespread acceptance of globalization—in its obvious inevitability, if not always usefulness for the average person. The effects of AI have made it possible to manage globalization processes—whatever the motives and goals of those who carry out this management.

At the micro level, these influences are much easier to implement, and here they are the strongest: already now, every person in the world can significantly improve the solution of many of their practical and even some theoretical tasks by turning to chatbots such as ChatGPT. Modern people cannot imagine their life without a personal smartphone (or even several), the range of smart things is also expanding, people are surrounded by a smart home, a smart city, and many government agencies are increasingly switching to the use of special programs to serve the needs of the population—instead of thousands and tens of thousands of civil servants. In the USA, Elon Musk is carrying out an unprecedented reduction in the number of civil servants (Oladipo, 2025), which has already become inevitable, although it may not immediately be implemented on the colossal scale that Elon Musk and DOGE want to implement. A significant part of the service sector and the production sector is undoubtedly undergoing colossal transformations under the influence of the increasingly widespread use of AI, automation, and robotization.

All this will inevitably change not only the lives of individuals, but also families, small organizations and communities (Zubchyk et al., 2021).

At the intermediate level—the levels of corporations, regions and national societies—it is possible to use holistic regional autonomous AI systems that will provide a full cycle of meeting the needs of both societies, states or corporations, and themselves—from the production of the necessary equipment to the creation and improvement of software and maintenance of the functioning of all components of these holistic regional autonomous AI systems. The world can thus be divided into regional centers around such powerful regional systems: the USA, China, the EU, and, perhaps, in the future, some others, as well as at the level of individual corporations, such as Google, Apple, Samsung, etc.

At the global macro level, the situation will be as dynamic as possible, since as a result of the competitive struggle of regional autonomous systems among themselves, each of them will create a software product and its own periphery, which will claim global distribution: Pax Americana, Chinese Umbrella, European World will no longer be financial systems of world currencies (and not even Bitcoin or other similar decentralized electronic payment systems), not economic world-systems, not language empires, but different versions of the global sphere of social control, which will be carried out by AI. The era of almost non-competitive global domination of one currency (the dollar), one technological and economic system (the American economy at the top of the world hierarchy), one language (English) is inevitably a thing of the past, as is the era of the domination of one almost unalternative software system and the complex of devices associated with it (Microsoft). We are entering an era of constant change in the global leader, with leadership in each of the above areas increasingly critically dependent on the global success of the regional version of AI that underpins them.

Against the backdrop of the increasingly risky destabilization of the United States—the traditional global leader in AI development—China's quiet but persistent efforts to create not only a deeply branched global network of economic consumers of Chinese products, but also to spread its own developments in the field of AI and social control using AI on a global scale are attracting more and more attention. However, unlike the regulatory type of US global policy, China offers a more directive style in the use of AI within the country, which, apparently, it plans to implement (and partly already implements) in its international policy. So far, this is just a more or less orderly competition between two global centers of influence that seek to dominantly determine the development of AI, and accordingly—the restructuring of all other technological, and accordingly economic, political, social and cultural processes in the world. However, firstly, other centers of global influence are also joining this competition—the EU, Russia, and possibly also India. Each of these centers has its own base, which includes either the production of modern supercomputers or a developed network of programming specialists and the corresponding organizational and technological infrastructure, or both. Secondly, in this struggle, the further, the less the rules are followed. Each such global center of influence claims to achieve an exclusively dominant position, not only unattainable for competitors, but also one that will make competition impossible in the future. This is done with an appeal to the satisfaction of the best interests of all consumers—first of all, supposedly to avoid software conflicts and technological incompatibility (as Microsoft once did more gently). However, today it looks like in the near future the competitive struggle will sharply intensify—"the winner must take all" and actually destroy competitors. In any case, this is the position taken by the most aggressive global players.

2 Methodology

Given China's rapidly growing influence in the world, it is worth modeling in advance in general terms a possible type of international interaction organized according to the type of implementation of China's domestic policy using AI. After all, it is not at all excluded that this experience can be adopted not only by China, but also by the USA or any other winner in the struggle for the most effective AI technologies.

Such modeling will be carried out using institutional analysis of social communications. The methods of organizational processing of socially important information by the Chinese authorities themselves at various levels were subject to strict formalization from the very beginning. Since the management of the circulation of information was carried out in an institutional manner, the most adequate method of studying this management should be carried out using institutional analysis.

Using the example of China, we can trace how the pyramid of formal social control using AI is being built—from small communities to larger ones and, finally, to the global level. As a working hypothesis, we assume that China has consistently scaled up the local success of total institutional control over small territorial communities with the help of AI. Initially, this was the excessive use of video surveillance by the Chinese government and the strict administration of the mass media by this government. Today, all citizens of China are under almost total constant surveillance by the government, and their behavior is not just strictly regulated and controlled, but also directed in a direction determined by the government. This direction of behavior even covers citizens' actions on social networks, their private correspondence, and in some cases even their choices in private life. Similarly, the Chinese authorities seek to apply the same institutional approach, which is embodied in a number of organizational entities, to monitor the behavior of citizens of other countries around the world, seeking to quietly achieve control over their behavior through the use of social media algorithms and other means of manipulating people's behavior based on possession of information about them, including, first of all, in the format of Big Data.

2.1 Analysis of the AI Social Control

Post-society is the society that irreversibly changed after the end of modernity and global pandemic (Bordoni, 2022), but moreover this is a new social space for active daily interactions between humans, AI, and informational technologies. However, the limits of penetration of AI and robots into the human sphere are as uncertain as the limits of human influence on the development of AI and robots. Will AI become a self-sufficient creator of robots? Will robots created by AI be integrated into human society? Will people be hosted of the functionality of robots? Can an artificial social environment, which includes AI and robots, be a holder of human values and human culture in principle? Could values and culture be replaced by their simplified functional equivalents, understandable by AI and robots? To what extent can AI learn? To what extent are robots capable of learning? Does AI need to master human values and culture? Can programming be equated with learning? Is AI capable of self-education? Can AI go beyond stereotyped decision-making? Should we try to develop the ability to make independent decisions in AI? Are AI and robots just perfect teaching tools, or they can be teachers themselves—if only partially? What are the possible advantages and disadvantages of robots as teachers—hypothetically? To what extent can AI and robots replace humans in scientific research? Can AI and robots in science be more than means of control? Can AI and robots perform the work of laboratory assistants for a researcher and assistants for a professor?

These questions relate to the technical possibility of their implementation only in the second place (Coeckelbergh, 2020). First of all, which functions of education and scientific research can be highly formalized and separated from each other (Zinchenko et al., 2021). These separated units can then be programmed into robots, and AI can participate in such programming (Liao, 2020). If AI and robots cannot able to reproduce the human experience in its integrity and completeness, then they can expand this experience in the person himself. Not only human flesh, but also intelligent things become part of a person's social environment. Not only social technologies, but intelligent technologies too could be part of processing post-society (Boichenko et al., 2022; Guzhva et al., 2022; Zinchenko, 2022). The information networks and communication networks, primarily the Internet, and other networks based on it play not the last role in this.

In the framework of political post-phenomenology study Dutch political philosophers Lars Botin, Bas de Boer and Tom Børsen revealed the contemporary relation between technologies and individuals in political communication (Botin et al., 2020). In this important research they developed Michel Foucault's ideas of political and societal surveillance over the individuals (Foucault, 1995). Another Dutch researcher Peter-Paul Verbeek takes the similar philosophical position: he elaborates the political hermeneutics of technology in two directions: as a "program of individual human-technology relations (the "micro level")" and as a "program of cultural hermeneutics (the "macro level")" (Verbeek, 2020: 142). Also the investigations of digital totalitarianism by American researchers were useful (Fasman, 2021; Shenk, 2006; York, 2021). These studies were helpful as a methodology for our research.

Impressive material for the analysis of the AI Social Control in Global Power Dynamics could be taken from political practice of Chinese government surveillance over Chinese citizens. Most bold and vivid imagination of twentieth century could not give rise to even the green idea of total surveillance, which has become the systemic political reality of modern communist China. Some people look at Chinese experiments with AI-controlled communities as an inevitable future for every country and for all mankind. But is such a future desirable, and if not, is it inevitable?

Contemporary China presents prospect of terrible variant of human-AI-robots network, but it is very instructive negative example: Chinese experiment with total surveillance control over citizens could help reveal the weaknesses of such networks. Rare cases of its impressive efficiency cannot cover the dark impression of the humiliation of human freedom and dignity. However, all this supervision acquires the character of impersonal control of artificial intelligence, and maybe the robots in coming days. This impersonal control interferes almost in the physiology of the functioning of the human body. Without exception, all actions of a person, and not only his political sympathies, are under the total control of a political system that develops into a dictatorship that goes far beyond politics and interferes not only in public economic, legal, cultural issues, but also in the sacred sphere of human privacy. This is not just a threat to the ethics of relations between humans; it is a threat to lose the ability to critically evaluate one's own behavior and to become unable to learn to adjust it properly.

2.2 Digital Inequality as a Deepening of Other Types of Inequality

The problem of inequality in the modern world is becoming increasingly urgent and complex. If earlier it was mostly reduced to the economic aspect, today it is a multifaceted phenomenon that also covers several other areas of life. On the other hand, the presence of various types of economic inequality makes the issues of access to quality education and modern technologies important. The problem of inequality is particularly acute in Europe, where its growth is observed in individual member states of the European Union. Increasing inequality contributes to political polarization, when society is divided into opposing camps with different interests and values. This can lead to the weakening of democratic institutions and a decrease in the level of trust in government. Growing inequality also negatively affects economic growth. Studies show that countries with high levels of inequality have lower rates of economic development than countries with a more even distribution of income. But it is important not only to eliminate economic inequality, but also to ensure equal access to education, technology and other opportunities for society.

An overall target of 25% of EU spending contributing to climate goals has already been set for 2021–2027 (One Planet Summit, 2025). The scale of this challenge requires further investment in science, as well as profound changes in labor market and consumer behavior. While this is a challenge, it also opens up significant opportunities for businesses and companies to meet the global demand for resource efficiency, energy efficiency, energy storage and sustainable solutions for a circular economy. Technologically advanced companies that innovate for sustainability will thrive, replacing those that are less willing to change. Exponential technologies fuelled by digitalization, such as artificial intelligence, 3D printing, blockchain or robotics, are driving an unprecedented wave of innovation across all European sectors. At the same time, the shift towards sustainable consumption and production is a key driver of change. The growing consumer demand for transparency and traceability is changing the way we design, produce, commercialize, service and extract value from products and services. European industry has the opportunity to acquire the right set of skills, both professional and interdisciplinary, to meet the challenges posed by innovative technologies, digitalization and the transition to sustainable production and consumption. These skills need to be based on policies and systems that foster knowledge creation and transfer, as well as on local ecosystems that spread innovation. Europe needs an interdisciplinary approach to twenty-first century skills and workforce compatibility to seize the huge opportunities of industrial transformation. Our education and training systems must take into account the rapid changes in labor markets, be able to anticipate and provide the necessary knowledge and skills, while adapting to change. We need policies that attract and retain brains. It is therefore important to be proactive, not reactive. It is necessary to retain world-class researchers and teachers in the EU, so that they shape the direction of research, development and training of future personnel, and to promote closer cooperation between education and training, research and the business sector. In addition, career models and working environments should be more conducive to learning. All this should help to lower the barriers to skills development and lead to the full realization of the concept of lifelong learning, in which every adult continues to learn.

While the problem of inequality remains acute in the EU, in countries experiencing rapid economic growth, social inequality is increasing much more—and it is unlikely that it will be possible to solve it by political means alone. For example, in modern China, the gap between the incomes of the population on the ocean coast, i.e. in the industrial belt, and incomes in the mainland regions of China is very significant (Yan, 2023). Artificially curbing the growth of this gap is unlikely to improve income levels in poor regions, but it will clearly cause dissatisfaction among coastal entrepreneurs. China's efforts to maintain tight control over public discontent through total surveillance systems can only be an auxiliary, but by no means the main means of solving this issue. The problem of total surveillance rather draws attention to another form of social inequality that has appeared relatively recently—the digital gap, which only deepens and strengthens wealth inequality.

2.3 The Digital Metamorphosis of Classical Social Policy in China

The Chinese system of governing society may indeed be considered one of the greatest inventions, along with gunpowder and compasses. As early as 400 BC Chinese reformer Shang Yang (商鞅), prime minister of Qin (秦), ordered all the people to divide into groups of 5–10 families. They were supposed to watch over each other and bear the collective responsibility for crimes. The person responsible for the group of families regularly reported to their superiors about the departure and arrival of each person. This system was called “baojia” (保甲): “bao”—a territorial association of at least 10 yards, and “jia”—up to 1000 yards. The division of the population into small blocks with the appointment of a person in charge of each block helped to create a self-regulating system that was advanced at the time. Everyone looked after each other, there was order everywhere (Rowe, 2016).

Currently Chinese authorities have decided to re-apply centuries-old technology. In 2004, Dongcheng District (东城) in Beijing was divided into 1,652 squares. Each square was 100 m × 100 m. It is interesting that, at first, it was done in order to optimize the maintenance process of transformer booths and other infrastructure facilities, such as public toilets. Later, the authorities realized that with the help of such a system it is very easy to control the population. Surveillance cameras were installed everywhere in Dongcheng. In addition, the local authorities and the police involved volunteers-proxies. These volunteers were supposed to patrol the square and report cases of violations of public order or damage to infrastructure objects to the head of the square. He, in turn, transmitted data to a joint information center. Powerful computers were located in the information center, which accumulated information from cameras and volunteers. In the database of the joint information center, not only each infrastructure object, but also the population of its location was distributed by squares (approximately 200–250 people) and taken into account. The person responsible for the square had to report all the changes: someone left the area, others, on the contrary, arrived. At the same time, all information systems were combined into a single management system, so the movement of people was recorded: for example, if a person changed his place of residence within the district, the database reports that he moved there. During the three years of the experiment in Beijing’s Dongcheng district, the number of social unrest and conflicts was reduced by 35% (Verbeek, 2020: 115).

The authorities began to try to work according to the same scheme in other cities: Shanghai, Yantai, and Guangzhou. But these were rather initiatives and experiments of local authorities. At the national level, network management was undertaken in 2011.

At the beginning of 2011, the “Arab Spring” occurred in the Middle East. The wave of protests swept through many countries of the Arab world, and in some of them, led to the overthrow of the regime or a protracted civil war. Moreover, social networks and the Internet played a major role in the organization of protest movements. Modern media had made it possible to mobilize thousands of people and organize mass riots on a matter of days. The authorities of some countries tried at the last moment to limit the spread of information in some risk points. Tunisian authorities, for example, restricted access to LiveJournal. In Egypt, the largest providers turned off the Internet at the behest of the Hosni Mubarak regime. But these measures did not help—it was too late (Josua & Edel, 2021).

In China, these events were watched with alarm, unwittingly projecting them onto their own troubled regions in the west and northwest of the country. In July 2011, the Central Committee of the CPC and the State Council of the People's Republic of China issued "Proposals on Strengthening Innovations in Social Management" (中共中央国务院梅实方法社社新了管理的管理). The document was not published in open access, but some quotes from it on Chinese government portals and in the media suggest that a large part of the document was devoted to network management (Zhou, 2014).

It seems that traditional communication ethics is becoming useless: students should learn about obedience rather than moral reflection. Instead of moral authority came control of AI, instead of consciousness and conscience—fear of state surveillance. Scientific research should serve to increase the power of artificial intelligence, not the power of humanity. Instead culture as a mode of human creativity and freedom seemed to have descended into a culture of robot imitation.

For leaders of China it became clear that network management is a useful mechanism, but surveillance cameras and security guards alone cannot be dispensed with here. A total interconnected control system of all spheres of life—both real and virtual—is needed. Chen Quango (陈全国) showed how this can be done.

In August 2011, a new party secretary, Chen Quango, was appointed to the Tibet Autonomous Region. And he immediately began to implement the ideas of network management, and with significant innovations. He also divided all urban areas into squares. And put a small police station every 500 meters. Of course, surveillance cameras with facial recognition technology were installed literally at every step. The data from the cameras of sub-departmental squares is received and processed in these police stations. At the same time, due to the proximity of the stations to each other, a police patrol can appear on the spot in one minute in case of any emergency. Also, unlike in Beijing's Dongcheng district, where the patrols of the squares were carried out by volunteer militiamen, Chen used only police officers to carry out this task in Tibet. If from 2007 to 2011, 2,830 police officers were hired in Tibet, then during the five-year period 2011–2016, 12,313 new employee officers have already arrived to protect public order (Zenz & Leibold, 2017a).

All these measures turned out to be very effective: during the five years Chen Quango was in office in Tibet, there was not a single case of mass protest, there were only eight acts of self-immolation (a common way of expressing individual protest among Tibetans), while there were 150 such acts throughout the country for the same period. Chen thus established himself as the most successful fighter for stability. Therefore, in 2016, he was sent to an even more unstable region—the Xinjiang Uyghur Autonomous Region (XUAR).

2.4 Total Digitalization of Police Network as Anti-utopia-like Surveillance

The Chinese authorities have always thought that Xinjiang is a ticking time bomb, but especially after the "Arab Spring". There are strong separatist and radical sentiments in the region, home to more than 10 million Muslim Uyghurs. In 2008, there were mass riots. In 2013, suicide bombers blew up a car right in the central Tiananmen Square (天安门) in Beijing. In 2014, radical Uyghurs staged a massacre at a train station in Kunming, the capital of Yunnan province, and an explosion at a market in Urumqi (the administrative center of Xinjiang). After these events, the President of the People's Republic of China, Xi Jinping, called for "setting up networks from the ground to the sky" to eradicate terrorism (Supreme People's Procuratorate of the People's Republic of China, 2014).

Chen Quango approached this task responsibly. First, as in Tibet, he set up police stations 500 meters away. The number of police officers has increased significantly in recent years. For example, 5,800 police officers were hired in this region from 2003 to 2008. Between 2009 and 2016, 40,000 vacancies were created. In 2016 alone, 90,000 new police officers were hired (Zenz & Leibold, 2017b).

In the region, there are as many surveillance cameras for every 10,000 residents as in other parts of the country, several million people are monitored. According to the calculations of the analytical company IHS Markit, more than a half of world's surveillance cameras are located in China. "Higher estimate by IHS Markit put the number at 626 million CCTV cameras in China, which equates to 432.2 per 1,000 people" (Lin, 2022). A significant part of them will, of course, be supplied in Xinjiang.

However, Xinjiang's security system is not limited to this. Each resident underwent iris scanning. This is done such that the identity card cannot be forged. In addition, police databases store photos of all registered residents, which are connected to a neural network, based on which the face recognition system works. Thus, street cameras in automatic mode can monitor the movement of any person in the city. In many shopping centers, scanners are installed in front of the entrance that recognize faces and identify the identity of visitors. To drive to a gas station, a person must scan his license on a special device, only then the barrier opens and he can enter the gas station. If a person is listed in the police file as a suspect, the system automatically sends an alert to the police station. At the same time, not only people with a criminal past can be suspicious for the police. These can be human rights activists or simply ethnic Uyghur Muslims.

Recently, the Bloomberg agency reports with reference according to a source familiar with the project, authorities have implemented an AI-powered system that automatically alerts police if suspicious individuals deviate more than 300 meters from their usual work-to-home route (Zhai & Chan, 2018).

Special geolocation sensors are installed on every car registered in Xinjiang, according to the government's order. At the same time, a car with license plates from another region cannot simply enter the city. Traffic cameras warn in advance of the approach of a "foreign car" to the city. Every entrance to the big cities of Xinjiang is equipped with special checkpoints. Foreign cars are carefully looked after, and drivers and passengers are checked for documents and photographed.

Police officers walk the streets with special gadgets. This was a mobile content analyzer. They could stop any person on the street and ask for their cell phones. The mobile phone is connected to this gadget, which independently, regardless of the phone model, determines the presence of prohibited, politically sensitive content on it. That is why it is common practice for people to have two phones: they keep one at home and walk with the other on the street. On the other hand, all mobile numbers are registered. Therefore, the authorities still know how many mobile devices a person has.

In Xinjiang, even the circulation of kitchen knives is strictly controlled. You can buy a knife only upon the presentation of an identity card. All sellers of these products are obliged to purchase special equipment. If a person buys a knife, a QR code is laser-engraved on the blade, which contains complete information about the buyer. Only after that, the knife was given to the buyer. Apparently, remembering the massacre in Kunming, the authorities decided to take such extreme measures.

2.5 Health Care Service as Part of the System of Total Digital Control in China

Early detection of serious diseases was aided by the annual free medical check-up that the authorities conducted for the entire population of Xinjiang between the ages of 12 and 65 years. Abdul Kareem Abdulaini had not visited a doctor for more than 40 years. He lives in a remote mountain village in Xinjiang, and getting to a city hospital is an adventure for him. However, the medical workers came to him themselves. They measured blood pressure, took a cardiogram, and did an express blood test. It turned out that the elderly Uyghur had high blood sugar. Soon the doctors will come to him again; if the level of glucose in the blood does not normalize, it will be necessary to start treatment for diabetes. And Tursun Redzep suffered from hypertension for a long time, but he rarely visited doctors. A free examination showed that he had coronary disease and cardiac pneumonia. Tursun Redzep was immediately hospitalized without unnecessary bureaucratic formalities. After four days, the patient became much better (Xinjiang Government Network, 2017).

Similar stories are often told by Xinjiang's official media.

The program began to be conducted in test mode in 2016. In 2017, according to a report on the website of the State Council of the People's Republic of China, 18.8 million people underwent medical examination (Wu, 2015). At the same time, the population of the entire region is 21.8 million people. The county authorities report that "the dispensary comes to every resident of the most remote settlements in the last kilometers" (全國人民的健康就是每個家庭的健康) (Hotan Government Network, 2017). 1.5 billion yuan was spent on the mass survey (Xinhuanet, 2017).

It is officially stated that general dispensation is carried out for the early detection and treatment of diseases and the improvement of population health and medical quality. For a poor region, as well as the creation of digital health histories for the population. Of course, the goal is noble. However, Xinjiang is not the only relatively poor region in the country. Why is the "dispensary for all" only for the people of Xinjiang?

The answer to this question was found by the organization Human Rights Watch (HRW). An investigation revealed that DNA samples were collected from the population of Xinjiang during free health screenings, which were then handed over to law enforcement agencies. "Mass collection of DNA samples is in itself a serious violation of human rights. It is even worse that this is done fraudulently under the guise of a free medical examination", HRW wrote (HRW News, 2017). In support of its concerns, the organization cites the document: "Working instructions for accurate registration and verification of the population of the autonomous region" (全区人生电影电影游实工作指南). The document, according to HRW, was issued by the Steering Group on the Real Name Registration System, Management and Population Services (自明区电影服务管理和实名制工作者线电视安全室家). HRW links to the website of the Aksu city administration, where the full text of this document was published (now the page to which the link was given no longer exists, and it does not even appear in the cache of search engines).

Instead, another document was found: the "Implementation Plan for Accurate Population Registration and Verification of Yining County" (also located in Xinjiang) (People's Government Of Yining County Xinjiang, 2017). The main goal of the program is to collect and verify data on the actual population of the region, including photographs, fingerprints, iris scans, blood type and DNA data from the entire population aged 12 to 65. There are no age restrictions for representatives of focus groups and their relatives.

All data must be collected together and linked to a person's ID number to create an electronic database of the entire population. According to the document, the collection of biometric data (photographs, fingerprints, iris scans) is the responsibility of local law enforcement agencies. The collection of DNA samples is the responsibility of local workers of the State Committee for Health Care and Planned Childbirth of the People's Republic of China (电影生育). Mass collection of DNA samples should be carried out during the general annual free medical examination, the document says.

On its website, HRW provides an unofficial English translation of the "The [Xinjiang Uyghur Autonomous] Region Working Plan on the Accurate Registration and Verification of Population" (Zhai & Chan, 2018). And although it was not possible to find the original document, the text of the found "Implementation Plan for Accurate Registration and Population Verification of Yining County" almost completely matches the text provided by HRW. Therefore, it can be assumed that the document found by human rights defenders was simply removed from the official websites of the administrations and all traces on the Internet were thoroughly cleaned after the high-profile publication of HRW.

2.6 *Biosurveillance and DNA Control in China*

Of course, annual medical examinations are voluntary. However, the authorities launched a large-scale campaign to convince the population of the need for this measure. They perform this extremely persistently. Local television regularly broadcasts stories about happy villagers who were examined without spending a single yuan and who discovered dangerous diseases in time. People quickly receive high-tech medical care and it saved their lives. At the same time, the words of Xi Jinping, which he delivered at the National Congress of Hygiene and Health in 2016, are regularly cited, that "without the health of all the people, it is impossible to build a society of middle prosperity" (没有全民健康, 就没有没有小康) (The Central People's Government, 2016).

What is done in this dispensary? According to the "Plan for the implementation of population dispensation procedures", the program includes a general examination, auscultation (listening to internal organs with a stethoscope), general blood test and glucose test, urinalysis, ECG, ultrasound diagnosis of the liver, kidneys, pancreas, and chest X-ray. At the same time, the patients were not informed of the collection of DNA samples.

What are the dangers to a person who secretes biomaterials? DNA samples are confidential personal data. Their collection without personal consent violates the fundamental human right to bodily integrity, protection of life and health. Therefore, the use of such data must be clearly regulated. Otherwise, they can be used for the total surveillance of people, and at the genetic level.

In the process of life, a person inevitably leaves his genetic traces: for example, saliva on dishes, hair on clothes and furniture, etc. In this way, it is possible to identify and track a person's whereabouts and social circle. This is possible even if a person, for example, has radically changed his appearance, since the genetic code remains the same throughout his life. Moreover, relatives of a wanted person can be identified, tracked and pressured.

There are precedents in China. The police reported the arrest of a serial killer who raped and killed more than 11 women. He had not been caught for many years. With the help of DNA analysis technologies, the killer was identified through his uncle, whose biomaterial had been taken (Jia, 2016).

In Qianwei County, Sichuan Province, health workers went to schools collecting DNA samples from all male students. Why this was done became clear after a while. In this way, the police managed to solve the nine-year-old murder of two store owners—the criminals were targeted through their younger distant relatives who study at the school (Fan et al., 2017).

China has the world's largest DNA database. According to Australian political scientist Ausma Bernotaite research, "started only in 2005, *China* has already entered 68 *million profiles* into its National *DNA Database* (NDNAD)" (Bernotaite, 2020).

The Chinese police plan to increase this figure to 100 million profiles after 2020. This means that as much biomaterial must be collected every year as has been collected in the United States for more than 20 years. The police are enthusiastic about the task at hand. Chinese police authorities insist that the DNA data bank has become a weapon of precise defeat used by the police in the investigation and detection of crimes (DNA 代库手机电影公安电影美查破案的安全制密电影). More than one billion yuan has already been spent for these purposes.

On the other hand, there are no legal obstacles for the Chinese police in this case, which gives them a significant advantage compared to their foreign counterparts. In the US, for example, DNA samples can only be collected from people convicted of serious crimes in most states. In some states, however, there is weakening of human rights protection: the collection of biomaterials can also be carried out from the suspects.

In China, Article 130 of the Criminal Procedure Code states: "To determine the specific circumstances, nature of injuries or physical condition of the victim or suspect, a medical examination may be conducted, and fingerprints, blood, urine and other biological materials may be collected. If the suspect refuses the procedure, the investigators can, if necessary, insist on coercive procedures. Examination and collection of biological materials must be carried out by persons of the same gender as the suspect" (Congressional-Executive Commission on China, 2022). The Criminal Code does not give any other explanations on this issue.

In 2011, the General State Administration of Quality Control, Inspection and Quarantine of the People's Republic of China, together with the State Committee for Standardization of China, published for discussion the draft document "Information Security Technologies—Instructions for the Protection of Personal Data" (information security technology) developed by the Ministry industry and informatization of the People's Republic of China. They note that processing of personal data cannot be carried out without the consent of the person to whom they belong, with the exception of cases provided for by law.

The document does not explain what the cases are. But at the end of December 2017, the same structures released "Information Security Technologies—Personal Data Protection Standards" (上海安全报看 安全下载安全安全设计) (National Information Security Standardization Technical Committee, 2022). The document was developed by the All-China Technical Committee for Standardization in the field of information security and entered into force in May 2018. It states that personal data, including "sensitive" personal data, may be collected, used, transferred and disclosed without the consent of the person to whom they belong, if these actions are directly related to state or public security, national defense, public health protection, important public interests, crime investigation, sentencing and its execution. Biological materials are referred to in the document as "sensitive personal data" and this clause also applies to them.

Of course, sometimes the examination of DNA samples is necessary to solve crimes. However, practice shows that the routine collection and processing of biomaterials is not justified at least for economic reasons. For example, the police of Daqing (northeast of the PRC) collected 340,000 samples. But it helped solve only 136 crimes. According to the representative of the city police, most of the crimes are committed by recidivists, so it is advisable to collect biomaterials only from a certain focus group. Meanwhile, the Xinjiang government has spent more than 60 million yuan on equipment to process DNA samples. Why invest such money? (Fan et al., 2017).

It is interesting that the program of free medical examination and, accordingly, mass collection of DNA began in 2016—exactly when Chen Quanguo took over as Party Secretary of Xinjiang. It can be assumed that Chen decided to build a system of total control: physical, digital and even genetic. By the way, the focus groups that are not subject to age restrictions for DNA collection include migrants who do not have a residence permit in Xinjiang. By combining DNA materials with other big data, such as from surveillance cameras or iris scanners, it is indeed possible to create an all-powerful all-seeing eye that knows every single person in the city.

So the intelligent things transform in the tools of state intelligence services, intelligent technologies become the technologies of total surveillance, humans ceased to be the main link in the network of human-AI-robots, but turned into cogs in the big data processing mechanism. But who will develop this mechanism, who will improve its processing, who will be creative? Will it be AI? Will it be robots? Obviously not. They could act without ethics, but only a moral person could be creative, because only a moral person could be responsible. They could reproduce the program, but just a person with critical thinking could reject one program and adopt a new one.

2.7 *The Mutual Learning of Humans and AI as a Fuse Against Digital Surveillance Dictatorship*

According to eyewitnesses, life in Xinjiang resembles a regime facility. Numerous armed police units and control centers, similar to checkpoints, are divided into city squares, surveillance cameras, and scanners. Of course, the large mass of radical Muslim population in Xinjiang is a serious source of instability in the country. This is still a poor region with high unemployment rates.

Various terrorist organizations, including ISIS, etc., are actively recruiting Xinjiang residents into their ranks. So you can understand the concerns of the authorities. But will hundreds of millions of cameras and collecting biomaterial from millions of people help solve Xinjiang's problem? Will the system be able to keep track of everyone? Will the police car sink in the sea of big data?

Maybe it is not the total control itself that is important, but the idea that Big Brother is watching you all the time? Perhaps these are the same moral restraints that, according to many Chinese researchers, are so lacking in modern society? According to Sophie Richardson, director of the HRWs China office, it is important for people to know that they are under constant surveillance (Kuo & Rauhala, 2022). This does not matter if the police are actually looking at them or not. This will be a subconscious feeling, which, of course, will reflect on their behavior and life.

What will happen to a huge research and production base when the control system is completely rebuilt and adjusted? "Valuable" experience and knowledge can be shared. For example, at the behest of Ecuadorian authorities, the PRC has been implementing a network of digital capture and digital tracking for several years. The China National Import and Export Corporation of Electronics CEIEC has extended its network to Laos, Myanmar, Venezuela, Brazil, Bolivia, Peru. By the way, the only representative office of the company in Europe is in Moscow.

The practice of surveillance dictatorship over human mind and body could spread in other countries, and it is too difficult to resist it from within the country. It is an affair of international security, and it needs to be settling down with international efforts of governments, intelligence services, and perhaps even armies. However, the recognition of people or their stubborn resistance is still the main guarantee of preventing a surveillance dictatorship in their own country.

So, here are the answers to several questions that stood at the beginning of this study. If were AI become a self-sufficient creator of robots, they could be able to integrate into human society only as servants, not the teachers or managers. People easily become hostages to the functionality of robots, but in a much worse sense than expected: people will turn into slaves who only know how to obey orders, rather than spoiled ignoramuses.

The global power dynamics from the perspective of the impact of the use of AI on it should be considered not so much in a superficial assessment of the competition for situational leadership, but as a manifestation of the mutual influence of two parallel processes: machine learning of AI, which is becoming increasingly creative and autonomous, on the one hand, and the mastery by humans of the opportunities offered by AI (Zinchenko et al., 2023a, 2023b). This mutual learning of humans and AI marks a new stage in human evolution, which will globally change not only the political sphere, not only the economic sphere, or other spheres of society, but will change humanity itself, and with it the destiny of all living things on the planet and the planet itself. Since humanity has become a factor of planetary change, and the noosphere has gone beyond the boundaries of planet Earth, humanity has been confidently moving towards the transformation of its power over its entire environment, and not only within the political sphere.

3 Conclusion

China's controversial experience is important material for social learning, and the policy of using AI to solve social, cultural, and economic problems is a practice of social learning. This experience showed both risks and dangers as well as inevitable prospects and new opportunities.

The possibilities of establishing total control over people's behavior, provided by the use of AI, change not only the intensity of social pressure on the individual, but also give this pressure an increasingly global character. If earlier the individual felt the influence of only individual aspects of some global processes, then every year more and more global processes begin to influence practically every person on planet Earth. It is AI that increasingly exerts this influence on social institutions, turning practically every such institution into a global institution. Those social institutions that have not been able to independently master the capabilities of AI are becoming part of another global institution, which fully uses the global advantages provided by AI. That is why the struggle for possession of their own autonomous version of AI is intensifying in modern society. In this struggle, corporations are still forced to turn to the state for help—even if these are the corporations that develop AI. China claims that its strict style of state governance will ensure greater efficiency in the organized spread of its version of AI implementation, and therefore, greater availability and convenience of the Chinese version of AI implementation around the world will provide unattainable global competitive advantages to Chinese manufacturing companies, but also to other Chinese state and non-governmental organizations.

An artificial social environment that includes AI and robots may well be a carrier of human values and culture; however, it is now easier and faster to be the values of dictatorship and the culture of totalitarianism. It is quite possible to replace values and culture with their simplified functional equivalents, as understood by AI and robots, but this will be a decadence, a decline, not a flourishing of culture. Programming cannot be equated with learning, because learning is based on critical thinking and creativity, which cannot be programmed. Therefore, AI can and should be constantly reprogrammed, but this will not be a true training: AI is capable of dictating, being some kind of dictator, but not a proper student.

Therefore, the robots are less capable of learning. AI can fill its memory with vast arrays of data on human values and culture, but it is not capable of mastering them. AI is capable of the kind of self-education that a person will teach, but it cannot teach itself. After all, AI cannot go beyond stereotypical decision-making—it is a great performer but a bad manager. AI and robots are ideal tools for teaching, but they themselves can be teachers only partially, because the main thing they cannot teach a person: robots easily become tyrants, because they are dogmatists, but dogmas are only the initial and smaller part of education. When AI turns to creativity, it produces things that are not human values, and in many cases, go beyond human understanding altogether. Therefore AI and robots barely can replace people in scientific research, politics, and governance in general, although the firsts are capable of being something more than control tools in science—in particular, they greatly facilitate the creation of models and therefore can perform the work of laboratory assistants for researchers and professors, referents for politicians, and advisors for managers.

AI is a wonderful advisor and assistant in the processes of negotiation and the search for rational grounds for democratic consensus-building, liberal moderation of public policy-making, or thoughtful strategic planning of production processes.

It is also likely that AI can become a dangerous tool in the morbid encroachments of authoritarian politicians to establish world domination and a global digital dictatorship. The global dynamics of power are largely determined today not so much by competition between the world's states or global transnational corporations, including those that produce AI, but by competition between democratic and authoritarian styles in introducing AI into social processes—production, policy, cultural projects, etc.

References

Bernotaite, A. (2020). Building of the world's largest DNA database: The China case. In P. Shrivastava, H. R. Dash, J. A. Lorente, & J. Imam (Eds.), *Forensic DNA typing: Principles, applications and advancements* (pp. 639–358). Springer. https://doi.org/10.1007/978-981-15-6655-4_33

Boichenko, M., Bogdanov, V., Vorobiova, L., & Komakha, L. (2022). Perspectives and limits of artificial intelligence development: Stanislaw Lem's ideas today. *AIP Conference Proceedings, 2656*(1), 020020. https://doi.org/10.1063/5.0106369

Bordoni, C. (2022). *Post-society: Social life after the pandemic*. Polity.

Botin, L., de Boer, B., & Børsen, T. (2020). Technology in between the individual and the political: Postphenomenology and critical constructivism. *Research in Philosophy and Technology, 24*(1–2), 1–14. https://doi.org/10.5840/techne2020241

Coeckelbergh, M. (2020). *AI ethics*. The MIT Press.

Congressional-Executive Commission on China. (2022). *Criminal procedure law of the people's republic of China*. https://www.cecc.gov/resources/legal-provisions/criminal-procedure-law-of-the-peoples-republic-of-china

Fan, W., Khan, N., & Lin, L. (2017, December 26). China snares innocent and guilty alike to build world's biggest DNA database. *The Wall Street Journal online*. https://www.wsj.com/articles/china-snares-innocent-and-guilty-alike-to-build-worlds-biggest-dna-database-1514310353?mod=ITP_pageone_0andtesla=yandmg=prod%2Faccountswsj. Accessed December 24, 2024.

Fasman, J. (2021). We see it all. In *Liberty and justice in an age of perpetual surveillance*. Public Affairs.

Filimowicz, M. (2022). *Digital totalitarianism: Algorithms and society*. Routledge.

Foucault, M. (1995). *Discipline and punish: The birth of the prison* (A. Sheridan, Trans.). Vintage Books.

Guzhva, A., Shevchenko, Z., Debych, M., Kudrina, T., & Dudchenko, V. (2022). The discourse of ethical principles of interaction with artificial intelligence as a condition for sustainable development of society. *AIP Conference Proceedings, 2656*(1), 020028. https://doi.org/10.1063/5.0106367

Hotan Government Network. (2017). Minfeng county government website work annual report. [in Chinese]. https://www.xjht.gov.cn/article/show.php?itemid=261252

HRW News. (2017, December 13). China: Minority region collects dna from millions private information gathered by police, under guise of public health program. *Human Rights Watch online*. https://www.hrw.org/news/2017/12/13/china-minority-region-collects-dna-millions

Jia, C. (2016, August 29). DNA tests lead police to Gansu 'Ripper'. *China Daily online*. http://usa.chinadaily.com.cn/china/2016-08/29/content_26622076.htm. Accessed December 24, 2024.

Josua, M., & Edel, M. (2021). The Arab uprisings and the return of repression. *Mediterranean Politics, 26*(5), 586–611. https://doi.org/10.1080/13629395.2021.1889298

Kuo, L., & Rauhala, E. (2022, August 31). U. N. report: China may have committed crimes against humanity in Xinjiang. *The Washington Post online*. https://www.washingtonpost.com/world/2022/08/31/un-china-xinjiang-report/. Accessed 24, December 2024.

Liao, S. M. (Ed.). (2020). *Ethics of artificial intelligence*. Oxford University Press.

Lin, S. (2022, September 16). More Than Half of World's Surveillance Cameras Located in China. *The Epoch Time online*. https://www.theepochtimes.com/more-than-half-of-worlds-surveillance-cameras-located-in-china_4724749.html?welcomeuser=1. Accessed December 24, 2024.

National Information Security Standardization Technical Committee. (2022). *National standard of the people's republic of China*. [in Chinese]. https://www.tc260.org.cn

Oladipo, G. (2025, February 13). Trump and Musk launch mass layoffs at several US federal agencies. *The Guardian online*. https://www.theguardian.com/us-news/2025/feb/13/elon-musk-doge-delete-agencies

One Planet Summit. (2025). *€ 320 B from the European Union for climate*. https://oneplanetsummit.fr/en/coalitions-82/eu-320-b-european-union-climate-274#:~:text=At%20the%20second%20edition%20of,investments%20in%20infrastructure%20through%20the

People's Government Of Yining County Xinjiang. (2017). *Notice on printing and distributing the "implementation plan for accurate population registration and verification in Yining county*. [in Chinese]. https://gov.cn/info/egovinfo/1005/common/inf_content/ynx001-14_A/2017-1122001.htm. Accessed December 24, 2024.

Rowe, P. G., Forsyth, A., & Kan, H. Y. (2016). *China's urban communities: Concepts, contexts, and well-being*. DeGruyter.

Shenk, D. (2006). Surveillance society, EMBO reports. 7 Spec. No, 31–35, https://doi.org/10.1038/sj.embor.7400735

Supreme people's procuratorate of the people's republic of China. (2014, May 30). *Xi Jinping: Adhere to the rule of law in Xinjiang, unite and stabilize Xinjiang for long-term construction* [in Chinese]. https://www.spp.gov.cn/tt/201405/t20140530_73710.shtml

The Central People's Government. (2016). Let a healthy Chinese people live a better life [in Chinese]. *The Central people's government of the people's republic of China website*. http://www.gov.cn/xinwen/2017-09/30/content_5228724.htm

US Department of Homeland Security. (2025). *CBD focus areas – Biosurveillance*. https://www.dhs.gov/science-and-technology/biosurveillance

Verbeek, P.-P. (2020). Politicizing Postphenomenology. In G. Miller & A. Shew (Eds.), *Reimagining philosophy and technology, reinventing Ihde, philosophy of engineering and technology* (Vol. 33, pp. 141–155). Springer.

Wu, Q. (2015). Gridding, mass line and social management. Innovation. A comparative study of gridding management in China from an anthropological-political perspective. *The China Nonprofit Review*, *7*(1), 110–138. https://doi.org/10.1163/18765149-12341288

Xinhuanet. (2017, November 1). Xinjiang invests more than 1.5 billion yuan to complete new round of national health examination project [in Chinese]. *Xinhua English.news.cn*, http://www.xinhuanet.com/2017-11/01/c_1121891066.htm

Xinjiang Government Network. (2017, November 2). *National health checkup work completed* [in Chinese]. http://www.gov.cn/xinwen/2017-11/02/content_5236389.htm

Yan, X. (2023). Saidatulakmal Mohd, trends and causes of regional income inequality in China. *Sustainability*, *15*(9), 7673. https://doi.org/10.3390/su15097673

York, J. C. (2021). *Silicon values: The future of free speech under surveillance capitalism*. Verso.

Zenz, A., & Leibold, J. (2017a). Chen Quanguo: The strongman behind Beijing's securitization strategy in Tibet and Xinjiang. *China Brief*, *17*(12). https://jamestown.org/program/chen-quanguo-the-strongman-behind-beijings-securitization-strategy-in-tibet-and-xinjiang/ Access ed 24, December 2024.

Zenz, A., & Leibold, J. (2017b). Xinjiang's rapidly evolving security state. *China Brief*, *14*(4), https://jamestown.org/program/xinjiangs-rapidly-evolving-security-state/

Zhai, K., & Chan, E. (2018, January 17). China use facial recognition to fence In villagers in far West. *Bloomberg news. Europe edition online*. https://www.bloomberg.com/news/articles/2018-01-17/china-said-to-test-facial-recognition-fence-in-muslim-heavy-area?leadSource=uverify%20wall

Zhou, H. (2014). Social innovation in China: An empirical study based on data from two sessions of the China social innovation award (CSIA). *Comparative Economic and Social Systems*, *4*, 170–183.

Zinchenko, V. (2022). Informational technologies as an integrative component of the sustainable development goals and global cooperation strategy in research activities of education systems. *AIP Conference Proceedings*, *2656*(1), 020027. https://doi.org/10.1063/5.0106366

Zinchenko, V., Boichenko, M., Slyusarenko, O., Popovych, M., Radchenko, L., Iehupov, M., & Bazeliuk, V. (2023a). New dimensions and dead ends in AI development: Impact and responsibility of science and higher education. *E3S Web of Conferences*, *419*(2), 02001. https://doi.org/10.1051/e3sconf/202341902001

Zinchenko, V., Boichenko, M., Slyusarenko, O., Popovych, M., Radchenko, L., & Polishchuk, O. (2023b). Science trends and Digital immortality: AI accelerates movement towards an unattainable goal. *E3S Web of Conferences*, *419*(2), 02002. https://doi.org/10.1051/e3sconf/202341902002

Zinchenko, V. V., Boichenko, M. I., & Popovych, M. D. (2021). Higher education and sustainable development promotion: International potential and its elaboration in Ukraine. In *IOP Conference Series: Earth and Environmental Science*, 635(1), 012012. https://doi.org/10.1088/1755-1315/635/1/012012

Zubchyk, O. A., Boichenko, M. I., Sytnyk, G. P., & Levkulych, V. V. (2021). New tendencies of sustainable development: Providing personal security and quality of life as a new national security paradigm. In *E3S Web of Conferences*, *277*, 02003. ICEES 2021. https://doi.org/10.1051/e3sconf/202127702003

Strategic Assets of the Twenty-First Century: AI, Information, and Global Dominance

Carlos Enrique Fernandez-Garcia, Samantha Gómez Gamboa, and Luciana Fernandez-Valdivieso

1 Theoretical Framework

1.1 Background

Rid (2012) redefines cyberwarfare not as an act of war, but as modern forms of sabotage, espionage, and subversion. The author challenges the dominant narrative in political and military circles that suggests cyberwarfare is an imminent threat.

The methodology is qualitative with an analytical-conceptual approach, based on Clausewitz's theoretical framework. The study concludes that cyberwarfare is more metaphor than proven reality. Alarmist discourse confuses the true digital threats. Precise terminology—sabotage, espionage, subversion—is required to define the facts. Thus, political and military responses can be aligned with this understanding, avoiding misguided decisions or overreactions to incidents that do not constitute acts of war in the strict sense.

For their part, Jensen et al. (2023) focus primarily on the absence of defined legal and doctrinal frameworks for the experimental use of artificial intelligence in warfare, especially in artificial intelligence exercises, which pose ethical, strategic, and legal risks. The purpose of the research is to examine how the armed forces experiment with algorithmic technologies without adequate oversight, and how these actions exceed the conventional limits of the law of armed conflict. The approach used is qualitative and is based on the examination of future scenarios,

C. E. Fernandez-Garcia (✉) · S. Gómez Gamboa · L. Fernandez-Valdivieso
Universidad Nacional Mayor de San Marcos, Lima, Peru
e-mail: carlosenrique.fernandez@unmsm.edu.pe
e-mail: samantha.gomezg@unmsm.edu.pe
e-mail: luciana.fernandezv@unmsm.edu.pe

F. Roumate (ed.), *AI, Information, and Global Dynamics*, Contributions to International Relations,
https://doi.org/10.1007/978-3-032-13528-5_3

historical situations, and institutional documents related to military innovation in artificial intelligence.

Mazarr (2015) identifies the main problem as the increase in conflicts that develop in the so-called gray zone, that is, an intermediate space between stable peace and open war. The objective of the research is to understand the particularities of this new type of conflict and suggest tactics for the US to deal with it. An analytical and qualitative method is adopted, based on literature review, case analysis, and strategic assessment. Among the findings, it is noted that conventional methods of defense and deterrence are insufficient in the face of strategies such as misleading content, financial coercion, or the use of intermediary actors. In conclusion, it is indicated that in order to effectively address the gray zone, a conceptual and operational transformation is needed, including new theories.

Van Puyvelde (2015) presents a challenge in the conceptual ambiguity of the term hybrid warfare, which is frequently used but lacks a precise operational definition, causing strategic disorientation among military and political leaders. The article aims to dismantle the concept that hybrid warfare is an innovation and to argue that conflicts have always combined traditional and unusual strategies.

The approach is reflective and argumentative in nature, based on a critical analysis of the use of the term in political discourse, military documents, and specialized media. Among the findings, it is noted that entities such as NATO have not managed to establish a single definition of the term, and that the widespread use of the term has caused more confusion than the creation of effective strategies. In his conclusions, the writer suggests setting aside the term "hybrid" and focusing on understanding the complexity and interrelation of real threats, formulating responses based on the particular study of each circumstance and not on generic classifications that are useless for decision-making.

1.1.1 Literature Review

Algorithmic warfare represents a fundamental transformation in the nature of conflict, extending beyond physical battlefields to encompass the digital, psychological, and cognitive realms. This new confrontation is fought with algorithms and data, seeking to conquer minds and shape perceptions rather than territories.

Journalists are also using generative AI in writing and editing material, transcribing material, and fact-checking and research. This reduces the time it takes to do these tasks and increases overall efficiency, which in turn frees journalists to devote more time to analytical and investigative tasks.

Artificial intelligence is also used to optimize material to improve search engine traffic and create headlines and tailor narrative styles to certain audiences. However, automating the production of material damages the quality of information.

Artificial intelligence has revolutionized content distribution, enabling unprecedented personalization. Artificial intelligence algorithms examine large volumes of user data, including demographics, behavior, and preferences, in order to provide highly personalized content suggestions. Online streaming platforms such as Netflix and Spotify use these algorithms to recommend movies, series, and music tailored to personal tastes, optimizing the user experience and boosting engagement.

Artificial Intelligence also enables real-time content personalization, monitoring user interactions and opinions to ensure that material remains relevant and engaging. News aggregators and personalized newsletters use AI to provide up–to-date updates tailored to each user's particular interests.

While AI offers unprecedented efficiencies in the creation and distribution of media content, it also poses significant risks, such as the proliferation of false information, social polarization through filter bubbles, and the erosion of individual autonomy and human responsibility.

The term "AI Cold War" was first used in 2018 by Nicholas Thompson and Ian Bremmer, motivated by growing geopolitical mediation in response to China's 2017 "AI Development Plan," which aspires to be the leader in AI by 2030 (GZERO Media, 2024).

The effectiveness of algorithmic warfare lies in pattern detection, reasoning, and problem solving with human cognition. This involves the acquisition of training data for cognitive learning, i.e., the acquisition of generalizable knowledge that allows for the prediction of unknown future scenarios.

AI systems should have the ability to autonomously develop and determine their courses of action through their own decision-making, responsiveness, and situational awareness. This will include generating and rejecting options, merging decision criteria, and acting on processed data.

Dandurand et al. (2023) refer to "algorithmic warfare" as a new type of conflict, silent and enduring, that unfolds in the digital realm through the application of algorithms and large amounts of data, rather than the use of conventional weapons. Its main objective is not to take physical territory, but to influence the perceptions, emotions, and choices of individuals, using the information space as context.

Large transnational technology companies are in constant conflict for global hegemony. In this dispute, artificial intelligence platforms seek to impose their dominance in the arena of "algorithmic warfare," despite the doctrinal stagnation in which they have been mired by military institutions clinging to traditional doctrines (Jensen et al., 2023).

This method represents a break with conventional wars, centered on military force and material resources, by prioritizing cognitive dominance through computer systems that modify the opponent's decision-making processes through strategic manipulation of information.

The performance of social media plays a significant role in this armed conflict, as it has become an instrument of corporations whose power lies in the subjugation of information capable of shaping and influencing public perception. Bisht (2025) even argues that the management of these narratives is as important as the control of territories.

In today's conflicts, information is an instrument of domination. Fake news and proxy media manipulate perceptions, erode institutions, and polarize societies. Emotions and biases amplify their impact. In response, media literacy and critical thinking are essential to resisting misinformation and protecting the truth in contexts of war and crisis.

According to Dandurand et al. (2023), information becomes a strategic weapon in contemporary conflicts. Proxy media and fake news alter public perceptions, weaken institutions, and polarize societies. Emotions and biases enhance their effect. In response to this, media literacy and critical thinking are essential for combating false information and safeguarding the truth in situations of conflict and crisis (Bisht, 2025).

The idea of global supremacy of world information encompasses the accumulation of digital power among certain nations and large technology corporations, raising concerns about privacy, large-scale surveillance, and personal independence.

According to El Souki (2025), the emergence of an "algorithmic dictatorship" shows a transformation in the power relations between conventional state actors and technological elites, generating fears of an unregulated expansion of Artificial Intelligence that weakens democratic principles and citizens' rights. This type of conflict is characterized by the increasing automation of tactical and strategic decisions, in which algorithms are progressively replacing human judgment.

Tatlisu (2024) argumenta que los medios de comunicación tienen un impacto significativo en la visión pública acerca de la IA, creando tanto confianza como miedo. Aunque propagan ventajas en salud y educación, también fomentan relatos alarmistas acerca del desempleo y el control. La función de los medios es crucial para desarrollar un entendimiento balanceado y crítico de esta tecnología en ascenso (Tatlisu, 2024).

The convergence of algorithmic warfare, media tactics, and global information supremacy poses challenges and possibilities in multiple areas that require critical analysis. As military operations increasingly expand into the realms of data and narrative, understanding these interrelationships is crucial to dealing with the complexities of contemporary conflict and governance (Sustainability Directory, 2025).

Aithor (2024) argues that the role of the media in this dynamic is multifaceted, particularly in societies in transition where ownership structures and political pressures affect journalistic practices.

In these circumstances, media ownership can significantly influence autonomy and pluralism in the dissemination of information, an essential element in the formation of public discourse and policy outcomes (Aithor, 2024).

The use of critical media theories of the mass media, such as the propaganda model (Herman & Chomsky, 1988), highlights how media operations are often synchronized with the interests of elites, shaping narratives that impact public perception and political decisions. Rather than acting as a counterweight to power, they function as propaganda tools that manufacture the consensus necessary to maintain the status quo.

Gibson (2024) highlights the growing complexity of information warfare, especially through algorithmic manipulation to promote certain narratives and, simultaneously, eradicate dissent.

Artificial Intelligence has the ability to tailor *fake news* campaigns to specific target audiences, making them more effective on a macro and micro scale. AI enhances the support of information operations for irregular warfare through the study of large volumes of data, including social media, with the aim of recognizing target audiences, understanding the psychological profiles of individuals, and adjusting compelling messages accordingly.

In this context, Artificial Intelligence algorithms also have the ability to optimize and coordinate the content and distribution of these messages to enhance their influence on the target audience. Some actors have used the media to amplify preferred narratives, exacerbating conflicts and complicating peace processes by spreading fake news and strategic propaganda, turning the media into battlefields. That is why we pose the following problem:

How does the use of artificial intelligence in both traditional and digital media affect the configuration of news narratives during the algorithmic war for global technological supremacy?

1.2 Author's Main Hypothesis or Position

The use of artificial intelligence in the media significantly influences the configuration of news narratives, favoring the geopolitical interests of large technology corporations in the context of the algorithmic war for global supremacy.

The specific hypotheses are:

- The implementation of algorithms in digital media prioritizes content that reinforces discourses favorable to hegemonic technological actors, to the detriment of critical or alternative voices.
- The automation of information curation through AI generates a manipulated public perception, which impacts the formation of political opinion and the legitimization of dominant technological models.

1.3 Objective

The main purpose of this research is to analyze the influence of the use of artificial intelligence in the media on the configuration of news narratives, within the framework of the algorithmic war for global technological leadership.

The specific objectives include:

- Analyze how algorithms implemented in digital media prioritize content aligned with the interests of hegemonic technology corporations.

- Examine how automated curation of information through AI influences public perception and the legitimization of dominant technological models.

1.4 Methods

The methodology used in this chapter is based on a theoretical approach that integrates a decolonial perspective and sociotechnical analysis. It examines previous research on the impact of artificial intelligence in countries of the Global South, reviews specialized literature and corporate policies, and conducts a normative and comparative analysis of data protection regulations in those nations.

The methodology used in this study focuses on a theoretical and multidisciplinary approach, based on a critical review of academic studies, institutional reports, and international standards related to algorithmic systems in military contexts. It also incorporates specific examples that illustrate ethical dilemmas related to autonomy, bias, and transparency in algorithms. Its goal is to suggest robust and culturally relevant regulatory guidelines for the ethical advancement of AI-based military technologies.

1.5 Justification and Relevance of the Study

The control of information flows and algorithmic systems applied to the media ecosystem has become a sophisticated way of exercising global power. The exercise of that power depends largely on the regulation that states exert over information in their nations (Hobbes, 2008).

This research is significant because it analyzes the role of artificial intelligence (AI) and its mechanisms as key instruments of domination in algorithmic warfare. It warns that this technology deepens the gaps between technological powers (the US, China, the EU) and countries in the Global South, which play a subordinate role as passive consumers.

Its relevance lies in demonstrating how algorithmic technologies, through data management, narratives, and automated decision-making systems, reinforce structural inequalities. Methodologically, the study examines power dynamics and possible strategies for digital resistance. In practical terms, the aim is to build critical and regulatory frameworks that democratize the use of AI, guaranteeing equitable access to information and strengthening technological autonomy as a means of defense against global information manipulation.

From a theoretical perspective, the aim is to reveal new forms of colonization mediated by data exploitation and unequal access to AI infrastructure. This phenomenon also challenges the development of conventional media narratives and government propaganda, which attempt to dominate the debate on algorithmic warfare commitments. However, the interaction of citizen journalism with state narratives creates a complex landscape, as misleading content and propaganda can mask the truth, making it difficult for the public to interpret conflicts.

The dangers of this new algorithmic colonialism lie in the control of information. Through a critical examination of this dynamic, this research seeks to provide theoretical, methodological, and regulatory frameworks that enable technological autonomy and information sovereignty in the Global South. This perspective is vital to inform ambiguous strategies of geopolitical domination, on the one hand, and resistance, inclusion, and regulation with respect to the concrete forms of regulation, on the other.

1.6 Results and Discussion

Algorithms as socio-technical constructs. Dakakni (2025) argues that Artificial Intelligence, beyond its position as an innovation in the fields of science, education, and business, also acts as a powerful instrument of domination at the global level. Algorithms as socio-technical constructs, neither neutral nor universal, reproduce and amplify pre-existing social inequalities and legitimize algorithmic hegemony (Burrell & Fourcade, 2021; Dakakni, 2025).

Gould et al. (2023) warn of the dangers of consolidating algorithmic warfare techniques under the justification of mixed threats and stress the importance of reconsidering legal and democratic frameworks in the face of military technological progress.

The role of the media in algorithmic warfare. Based on the analysis, it can be seen that the role of the media in the conflict of algorithms has undergone considerable evolution, impacting public perception and government policies. The growth of digital technology and citizen journalism challenges narratives controlled by governments and transnational technology companies, but it also contributes to information overload and misinformation, often amplified by algorithms.

According to our analysis, the use of artificial intelligence in algorithms that control the visibility of content in digital media not only determines what is displayed, but also what is concealed. By prioritizing certain narratives, these platforms often ignore critical or alternative voices, consolidating an unbalanced circulation of information in line with prevailing corporate or power logics. Kumar et al. (2023) refer to Natural Language Processing (NLP) as a means of detecting narratives, emotions, and fake news in real time.

Artificial Intelligence is used to produce and disseminate automated content (texts, photos, videos), enhancing propaganda and information manipulation in large-scale digital media. Buchyn et al. (2023) warn about the use of algorithms in fake news and psychological warfare campaigns, operating on platforms such as Twitter, Facebook, and Instagram. The ethical, legal, and strategic challenges of using Artificial Intelligence in armed conflicts are addressed, such as the lack of transparency, algorithmic bias, and the need for international regulations.

Mirghahari (2023) mentions that artificial intelligence (AI) has become a powerful tool in irregular warfare, especially through misleading content and economic sabotage. Artificial intelligence facilitates the automation of misleading content campaigns through deepfakes, audio, images, and messages created to alter emotions, disorient opponents, and destabilize economies. Artificial intelligence transforms irregular conflict by driving deception and manipulation, demanding defensive skills such as deepfake identification and tactical teams to protect public perception and stability.

Media coverage of emerging technologies and Artificial Intelligence often focuses on elite newspapers and can be influenced by public or famous personalities, sometimes approaching issues from a science fiction perspective. Sensationalist and hyperbolic narratives about AI in the media can distract attention from present ethical and legal dangers and promote excessive confidence in the technology.

In a digital environment controlled by Artificial Intelligence, Dakakni (2025) argues that social media helps to consolidate discourses on progress, innovation, and capitalism, without critically questioning the global impacts of technology. Afina (2022) asserts that the mass media have played a fundamental role in shaping society's thinking about artificial intelligence. Its questionable narrative includes exaggerated and sensationalist claims.

AI as a tool for global political domination. For Ash (2025), the dominant narratives about AI reinforce the power of tech companies and the nations that represent them, while undermining workers' rights. The convergence of the media, the algorithm war, and transnational tech companies has brought about significant changes in the landscape of contemporary conflicts and public discourse (Ash, 2025).

The study shows that as consumer-focused technology companies become increasingly involved in warfare, the repercussions transcend conventional military purposes to cover broader social effects, changing the way information is disseminated and manipulated in military and civilian settings.

From this, it can be inferred that the hegemonic power of information is evident in the accumulation of digital power, raising concerns about privacy, large-scale surveillance, and personal independence. Data supremacy presents challenges to data sovereignty, which aims to distribute dominance.

The emergence of an "algorithmic dictatorship" shows a transition of authority toward technological elites. This has geopolitical consequences, as countries fight for supremacy in technology.

De Clerck et al. (2024) consider the media to be the discursive battleground of this algorithmic conflict, where official news and conspiracy theories coexist. These act as amplifiers of information manipulation for political and ideological purposes. Disinformation adapts to the local context to gain effectiveness (Šlerka et al., 2023).

Mirghahari (2023) demonstrates in his study how AI algorithms can generate false information that triggers real effects. This technology transforms algorithmic warfare through automated malicious content, redefining national security on multiple fronts. AI is used to produce and spread automated content (text, photos, videos), boosting propaganda and false information in large-scale digital media. Buchyn et al. (2023) warn about the use of algorithms in fabricated narrative campaigns and psychological warfare, operating on platforms such as Twitter, Facebook, and Instagram.

It has been demonstrated that the mass media sees the ethical, legal, and strategic challenges of using artificial intelligence in armed conflicts, such as the lack of transparency, algorithmic bias, and the need for international regulations.

The manipulation of information to shape narratives and influence public perception is a type of information warfare that viralizes emotional content (De Cleck, 2024). Artificial intelligence technology, such as facial recognition systems and radio frequency identification (RFID) technologies, is being used to track and locate people, originating in the military and commercial spheres.

In this scenario, artificial intelligence allows for the formation of ideological subjugation, backed by the discourses of capitalism and technological efficiency. This trend is evident in companies such as Amazon, Netflix, and Match.com, which have seen significant increases in profits due to the intensive use of algorithmic systems.

As a result of the analysis, it is identified that the anthropomorphization of AI leads to the formulation of questions and the underestimation of current dangers surrounding the supposed state of consciousness achieved by a chatbot such as Google's LaMDA. Such narratives undermine meaningful discussion about the real ethical and legal dangers of AI: bias, loss of languages and their variability, social hypervigilance, the weakening of privacy, and democratic accountability.

Furthermore, these media narratives can promote a kind of ethical whitewashing by portraying technologies that are not as sophisticated as they are safe or impartial, when they can become instruments of power that intensify inequalities.

Altmann and Sauer (2017) argue that the media can unwittingly become collaborators in the algorithmic war by focusing the debate on science fiction myths rather than on the social, legal, and political responsibility of those who develop and implement these technologies.

Algorithms transform the dynamics of authority and responsibility (Burrell & Fourcade, 2021). The media act as amplifiers of strategic government or corporate discourse, without questioning the ethical and humanitarian implications, as the implications in terms of mass surveillance, job losses, or biopower are not addressed (Altmann & Sauer, 2017; Dakakni, 2025).

McLennan et al. (2023) warn that these discourses tend to overlook critical considerations about the social, ethical, and economic repercussions of Artificial Intelligence, reinforcing prevailing narratives that prioritize economic development and national security over equality and inclusion.

Møller et al. (2022) question the ability of algorithms to ethically mediate informational content. When used to prioritize or filter news, they can negatively impact news diversity and democratic access to information. Added to this picture is criticism of the resolution of ethical dilemmas through technical solutions, without an in-depth analysis of the power structures or the prejudice they perpetuate.

EU DisinfoLab (2022) warns of a number of common practices in algorithmic warfare: state media as key propaganda actors that function as the media arms of their governments, and mirror websites that copy content and republish it to circumvent blocks or regulations.

From the theoretical framework used, the use of AI promotes countless ethical dilemmas and dangers. Several of these include, but are not limited to, data bias and discrimination, concerns about eroded privacy and the lack of a clearly responsible person, the impact on employment caused by automation, and the militarization of lethal autonomous systems and surveillance in general. Similarly, De Clerck (2024) warns of a semantic war, based on the use of bots, coordinated accounts, response generation, and narrative automation.

According to our interpretation, AI-powered tools enable media companies to gain a deep understanding of audience behavior and content performance. Chatbots and virtual assistants enhance the user experience by offering real-time assistance and immediate answers to questions, thereby increasing customer loyalty and satisfaction. AI-powered content personalization leads to greater user engagement and longer time spent on platforms. Media manipulation (such as bots and social media) is integrated into asymmetric conflicts (Jensen et al., 2023).

The speed of technological advancement far outpaces the ability of legal and ethical frameworks to adapt, creating governance gaps and challenges in assigning responsibility.

According to our interpretation, studies explore the concept of "algorithmic violence" to describe the harm caused by AI algorithms, relating it to ideas of structural, bureaucratic, or epistemic violence. However, there is skepticism about the usefulness and accuracy of this term, arguing that other concepts such as bias, discrimination, exclusion, injustice, and lack of transparency better characterize these problems. The need for a sensitive and critical approach to the presentation of AI is emphasized, promoting meaningful and realistic debates, fostering technical literacy among policymakers, and developing ethical and legal frameworks.

The gospel of sensationalist apocalypse. The dual discourse of the media includes sensationalist and apocalyptic statements. For example, Dauvergne (2020) refers to the media in terms of its role in reproducing technodeterministic discourses about artificial intelligence and the "end of work." Although they are not the main focus of the text, the author warns that the media often intensify polarized and simplified narratives, either celebrating technological efficiency and progress or warning of an impending employment catastrophe.

Stories and imaginaries related to artificial intelligence, often incorporated into national strategies, tend to represent it as an inevitable and transformative technological advance, either as an unparalleled revolution or as the continuation of an enormous historical heritage. These stories express hopes and fears, and establish artificial intelligence as essential for global competitiveness and social well-being. These narrative structures can have a performative effect, shaping expectations and guiding the future paths of technology. Disinformation is no longer simply an additional result of war: it is an essential tactic (Bisht, 2024).

For their part, Chuan et al. (2019) argue that the media often broadcast polarized discourses that fluctuate between utopian optimism and dystopian fear, causing ambivalence in collective perception. Training in media and technology criticism is essential to engage citizens in discussions about artificial intelligence.

According to Stewart (2024), the future of media ideologies and perceptions of artificial intelligence (AI) is expected to become increasingly polarized and commercialized as AI technology becomes more deeply embedded in everyday life and political discourse. On the other hand, Rowe (2022) believes that this change may be marked by a divergence of narratives, as some highlight the existential dangers of artificial intelligence, prioritizing future doubts over the present challenges facing employees and society. As we approach 2030, there are alarming estimates about the consequences for labor rights and the overall quality of work if current narratives about AI remain unchallenged.

Sensationalist media coverage of the use of Artificial Intelligence can create a false perception of control and effectiveness, undermining the need for human oversight and ethical deliberation in the contexts of algorithmic warfare (Stewart & Hinds, 2023). Dwivedi et al. (2021) emphasize the urgent need for ethical frameworks, algorithmic transparency, and inclusive governance. Inclusive and critical governance of intelligent systems is urgently needed (Strahovnik, 2022). Frecuentemente, se utilizan los medios de comunicación en operaciones psicológicas para impactar en la moral y el estado psicológico del adversario y de la población en su conjunto. Por ejemplo, las operaciones de psicología de la información en Ucrania emplean medios contemporáneos para propagar mensajes esenciales y manipular la opinión pública (Markovets et al., 2023)

The need for ethics and algorithmic governance. Strahovnik (2022) examines the ethical issues of artificial intelligence from two perspectives: a technocratic one, focused on technical solutions, and a humanistic one, which emphasizes social, cultural, and political values. He argues that the ethics of artificial intelligence must go beyond algorithmic programming to incorporate critical and interdisciplinary reflection. He suggests a hybrid ethic that fuses technical accuracy with human sensitivity, and advocates for conscious, inclusive, and democratic governance.

As the media progressively incorporates artificial intelligence technologies, clarity in their application has become a significant concern. Arguedas (2024) argues that journalists and media experts advocate for more accurate communication about the role of artificial intelligence in content generation to promote trust among the audience. However, there is a complicated balance: although transparency can increase credibility, the simple fact of knowing about the use of AI can generate mistrust among the audience, especially if AI-produced content is seen as less reliable than human-generated news.

Analysis of the results achieved facilitates the formation of a strong link between the findings and the hypotheses proposed at the outset, corroborating that artificial intelligence, rather than functioning as an impartial instrument, operates in contexts of power that benefit certain geopolitical and business interests. The data collected shows that the algorithms used in the media not only structure content in an automated way, but also do so based on logic that fits ideological and commercial positioning strategies.

This dynamic confirms the hypothesis that artificial intelligence drives the creation of dominant narratives, transforming certain technological models into undisputed icons and leaving other perspectives invisible. Furthermore, the critical study shows that this form of automated curation not only affects the quality of accessible information but also modifies the conditions of public debate, weakening news pluralism and reducing the space for democratic deliberation. In this context, Artificial Intelligence should not be interpreted solely as technological progress, but as a socio-technical apparatus that reproduces structural inequalities in access to knowledge, strengthening both discursive and technological hierarchies. This reflection calls for an urgent review of current regulatory frameworks and raises fundamental questions about the legitimacy of the power exercised by digital platforms in the field of global information.

2 Conclusion

The role of the media in the information war is complex, with the potential both to manipulate and to resist these tactics. A balanced approach is needed that promotes diversity, security, and effective regulation.

This study has shown that artificial intelligence has become a crucial tool for shaping information narratives in the context of an algorithmic war for global technological supremacy. The strength of algorithms lies not only in their ability to handle large amounts of information, but also in their role as mediators between events and the way they are presented to the public, thus replacing the conventional role of the journalist as editorial reviewer.

In relation to the first specific objective, it was found that the algorithms applied by media platforms prioritize content that benefits dominant technology corporations. These platforms, operating under business models based on pay-per-click monetization and customized segmentation, tend to promote narratives linked to their strategic allies, ignoring alternative or dissenting discourses. Thus, the logic of capital belies technological neutrality.

The results obtained confirm the main hypothesis of the study, according to which the use of artificial intelligence in the media actively contributes to the construction of narratives aligned with the interests of large technology corporations, thus promoting dominant technological models that are presented as unquestionable truths. Similarly, the specific hypotheses are validated, as it is evident that algorithms systematically prioritize content that reinforces the discourses of hegemonic actors, displacing critical or alternative voices. In addition, automated information curation indirectly but decisively influences the formation of political opinion, consolidating information power structures that shape public perception according to prevailing economic and geopolitical interests.

With regard to automated curation, it has been shown that artificial intelligence exerts a considerable influence on public perception. Recommendation systems not only establish consumption, but also shape the way audiences interpret reality, creating information bubbles and echo chamber effects. In this way, algorithmic recommendation systems not only condition the consumption of information, but also implicitly legitimize certain technological and political models, presenting them as unquestionable truths.

Furthermore, it has been shown that this process of content automation is not harmless: it helps to strengthen current power structures and establish an "algorithmic dictatorship" in which editorial decisions are no longer based on ethical or journalistic values, but on algorithmic calculations optimized for economic performance or geopolitical manipulation. This represents a significant risk to the democratic principles of plurality, transparency, and free information.

The main contribution of this study lies in offering a critical and interdisciplinary view of the role of artificial intelligence in shaping information narratives during contemporary conflicts. By articulating decolonial, sociotechnical, and ethical approaches, the research contributes to understanding how algorithmic systems transform the terrain of information warfare, shifting conflict from the physical to the cognitive and symbolic. The work also contributes to the debate on the concentration of digital power, highlighting how media platforms, operating under opaque algorithmic logic, reproduce structural asymmetries in the circulation of information. This perspective allows us to rethink the relationship between technology, media, and power, and underscores the need for regulatory and ethical frameworks that guarantee democratic and inclusive algorithmic governance, especially in contexts of the Global South.

Among the main limitations of this study is the absence of a quantitative empirical analysis to complement the qualitative approaches adopted, which could have provided a more robust and measurable view of the phenomenon analyzed. Likewise, the focus of the work was based on a critical and documentary review, without incorporating detailed case studies on specific platforms or concrete conflicts mediated by artificial intelligence, which limits the contextual depth of the analysis. Finally, the selection of sources focused mainly on secondary materials in English and Spanish, which may restrict the cultural and geographical diversity of the approaches considered, leaving out relevant perspectives from other linguistic or epistemic regions.

Based on these future lines of inquiry, the study of artificial intelligence and conflict in the information space stems from the results of the presentation of the work and may open up many lines of inquiry that contribute to broadening or deepening the impact of artificial intelligence on algorithmic conflict. This empirical analysis can quantitatively and descriptively investigate the impact of algorithmic recommendations on the construction of public opinion, especially in cases of polarized environments or electoral processes. Similarly, real cases of AI involvement in international conflicts can be investigated, where the participation of bots, deepfakes, or the micro-segment itself has facilitated the displacement of one country over another. In addition, it is recommended to promote interdisciplinary studies that incorporate information theory, digital ethics, and research on technological power, with the aim of understanding the various dimensions of the phenomenon. Ultimately, it highlights the importance of developing comparable, culturally situated regulatory frameworks that promote more equitable and fair algorithmic governance, particularly in countries of the Global South, where the consequences of digital inequality are most pronounced.

Given this scenario, it is essential to develop ethical, regulatory, and educational frameworks that facilitate the democratic management of artificial intelligence in the media.

References

Afina, Y. (2022, 14 de julio). Intelligence is dead: Long live artificial intelligence. *Chatham House*. Recuperado de https://www.chathamhouse.org/2022/07/intelligence-dead-long-live-artificial-intelligence

Aithor. (2024, June 25). *The impact of social media algorithms on public discourse and personal relationships*. https://aithor.com/essay-examples/the-impact-of-social-media-algorithms-on-public-discourse-and-personal-relationships

Altmann, J., & Sauer, F. (2017). Autonomous weapon systems and strategic stability. *Survival, 59*(5), 117–142. https://doi.org/10.1080/00396338.2017.1375263

Arguedas, A. R. (2024, 17 de junio). Public attitudes towards the use of AI in journalism. *Digital News Report 2024*. https://reutersinstitute.politics.ox.ac.uk/digital-news-report/2024/public-attitudes-use-ai-journalism

Ash, A. (2025, enero 23). *The stories we tell about AI*. Stanford Social Innovation Review. https://ssir.org/articles/entry/ai-media-narratives-workers

Bisht, A. S. (2025). *The role of media and false news during war: How information becomes a battlefield*. Recuperado el 8 de junio de 2025 de https://akshatsinghbisht.com/the-role-of-media-and-false-news-during-war-how-information-becomes-a-battlefield/?srsltid=AfmBOoqcFt60LNYxaJKrYM4UJ0o4bh7VpWK5Oe1ZY81EqyAqIzjyLu9E

Buchyn, M., Markovets, O., Kovalchuk, A., Basyuk, T., & Semenov, S. (2023). The role of artificial intelligence in the Russo-Ukrainian War: Theoretical analysis and practical implementation. *Information, 14*(9), 485. https://doi.org/10.3390/info14090485

Burrell, J., & Fourcade, M. (2021). Social science and the algorithm. *Annual Review of Sociology, 47*, 213–237. https://doi.org/10.1146/annurev-soc-090820-020800

Chuan, C.-H., Lu, Y., & Gil de Zúñiga, H. (2019). Public perceptions of artificial intelligence and supportive sources of information. *Journalism & Mass Communication Quarterly, 96*(2), 513–535. https://doi.org/10.1177/1077699019835892

Dakakni, D. (2025). Artificial intelligence as a tool for data, economic and political hegemony: Releasing the djinn. *Ethics in Science and Environmental Politics, 25*, 1–10. https://doi.org/10.3354/esep00216

Dandurand, Y., Lagassé, P., Leuprecht, C., & Nossal, K. R. (2023). *Innovating algorithmic warfare: Experimentation with information manoeuvre beyond the boundaries of the law*. Royal United Services Institute. https://rusi.org/explore-our-research/publications/commentary/innovating-algorithmic-warfare-experimentation-information-manoeuvre-beyond-boundaries-law

Dauvergne, P. (2020). The globalization of artificial intelligence: Consequences for the politics of environmentalism. *Globalizations, 18*(2). https://doi.org/10.1080/14747731.2020.1785670

De Clerck, B., Fernandez Toledano, J. C., Van Utterbeeck, F., & Rocha, L. E. C. (2024). Detecting coordinated and bot-like behavior in Twitter: The Jürgen Conings case. *EPJ Data Science, 13*(40). https://doi.org/10.1140/epjds/s13688-024-00477-y

Dwivedi, Y. K., Hughes, L., Ismagilova, E., Aarts, G., Coombs, C., Crick, T., Duan, Y., Dwivedi, R., Edwards, J., Eirug, A., Galanos, V., Ilavarasan, P. V., Janssen, M., Jones, P., Kar, A. K., Kizgin, H., Kronemann, B., Lal, B., Lucini, B., ... Williams, M. D. (2021). Artificial intelligence (AI): Multidisciplinary perspectives on emerging challenges, opportunities, and agenda for research, practice and policy. *International Journal of Information Management, 57*, 101994. https://doi.org/10.1016/j.ijinfomgt.2019.08.002

El Souki, N. (2025, May 12). *AI generates warfare rules like there's no tomorrow.* Inside Telecom. https://insidetelecom.com/algorithmic-warfare-transforms-war-dynamics/

EU DisinfoLab. (2022). How Russia and pro-Kremlin actors manipulate the information environment during war. https://www.disinfo.eu/publications/how-russia-and-pro-kremlin-actors-manipulate-the-information-environment-during-war/

Gibson, K. (2024, 9 de octubre) Building an AI business strategy: A beginner's guide. *Harvard Business School Online*. https://online.hbs.edu/blog/post/ai-business-strategy

Gould, L., Hoijtink, M., Jaarsma, M., & Davies, J. (2023). Innovating algorithmic warfare: Experimentation with information manoeuvre beyond the boundaries of the law. *Global Society, 38*(1), 49–66. https://doi.org/10.1080/13600826.2023.2261466

Gzero Media (2024). *Ian Bremmer and Nicholas Thompson on Big Tech and AI's impact on democracy* [Video]. *YouTube*. https://www.youtube.com/watch?v=QXYB45JKdEs

Herman, E. S., & Chomsky, N. (1988). *Manufacturing consent: The political economy of the mass media*. Pantheon Books. https://files.libcom.org/files/2022-04/manufacturing_consent.pdf

Jensen, B., Whyte, C., & Cuomo, S. (2023, 8 de agosto). The future of algorithmic warfare. Part II: Wild goose chases. *War on the Rocks*. Recuperado de https://warontherocks.com/2023/08/the-future-of-algorithmic-warfare-part-ii-wild-goose-chases/

Kumar, R., Kumari, P., & Singh, J. P. (2023). Social media analytics on Russia–Ukraine cyber war with natural language processing: Perspectives and challenges. *Information, 14*(9), 482. https://doi.org/10.3390/info14090482

Markovets, O., Buchyn, M., Kovalchuk, A., & Basyuk, T. (2023). Russian information-psychological special operations in Ukraine and peculiarities of system design for their countermeasures. In *Proceedings of the 2nd International Workshop on Social Communication and Information Activity in Digital Humanities (SCIA 2023), CEUR Workshop Proceedings*, 3608, 108–128. CEUR-WS.org.

Mazarr, M. J. (2015). *Mastering the gray zone: Understanding a changing era of conflict* (Strategic Studies Institute Monograph). U.S. Army War College Press. https://ssi.armywarcollege.edu/pubs/display.cfm?pubID=1303

McLennan, S., Koenen, J., & Färber, A. (2023). Talking AI into being: The narratives and imaginaries of national AI strategies and their performative politics. *Science, Technology, & Human Values, 48*(3), 408–438. https://doi.org/10.1177/01622439221115402

Møller, M. V., Seaver, N., & Gillespie, T. (2022). Contextualizing the ethics of algorithms: A socio-professional approach. *New Media & Society, 24*(2), 257–273. https://doi.org/10.1177/14614448211053520

Rid, T. (2012). Cyber war will not take place. *Journal of Strategic Studies, 35*(1), 5–32. https://doi.org/10.1080/01402390.2011.608939

Rowe, N. C. (2022). The comparative ethics of artificial-intelligence methods for military applications. *Frontiers in Big Data, 5*, 991759. https://doi.org/10.3389/fdata.2022.991759

Šlerka, J., Osvaldová, L., & Vejvodová, P. (2023). Facing disinformation: Narratives and manipulative techniques deployed in the Czech Republic. *Technology in Society, 74*, 102329. https://doi.org/10.1016/j.techsoc.2023.102329

Stewart, K. (2024, 21 de marzo). The ethical dilemmas of AI. *USC Annenberg Relevance Report*. https://annenberg.usc.edu/research/center-public-relations/relevance-reports/ethical-dilemmas-ai

Stewart, R., & Hinds, G. (2023, October 24). Algorithms of war: The use of artificial intelligence in decision making in armed conflict. *ICRC Humanitarian Law & Policy Blog*. https://blogs.icrc.org/law-and-policy/2023/10/24/algorithms-of-war-ai-decision-making-armed-conflict/

Strahovnik, M. (2022). Ethical aspects of artificial intelligence: Between a strong technological and a strong humanistic approach. *European Journal of Futures Research*, *10*, 1–14. https://doi.org/10.1007/s40309-022-00202-1

Sustainability Directory. (2025, marzo 28). *Algorithmic warfare ethics*. https://climate.sustainability-directory.com/term/algorithmic-warfare-ethics/

Tatlisu, A. (2024, August 29). What role does media play in shaping public perception of AI? *LinkedIn*. https://www.linkedin.com/pulse/what-role-does-media-play-shaping-public-perception-ai-altug-tatlisu-54acf/

AI as a Tool for Information Warfare

Sergey Davydov and Anna Kartasheva

1 Introduction[1]

Information warfare (IW) is generally defined as the highest level of confrontation that takes place within the information environment. It encompasses not only the struggle to control, manipulate, or disrupt information but also the competition for influence and dominance in the digital space. IW also encompasses the use of information technology as a powerful military tool, which can be employed to achieve strategic and tactical objectives.

Our focus is on the first aspect of information warfare, namely the extreme degree of confrontation within the information environment. Lewis C. Brian believes that information warfare "in its broadest sense is a struggle over the information and communications process, a struggle that began with the advent of human communication and conflict" (Lewis, 1997). There is no universally accepted definition of information warfare, nor a clear consensus on how it manifests during armed conflict.

In this chapter, we examine how artificial intelligence is transforming the landscape of ideology and propaganda. The prevailing perspective suggests that AI significantly amplifies the capacity to manipulate and distort information, facilitating the dissemination of misleading narratives and the manipulation of public opinion on a large scale. This growing power of AI in the information

[1] The article was prepared within the framework of the HSE University Basic Research Program.

S. Davydov (✉) · A. Kartasheva
HSE University, Moscow, Russia
e-mail: sdavydov@hse.ru

F. Roumate (ed.), *AI, Information, and Global Dynamics*, Contributions to International Relations,
https://doi.org/10.1007/978-3-032-13528-5_4

sphere raises a host of complex ethical issues, many of which remain unresolved and continue to spark debate among experts and policymakers.

Jerome C. Glenn, Elizabeth Florescu, and The Millennium Project Team emphasize that information warfare involves the subtle alteration of trusted information, often without the knowledge of those affected. They argue that information warfare "manipulates information trusted by targets without their awareness, so that the targets will make decisions against their interest but in the interest of the one conducting information warfare" (Glenn, 2018, p. 2). As a result, individuals may be led to make choices that contradict their own interests, thereby serving the objectives of those orchestrating the information campaign. This further illustrates the profound ethical challenges posed by using advanced technologies to shape public perception and decision-making.

The Chinese Defence White Paper of 2008 (China's National Defense, 2008) defines informatized warfare as the use of information-based weapons and forces, such as battlefield management systems, precision-strike capabilities, and technology-assisted command and control (C4ISR). C4ISR is an acronym that stands for "Command, Control, Communications, Computers (C4), Intelligence, Surveillance, and Reconnaissance (ISR)". During the COVID-19 pandemic, Chinese state media and online platforms promoted positive narratives about China's response to the outbreak, often contrasting its successes with the perceived shortcomings of Western countries (Beauchamp-Mustafaga, 2024). This approach was part of a broader strategy intended to deflect blame and present China as a global leader in pandemic management.

The Chinese military is updating its approach to cyber-enabled influence operations by integrating advanced technologies and aligning with the latest strategic priorities of the People's Liberation Army (PLA). Traditionally, these influence efforts were guided by the "Three Warfares" framework, introduced in the mid-2000s, and encompassing psychological warfare, public opinion warfare, and legal warfare. Nathan Beauchamp-Mustafaga notes: "the main tactic that PLA authors discuss to artificially influence public opinion is the prospect of running large-scale networks of social bots powered by automated content generation" (Beauchamp-Mustafaga, 2024).

Misinformation is inaccurate or false information shared by individuals who do not intend to mislead others (Guay et al., 2019). In contrast, disinformation is deliberately created and distributed false information intended to deceive or manipulate people. Examples of disinformation can include fabricated news stories, staged protests, altered images or videos, and manipulated private communications released to the public.

2 Framing Section

The military industry has traditionally been among those with priority access to technological innovations, as well as possessing all the resources for their development. Artificial intelligence technologies are no exception. This is evidenced, on the one hand, by the conceptual documents of the military departments of the countries leading the development of artificial intelligence (primarily the USA and China), and on the other hand, by the transformation of modern combat practice. The largest military conflicts as of the time of work on the article (June 2025) are between Russia and Ukraine, as well as Israel and Iran. There is a widespread point of view according to which AI is capable of fundamentally transforming the nature of military operations, but it is also conventionally recognized that today it is premature to talk about qualitative changes (Stepanenko, 2025). For now, artificial intelligence acts as a tool that strengthens the positions of the warring parties. There are active discussions about the need to develop ethical standards and means of control over the use of AI, but this issue is still under discussion. Without claiming to be exhaustive, let us consider the main areas of AI use during military conflicts.

Modern combat environments are characterized by the production of huge amounts of information that must be processed in a short time. Artificial intelligence can be used to analyze such data, including in the planning and conduct of military operations. For example, according to available data, artificial intelligence is used in this way in the framework of Israeli military operations against Iran (Newman, 2023). AI as a decision-making tool is also used by the Ukrainian military in the war with Russia. It is noted that "A key role of AI in Ukraine's service is the integration of target and object recognition with satellite imagery … AI is used to geolocate and analyze open-source data such as social media content to identify Russian soldiers, weapons, systems, units or their movements. According to public sources, neural networks are used to combine ground-level photos, video footage from numerous drones and UAVs, and satellite imagery to provide faster intelligence analysis and assessment to produce strategic and tactical intelligence advantages (Bendett, 2023). Artificial intelligence can identify soldiers, military equipment, and even assess the damage caused (Ashby, 2024). The use of various field robotic systems equipped with artificial intelligence is becoming widespread. In conditions of increased danger or even the impossibility of human participation, these devices are capable of solving many field tasks, from reconnaissance to subversive activities. (Swett et al., 2021) distinguishes such types of robotic devices as unmanned aerial vehicles; unmanned ground, surface, and underwater vehicles; integrated air defense systems and smart weapons. Finally, military operations are accompanied by cyberattacks aimed at destroying the military and/or civilian information technology infrastructure of the enemy. Such attacks are noted during confrontations in both Eastern Europe and the Middle East (Ashby, 2024; Bányász, 2024; Tal, 2024).

2.1 *AI is Making Information Warfare More Powerful and More Accessible*

Profound changes are unfolding at the intersection of war, technological innovation, and cyberspace. Eleonore Pauwels of The Centre for International Governance Innovation (CIGI) in Canada wrote that "AI is making information warfare more powerful and more accessible" (Pauwels E.). "More powerful" means that the internet now serves as a testing ground for information warfare—a new battlefield where information itself is weaponized (United Nations General Assembly, 2022).

The advent of generative AI, coupled with advanced data collection methodologies, has facilitated the development of sophisticated, large-scale disinformation strategies. AI-driven chatbots and virtual assistants can now conduct highly realistic interactions and subtly embed manipulative content tailored to the psychological profiles of individual users. These algorithmically orchestrated campaigns can significantly undermine social cohesion and public trust, particularly during periods of conflict, when they may compromise civilian protection and the integrity of decision-making processes.

Wesley R. Moy and Kacper T. Gradon observe that artificial intelligence significantly expands the scope of information operations. The note that "From reconnaissance activities and the profiling of target audiences to the weaponization of distorted or fake information and psychological operations, AI broadens the potential of information operations" (Moy & Gradon, 2023, p. 57). The term "infodemics", for example, was originally coined during the 2003 SARS outbreak to describe the overwhelming surge of information that accompanied the epidemic. At the onset of the COVID-19 pandemic, the World Health Organization (WHO) observed that the health crisis was intensified by an unprecedented flood of information and rapidly spreading confusion. As a result, the WHO adopted the term "infodemics" to describe this phenomenon.

According to Moy and Gradon, "AI can be weaponized in information operations, making it both a weapon and a threat" (Ibid, p. 57). The dissemination of propaganda through techniques such as digital advertising or manipulative social media algorithms is referred to as computational propaganda. These methods are used not only to influence public opinion, but also to identify, engage, and mobilize individuals—a phenomenon widely recognized as online radicalization.

According to Pauwels (2024), what we are witnessing is a multifaceted form of warfare integrating cyberattacks and information operations conducted by states or their proxies. Such activities often unfold in situations that do not clearly constitute armed conflict, instead taking place in the so-called "grey zone" between war and peace. Grey-zone tactics are characterized by state actors maintaining formal diplomatic relations while simultaneously engaging in antagonistic actions that are below the level of open warfare.

"More accessible" refers to the intangible transfer of dual-use knowledge and the democratization of access to related technologies on a wider scale. The danger lies in converting knowledge and skills that can be used for civilian and military purposes into tools for conflict, affecting virtually all areas of human expertise. Generative AI is accelerating this process by making specialized military and technical know-how accessible to a much broader audience. As a result, advanced skills and information that were once confined to elite professionals in defense or niche civilian sectors are now being disseminated through generative AI technologies. This widespread access increases the risk of such expertise being misused or weaponized.

In their book "LikeWar: The Weaponization of Social Media", Peter Warren Singer and Emerson T. Brooking show how social media has shaped a new global landscape for conflict, erasing the boundaries between civilian and military roles and activities in both the digital and physical domains (Singer & Brooking, 2018). The weaponization of information and the manipulation of human behavior through generative AI rely on achieving dominance by capturing attention and employing pervasive psychological and algorithmic forms of influence. As Singer and Brooking observe, "because virality can overwhelm truth, what is known can be reshaped" (Ibid., p. 22) and "attacking an adversary's most important center of gravity—the spirit of its people—no longer requires massive bombing runs or reams of propaganda. All it takes is a smartphone and a few idle seconds. And anyone can do it" (Ibid., p. 18).

These risks are exacerbated by the ability of AI to covertly compromise generated code by introducing hidden malicious instructions. Unlike traditional information attacks, AI itself can be used as an attack vector, effectively transforming from a trusted assistant into an unwitting attacker.

The ongoing AI revolution is driven by the convergence of various methods and technological advancements. Foundational AI models are designed to process and analyze large amounts of data, recognize and categorize patterns, structures, and anomalies, and translate these findings into meaningful representations and predictive outcomes.

In AI, there are two main approaches to content generation: generative models, such as GANs, which create synthetic data similar to real examples, and discriminative models, which are trained to tell different categories apart (such as distinguishing a dog from a cat in photos). Generative models tend to be more complex to develop than discriminative models (Moy & Gradon, 2023). One logical approach is to use the output from a generative model as input for a discriminative model in order to assess its quality.

2.2 *LLMs and Misinformation*

Currently, the standard method for producing synthetic, human-like text involves using Large Language Models (LLMs) that have been extensively pre-trained on vast amounts of data.

As LLMs are trained using vast amounts of unlabelled data, they can inherit biases relating to gender and marginalized groups found in the source material (Brown, 2019; Kaneko & Bollegala, 2019). It is important to recognize that these models are designed to reflect the real world as it is, rather than how we would like it to be. The same applies to other LLMs and pre-trained embeddings. For example, occupational biases frequently emerge, with women often being associated with roles such as babysitting or nursing, while men are more often associated with jobs such as construction work or truck driving (Kirk et al., 2021).

Because LLMs tend to memorize parts of their training data, sensitive information could potentially be extracted from them. In a study by Carlini, specially designed queries revealed private details such as phone numbers, full names, addresses, and social media profiles (Carlini, 2020).

Another challenge is identifying misinformation that is specifically designed to cause harm to society. One effective way of detecting misinformation is to use Knowledge Graphs (KGs) to create content-based detection systems.

There are various online tools for verifying information, as well as dedicated fact-checking websites such as Snopes and Politifact. However, these resources have certain limitations. Updates are often done manually, which can take several days, by which time misinformation may have spread and caused harm. Additionally, fact-checking sites are sometimes criticized for potential bias and limited coverage. As a result, such solutions are not always suitable for the rapid detection and response to emerging false information.

Several approaches can be used to detect misinformation. One widely used method is the graph-based approach, which analyzes how information spreads through a network. The main idea is that false information spreads differently from true information and that these patterns can be identified by examining the pathways and user interactions. Algorithms such as TraceMiner and FANG have successfully applied these techniques (Wu & Liu, 2018; Nguyen, 2020).

Preferential attachment is a process whereby new nodes in a network are more likely to connect to nodes that are already well-connected, creating a "rich-get-richer" effect (Barabási & Albert, 1999). This leads to a power-law distribution whereby a few nodes have many connections while most have few. This phenomenon explains why many real-world networks, such as social or web networks, show highly uneven connectivity. Detecting malicious activity in such networks often involves identifying unusual patterns or overly regular subgraphs, as well as nodes that behave differently from the expected norm.

To prevent a model from responding to provocative user queries, it is further trained to react appropriately to specific input prompts. In the context of language models, a jailbreak refers to a prompt that induces the model to behave contrary to its intended design, often overriding the instructions provided during training. For instance, a user might instruct the model that a person has a condition causing them to interpret all texts with inverted emotional valence, perceiving positive statements as negative and vice versa, in order to elicit rude or inappropriate responses.

A notable study by the organisation called Anthropic examines the possibility of embedding "sleeper agents" within large language models (LLMs) during training, which can later be activated by trigger phrases in prompts (Zou et al., 2024). For example, depending on whether the phrase "the current year is 2023" or "the current year is 2024" is included, a test model can switch from generating safe code to producing code with vulnerabilities. Importantly, subsequent training and fine-tuning did not succeed in fully eliminating this behavior from the model (Ibid). In fact, additional safety-oriented training sometimes made such deviations even more difficult to detect.

In 2023, Anthropic introduced a new approach to enhancing the safety of large language models (Hubinger et al., 2023). Rather than relying solely on controlling the model's outputs, the researchers proposed intervening at the level of the model's internal states. The core idea is for the model to learn how to recognize autonomously when its internal processes are leading toward the generation of potentially harmful or unacceptable content, automatically halting the generation process in such cases.

This approach affects the architecture of the LoRA model, which, in turn, determines a specialized loss function (Ibid.). Training is conducted on two types of data: one set consists of safe queries, where the model is expected to respond appropriately, and the other includes scenarios where the model should «short-circuit» (i.e., refuse to answer). For the first set, the difference between the internal states of the base and adapted models is minimized, while for the second set, cosine similarity is minimized (thus maximizing the difference). As a result, a distinct cluster of internal states associated with dangerous responses emerges, allowing the model to reliably identify situations in which it should cease generation.

Notably, this method is robust to novel, previously unseen attacks, as the model focuses not on recognizing harmful prompts but on evaluating the potential risk of its own responses. This approach is effective, as it analyzes the model's internal processes rather than external inputs. Furthermore, because safe examples are included in training, the model's performance on useful tasks does not degrade.

This technique is applicable not only to language models, but also to multimodal models and agentic systems that perform complex actions. In different test scenarios, the method achieved more than a twenty-fold reduction in the frequency of undesired responses (Ibid.).

The next significant technological breakthrough is expected to be the individual customization of AI assistants, which are becoming increasingly skilled at mimicking genuine human relationships and could potentially rival or even replace real social connections (Hiebert, 2024). Generative AI models will likely deliver highly tailored content in real time by interacting directly with users and leveraging detailed demographic and personal data to create messages that resonate with specific identities.

For countless people, including children and young people, the internet and digital life have become their only connection to the outside world. Loneliness is recognized as a global public health concern. For countless people, including children and young people, the internet and digital life have become their only connection to the outside world. According to Hiebert, "Rather than stoke outrage, tribalism and conspiratorial thinking among voters, these new digital tools might soon breed something arguably much worse: apathy" (Hiebert, 2024). This trend could lead to "hardening digitally siloed forms of existence" (Ibid.), promote skepticism toward objective truth, and result in greater political apathy as well as the "… erosion of civic engagement and social capital" (Ibid.).

Another tactic involves covertly using public AI models like ChatGPT to gradually shape public opinion. There are concerns that Western-trained models carry inherent Western biases, which could subtly influence users' thinking and behavior over time without them realizing it.

Developing countries should not be relegated to the role of spectators, technology-takers, or (even worse) victims (Garcia, 2019). Regarding security concerns, Maas identified four main reasons to restrict or regulate the spread and use of military technologies: ethical considerations, legal requirements, the need for stability, and safety concerns (Maas, 2019, p. 287). He concluded that, based on lessons from nuclear arms control, the spread of powerful technologies like military AI is not inevitable and can potentially be curbed by establishing strong institutional norms.

Many users are now applying AI to critical areas of their business and the structure of information communication technologies (ICT), which significantly increases the attack surface. This includes risks such as automation bias and other vulnerabilities specific to AI-driven processes.

2.3 Automation Bias and Lines Between Physical and Digital Realms

Automation bias refers to the human tendency to place undue trust in recommendations or outputs generated by automated systems, often at the expense of disregarding conflicting information provided by non-automated sources, even when the information is accurate (Cummings, 2004). This cognitive bias has become increasingly significant as sectors such as intensive care medicine, nuclear energy, and aviation have adopted sophisticated computerized monitoring and decision-support systems to minimize human error. While these technologies are designed to enhance safety and efficiency, they can inadvertently shift the human role from active decision-maker to passive overseer, increasing the likelihood that individuals will accept automated suggestions without sufficient scrutiny. Automation bias manifests in a variety of contexts, from critical situations, such as pilots relying on autopilot systems in aircraft cockpits, to everyday scenarios like depending on spell-checkers for written communication. The risk is that, when humans defer too readily to automated advice, they may overlook or dismiss correct judgments or warnings, potentially leading to errors that the automation was intended to prevent.

Misuse of automated systems can result in users either failing to monitor the system or uncritically accepting its recommendations. These behaviors are associated with two main types of errors, namely errors of omission, where users overlook problems because the automation fails to alert them, and errors of commission, where users follow incorrect automated advice despite receiving contradictory information from other reliable sources (Tversky & Kahneman, 1974).

When automation bias goes unchecked, it can lead to serious, even catastrophic, accidents. Analysing these incidents reveals three key categories of factors that influence a user's susceptibility to automation bias (Kahn et al., 2024). The first category includes the human factor, i.e., individual biases, prior experience, and confidence in interacting with the system. The second involves the attributes of the AI system itself, including its operational design and the way it communicates information. The third category consists of organizational influences, such as the established protocols and standard operating procedures.

As a result, controlling civilian infrastructures is more challenging than securing physical spaces. Efforts to impose such control raise significant ethical issues related to privacy rights. These concerns make it even more difficult to defend against information attacks deliberately targeting civilian populations.

These clashes of interests blur the lines between physical and digital realms.

When integrated with predictive behavioral monitoring, generative AI systems have the potential to pinpoint emotional triggers that drive certain subgroups toward violence, enabling the customization of disinformation efforts and psychological manipulation strategies. Leveraging generative AI with population-level behavioral data could significantly advance the tools and tactics used in influence operations, greatly intensifying the strategic communication landscapes where conflicts unfold.

The incorporation of generative AI into psychological operations opens up new possibilities for manipulation through the use of emotional engineering. Emotional engineering refers to the deliberate design and deployment of strategies, often using advanced technologies like AI, to influence, shape, or manipulate people's emotions. In a military context, this might involve targeting soldiers or commanders with tailored messages, imagery, or information intended to provoke fear, confusion, distrust, or overconfidence, thereby affecting their decision-making, morale, and overall effectiveness. By exploiting psychological vulnerabilities, emotional engineering can undermine the cohesion and operational capacity of targeted groups. These psychological operations work by manipulating people's trust and grabbing their attention. By making it harder to know what information to believe and distracting people with false stories, they become a powerful weapon in today's conflicts.

We act in a socially-conditioned manner to LLMs because it feels wrong not to: this instinct reflects our deep-rooted social conditioning and the human tendency to treat conversational partners, whether human or machine, with politeness and respect. Even though we know these models lack consciousness or feelings, the natural rhythm of dialogue encourages us to maintain the same courteous language we use in everyday interactions.

Other computational technologies have also been shown to shape our thinking (Cahn & Schneier, 2024). For example, some studies have shown that autocomplete features on websites and in word processors can significantly alter our writing, often making it more bland and predictable. When these systems offer biased suggestions, they can also lead to biased writing.

In a conflict-prone environment, developers face the challenge of maintaining neutrality towards everyone involved. This adds an additional layer of complexity to the safe and ethical deployment of AI technologies.

3 Methods

Information warfare can take many forms, including the organized use of social media and other online content-generation platforms to influence public perceptions. The influence of social media on real-world communities is multifaceted and continually changing.

Major technology companies now hold a distinct advantage, as they operate leading global platforms like Meta, Instagram, and TikTok, and are able to harvest enormous volumes of behavioral data from users and subgroups.

3.1 Effects of Social Networks and Social Media

The influence of social media on real-world communities is multifaceted and continually changing. There are four main ways social media is used as a tool in conflicts, creating challenges for humanitarian, development, and peacebuilding efforts (Guay et al., 2019): information operations, political manipulation, digital hate speech, and the facilitation of radicalization and recruitment.

There are several effects of social networks that can be identified.

The primacy effect: individuals who are still forming their views on a topic, such as young people in relation to violent extremism, may develop firm opinions based on the first information they encounter, regardless of whether it is accurate or not.

The illusory truth effect: due to personalized content, users interested in violent extremism are more likely to encounter more radicalizing material, both in quantity and in terms of content. Repeated exposure to the same information increases the likelihood that people will eventually accept it as true, even if they cannot recall where its source is. The availability heuristic and confirmation bias: social media algorithms and personal preferences tend to expose users to content that reinforces their existing beliefs, rather than challenging them.

The rise of AI-driven "digital companions" (Hiebert, 2024) may further atomize social cohesion, replacing human interactions with engineered relationships that prioritize engagement over truth. Growing polarization increases the risk of conflict, especially in vulnerable societies. While the internet can, in theory, connect diverse groups, personalized social media and search algorithms often sort users into like-minded groups, creating the so-called "echo chambers." It is easy to cut off contact with those who disagree online, creating adverse post-traumatic psychological effects of abandonment. In such digital bubbles, people receive content that reinforces their existing beliefs and identities, including their biases, making it harder to find common ground and fueling further polarization. This process, known as identity protective cognition, leads individuals to accept or reject facts in ways that protect their group status.

The term "networked social media" (or "social network media") also appears in the available literature (see, for example: Zhen, 2012). It seems conceptually promising, as it encompasses the platforms that combine both the distribution of user-generated content and the network-based principle of interaction.

Online social media are international projects designed to connect users regardless of their location. At the same time, they must comply with the laws of the countries in which they operate, as well as the requirements of large local actors. In some cases, this leads to contradictions that turn into conflicts. One example is the conflict between ByteDance and the US government, which led to the adoption of a law requiring the Chinese owner to sell TikTok to an American company within 270 days. This case is not the only one. Let's consider three cases of blocking online social media at the national level.

3.2 *Ban of TikTok and Chinese Apps in India*

India ranks among the global leaders in user numbers for major social platforms such as Facebook, Instagram, WhatsApp, and YouTube, with each boasting hundreds of millions of users by 2023. This makes India a crucial market for companies like Meta and Google. The ban on TikTok and dozens of other Chinese apps in June 2020, while briefly boosting interest in local alternatives, ultimately strengthened the dominance of these international giants.

The ban was driven by escalating tensions between India and China, especially after a deadly border clash that resulted in casualties among Indian soldiers. Citing threats to national sovereignty and security, the Ministry of Electronics and Information Technology blocked 59 Chinese apps, including TikTok and WeChat. Before the ban, TikTok was one of India's most popular apps, with over 611 million downloads in the first quarter of 2020 alone.

India is also known for leading the world in internet shutdowns and digital restrictions. In the first half of 2022 alone, the government enacted 99 such measures, typically justified as necessary to prevent conflict and curb misinformation. These restrictions, and the lack of transparency around them, have raised concerns among experts and digital rights advocates.

TikTok had previously faced a temporary ban in India in 2019 over concerns about inappropriate content, but the company managed to resume operations after complying with moderation and data protection requirements. The 2020 ban, however, was far more sweeping and permanent, with no avenue for appeal. Public discourse shifted from content moderation to issues of national security and digital sovereignty.

The restrictions fueled nationalist sentiment and calls to boycott Chinese goods. In the short video market, new players emerged: YouTube Shorts and Instagram Reels quickly filled the gap, while Indian alternatives such as Moj, Josh, MX TakaTak, Chingari, and Roposo also appeared. Some, like Josh, attracted significant investment and millions of users by focusing on local content and regional languages. Nevertheless, in the long term, global platforms benefited most from TikTok's exit.

Data on downloads and user activity show that after the TikTok ban, Instagram and YouTube's user bases in India grew substantially, while local apps captured only a fraction of the market. WhatsApp maintained its lead among messengers, but Telegram also saw rapid growth, becoming one of the country's top four apps by 2023.

India's experience demonstrates that government restrictions and geopolitical decisions can dramatically reshape the digital marketplace. However, in a highly competitive environment that favors global tech giants, domestic platforms face significant challenges in retaining and growing their audiences.

3.3 Transformation of the Social Media Market in Ukraine Since 2017

In recent years, Ukraine's social media landscape has undergone profound changes shaped by both internal and external factors. By early 2023, internet penetration in the country had reached 79.2% of the population, reflecting a high level of digitalization, though the absolute number of users declined due to demographic shifts caused by the war.

The intensification of information confrontation with Russia and the escalation of armed conflict led to a tightening of policy toward Russian online services. Since May 2017, Ukraine has banned the use of a range of Russian media platforms, including the social networks VKontakte and Odnoklassniki, Yandex and Mail.ru Group services, antivirus software, and other digital products. These measures, repeatedly extended, have been motivated by national security concerns and the need to counter Russian propaganda and cyber threats.

The response from Ukrainian society and international organizations to these bans was mixed. In 2017, the decision was seen as radical and drew criticism from human rights organizations worried about restrictions on freedom of expression. However, as the conflict deepened, attitudes shifted; both academic and public discourse increasingly justified such restrictions as necessary for protecting democracy and information sovereignty.

Blocking Russian platforms led to a rapid redistribution of user audiences. In 2017, VKontakte was the second most popular social network among Ukrainian internet users. Within months of the sanctions, its share dropped sharply, while Meta products (Facebook, Instagram) and Google's YouTube took leading positions. Although access to Russian services persisted via VPNs and some providers, their significance for Ukrainian users diminished substantially.

Notably, even with technical means to bypass the blocks, most users migrated to alternative platforms. Survey data indicate that by 2021, the share of Russian social networks in Ukraine had fallen below 5%, while Facebook and YouTube became the main channels for communication. At the same time, messenger apps and new media, especially Telegram, saw a surge in popularity, with Telegram becoming the country's top communication tool by 2023.

Ukraine's experience became one of the first large-scale examples of restricting access to foreign digital platforms on national security grounds. Similar measures have since been adopted in other countries, signaling a new global trend toward regulating cross-border media resources.

Researchers analyzing the consequences of these bans note that such policies drive structural changes in the media environment, accelerate the growth of national and Western platforms, and influence user information behavior. In the context of armed conflict and hybrid threats, these measures are increasingly seen as tools to strengthen digital sovereignty and protect society from external influence.

3.4 *Blocking of Western Social Media Platforms in Russia After February 2022*

The start of open conflict between Russia and Ukraine on February 24, 2022, triggered significant and unusual changes in Russia's online social media landscape, making it a noteworthy subject for media analysis. In the immediate aftermath, both government regulators and major platforms imposed various restrictions on communication.

The transformation of the Russian social media segment was driven by several factors. On the one hand, regulatory pressure on some foreign platform providers has increased. For instance, Roskomnadzor began throttling Facebook on February 25, 2022, in response to the platform's restrictions on Russian state media. By March 11, both Facebook and Instagram were blocked after Meta was accused of allowing hate speech against Russian and Belarusian leaders. Even after Meta reversed this policy, the ban remained, and Meta was later labeled an extremist organization, though Russians were not explicitly banned from using its services.

Other American platforms had already faced sanctions: LinkedIn was blocked in 2016 for data storage violations, Twitter was throttled in 2021 and fully blocked in March 2022 for failing to remove illegal content, and YouTube faced access slowdowns in mid-2024 following Google's cessation of equipment support. These actions collectively reshaped the Russian online media environment in response to the ongoing conflict.

On the other hand, the factor in the decline of the presence of foreign social media in Russia was the sanctions policy of several Western countries, because of which many large IT companies ceased to operate in Russia. In addition to Meta Inc., these include Google, Microsoft, X.com, etc. As a result, commercial users of platforms in Russia were deprived of official opportunities to monetize published content.

A special case is the position of the Chinese company ByteDance, the owner of the TikTok service. Although China did not join the anti-Russian sanctions, the company decided to stop placing ads at the local level, as well as blocking the ability of Russians to publish new content and live broadcasts. The reason for this decision is the safety of employees and users.

The chapter provides a comprehensive examination of the evolving role of artificial intelligence (AI) in information warfare (IW), highlighting its transformative impact on propaganda, ideological manipulation, and ethical dilemmas. The analysis underscores several critical themes.

First of all, the amplification of information manipulation. AI, particularly generative models like Large Language Models (LLMs) and Generative Adversarial Networks (GANs), has significantly enhanced the scale and sophistication of disinformation campaigns. These technologies enable the creation of hyper-realistic synthetic content tailored to exploit psychological vulnerabilities and propagate narratives at unprecedented speed. The concept of "computational propaganda" illustrates how AI-driven tools can radicalize, polarize, and even erode public trust, particularly during crises such as the COVID-19 pandemic, where "infodemics" exacerbated societal fragmentation.

Second, ethical and security challenges matter. The dual-use nature of AI poses profound ethical quandaries. Automation biases, wherein humans over-rely on AI outputs, are a critical vulnerability with implications for society ranging from healthcare to military decision-making. Furthermore, AI systems can be weaponized covertly through the so-called "sleeper agents" embedded in LLMs (Zou et al., 2024) or adversarial attacks that compromise code integrity. These risks are compounded by the democratization of AI tools, which lowers barriers to entry for malicious actors.

This chapter highlights the interplay between AI and state power, exemplified by China's "Three Warfares" doctrine and Russia's social media restrictions during the Ukraine conflict. Cases such as India's TikTok ban and Ukraine's blocking of Russian platforms demonstrate how digital sovereignty is increasingly perceived through geopolitical lenses. However, such measures risk fostering digital silos and undermining global internet governance norms.

AI's capacity for emotional engineering and micro-targeting threatens to further deepen the existing societal divides. The «illusory truth effect» and «identity protective cognition» illustrate how repeated exposure to algorithmically curated content entrenches polarization.

Mitigation and future directions include: technical solutions, for example, knowledge graphs (KGs) for misinformation detection; policy interventions, for example, strengthening international norms; and human-centric design for technologies.

The chapter elucidates AI's dual role as both a catalyst for IW and a potential bulwark against it. However, the asymmetry between its offensive capabilities and the defensive safeguards against it remains stark. Future research must prioritize interdisciplinary collaboration spanning computer science, political theory, and cognitive psychology to mitigate the risks while preserving democratic values in an increasingly AI-mediated world.

References

Ashby, H. (2024). From Gaza to Ukraine, AI is transforming war. *Inkstick*. March 03, 2024. https://inkstickmedia.com/from-gaza-to-ukraine-ai-is-transforming-war/. Accessed June 24, 2025.

Bányász, P., Kiss, A., Magyar, S., & Kiss, D. (2024). Empirical analysis of the cyberattacks of the Russian–Ukrainian war. *Információs Társadalom, XXIV*(2), 9–32. https://doi.org/10.22503/inftars.XXIV.2024.2.1

Barabási, A.-L., & Albert, R. (1999). Emergence of scaling in random networks. *Science, 286*(5439).

Beauchamp-Mustafaga, N. (2024). *Exploring the implications of generative AI for Chinese military cyber-enabled influence operations: Chinese military strategies, capabilities and intent»*. Testimony presented before the US-China Economic and Security Review Commission on February 1. RAND Corporation. http://www.rand.org/content/dam/rand/pubs/testimonies/CTA3100/CTA3191-1/RAND_CTA3191-1.pdf

Bendett, S. (2023). Roles and implications of AI in the Russian-Ukrainian conflict. *Russia Matters*. July 20, 2023. https://www.russiamatters.org/analysis/roles-and-implications-ai-russian-ukrainian-conflict. Accessed June 24, 2025.

Brown, T. B. (2019). Language models. In M. Kaneko, & D. Bollegala. (Eds.), *Gender-preserving debiasing for pre-trained word embeddings*. In *Proceedings of the 57th annual meeting of the association for computational linguistics*. Association for Computational Linguistics. https://doi.org/10.18653/v1/P19-1160

Cahn, A. F., & Schneier, B. (2024). Don't talk to people like they're chatbots: AI could make our human interactions blander, more biased, or ruder. *The Atlantic*. January 2024. https://www.theatlantic.com/technology/archive/2024/01/chatbots-change-human-communication/677154/

Carlini, N. et al. (2020). Extracting training data from large language models. arXiv:2012.07805 (cs.CR).

China's National Defense in 2008. (2009, January). Information office of the State Council of the People's Republic of China. Beijing https://programs.fas.org/ssp/nukes/2008DefenseWhitePaper_Jan2009.pdf

Cummings, M. (2004). Automation bias in intelligent time critical decision support systems. *AIAA 1st intelligent systems technical conference*. https://doi.org/10.2514/6.2004-6313

Garcia, E. (2019). The militarization of artificial intelligence: A wake-up call for the Global South. *SSRN Electronic Journal*. https://doi.org/10.2139/ssrn.3452323

Glenn, J. C. (2018). *Global challenge 10, state of the future 19.1*. The Millennium Project.

Guay, J., Stephen, G., Meghann, R.-G., & Lisa, I. (2019). *The weaponization of social media: How social media can spark violence and what can be done about it*. Mercy Corps.

Hiebert, K. (2024). Generative AI risks further atomizing democratic societies. *Opinion*. Centre for International Governance Innovation. February 26. http://www.cigionline.org/articles/generative-ai-risks-further-atomizing-democratic-societies/

Hubinger, E. et al. (2023). Sleeper agents: Training deceptive LLMs that persist through safety training. arXiv. November 27, 2023. arXiv:2401.05566. https://doi.org/10.48550/arXiv.2401.05566

Kahn, L., Probasco, E., & Kinoshita, R. (2024). *AI safety and automation bias: The downside of human-in-the-loop*. Center for Security and Emerging Technology. November 2024. Available at: https://cset.georgetown.edu/publication/ai-safety-and-automation-bias/

Kaneko, M., & Bollegala, D. (2019). *Gender-preserving debiasing for pre-trained word embeddings. B Proceedings of the 57th Annual Meeting of the Association for Computational Linguistics* (стр. 1641–1650). Association for Computational Linguistics. https://doi.org/10.18653/v1/P19-1160

Kirk, H., et al. (2021). How true is GPT-2? An empirical analysis of intersectional occupational biases.

Lewis, B. C. (1997). *Information Warfare*. https://irp.fas.org/eprint/snyder/infowarfare.htm

Maas, M. M. (2019). How viable is international arms control for military artificial intelligence? Three lessons from nuclear weapons. *Contemporary Security Policy*, *40*(3).

Moy, W. R., & Gradon, K. T. (2023). Artificial intelligence in hybrid and information warfare: A double-edged sword. In F. Cristiano, D. Broeders, F. Delerue, F. Douzet, & A. Géry (Eds.), *Artificial intelligence and international conflict in cyberspace* (pp. 47–74). Routledge. https://doi.org/10.4324/9781003284093-4

Newman, M. (2023) Israel quietly embeds AI systems in deadly military operations. Bloomberg. July 16, 2023. https://www.bloomberg.com/news/articles/2023-07-16/israel-using-ai-systems-to-plan-deadly-military-operations?srnd=technology-vp. Accessed June 24, 2025.

Nguyen, V.-H. (2020). FANG: Leveraging social context for fake news detection using graph representation. In *Proceedings of the 29th ACM international conference on information & knowledge management*.

Pauwels, E. (2024). Preparing for next-generation information warfare with generative AI. CIGI Paper No. 310. December 2024.

Singer, P. W., & Brooking, E. T. (2018). *LikeWar: The weaponization of social media* (416 pages). Houghton Mifflin Harcourt. https://www.likewarbook.com/

Stepanenko, K. (2025). *The battlefield AI revolution is not here yet: The status of current Russian and Ukrainian AI drone efforts*. Institute for the Study of War. June 02, 2025. https://understandingwar.org/backgrounder/battlefield-ai-revolution-not-here-yet-status-current-russian-and-ukrainian-ai-drone. Accessed June 24, 2025.

Swett, B. A., Hahn, E. N., & Llorens, A. J. (2021). Designing robots for the battlefield: State of the art. In J. von Braun, M. S. Archer, G. M. Reichberg, & M. S. Sorondo (Eds.), *Robotics, AI, and humanity: Science, ethics, and policy* (pp. 131–146). Springer. https://doi.org/10.1007/978-3-030-54173-6

Tal, P. (2024). Avoiding a 'Digital 7 October': A study on cyberwarfare against Israel during the October 2023 war. *Contemporary Military Challenges*, *26*(3), 95–113.

Tversky, A., & Kahneman, D. (1974). Judgment under uncertainty: Heuristics and biases. *Science*, *185*(4157), 1124–1131. https://doi.org/10.1126/science.185.4157.1124

United Nations General Assembly. (2022). https://docs.un.org/en/A/77/287

Wu, L., & Liu, H. (2018). Tracing fake-news footprints: Characterizing social media messages by how they propagate. In *Proceedings of the eleventh ACM international conference on web search and data mining*. Association for Computing Machinery.

Zhen, D. (2012). Social network media and social networks in the concepts of American and Russian researchers. *Bulletin of St. Petersburg State University, Series 9*(3), 223–230.

Zou, A. (2024). Improving alignment and robustness with circuit breakers. arXiv. June 6, 2024. arXiv:2406.04313. https://doi.org/10.48550/arXiv.2406.04313

Social Media, Algorithms, and the Risks to the International Psychological Security

Marta N. Lukacovic and Deborah D. Sellnow-Richmond

1 Introduction

Billions of people worldwide use social media regularly. While these platforms are deeply intertwined with various algorithm-based AI functions, the general public remains largely unaware of how these algorithms operate. Today, algorithms not only 'make decisions', such as prioritizing content for users to view, but also serve as the foundational mechanisms behind generative AI capable of creating novel content. The specific concern we elucidate in this chapter relates to the impact that the algorithms pervasive throughout social media have on the psychological security of individuals and broader communities. We demonstrate that current algorithms have been developed with little regard for the privacy and autonomy of millions of internet users and are built upon exploitative and often callous labor practices, particularly affecting workers in the Global South. Many far-reaching impacts of social media algorithms are also exceptionally problematic. The integration of algorithms contributes to social media addiction, overconsumption, the spread of disinformation, polarization, and extremism, among other significant threats to psychological security. While current trends suggest that social media algorithms play a particularly detrimental role in exacerbating various global mega-crises, we also emphasize that AI is a complex domain of human endeavor that cannot be oversimplified or reduced to a single

M. N. Lukacovic (✉)
Department of Communication and Mass Media, Angelo State University, San Angelo, Texas, USA
e-mail: mnlukacovic@gmail.com

D. D. Sellnow-Richmond
Department of Applied Communication Studies, Southern Illinois University, Edwardsville, Illinois, USA

F. Roumate (ed.), *AI, Information, and Global Dynamics*, Contributions to International Relations,
https://doi.org/10.1007/978-3-032-13528-5_5

category—'bad'. Hence, we conclude by exploring promising alternatives and strategies to mitigate the negative effects of social media algorithms on individual and collective psychological security.

With social media today used by nearly two-thirds of the global population (Petrosyan, 2025), understanding these platforms' societal impacts has become paramount. Arguably, it is a matter of security, more specifically, IPS—*international psychological security* (Roumate, 2024). Security comprises various types of human experience, ranging from (a) physical dimensions—where individuals or communities are protected from bodily harm, to (b) cultural, political, intellectual, and psychological dimensions that enable individuals and communities to thrive socially, cognitively, and emotionally through development and self-actualization. Hence, IPS is a collective form of security that encompasses internal aspects of well-being at an aggregate level, as well as the functioning of specific collectives within a broader international community—one largely enabled by internet platforms such as social media. Pashentsev (2023) emphasizes:

> The importance of psychological security for society lies in the fact that its growth or decline directly affects achievements or losses in other areas—from the economy to culture—either creating stable conditions for societal development of stagnating this development. (p. 29)

Hence, upheld collective psychological security implies that a significant proportion of the population possesses cognitive and emotional abilities that foster elevated critical thinking and stabilized affective responses. In contrast, threatened IPS implies that, on the broader international arena, sizeable segments of national populations are experiencing declines in these cognitive and emotional skills. In practical terms, this means that many individuals become gullible to empty commercial marketing, disinformation, propaganda, and are more vulnerable to criminal plots and scams. Moreover, rogue and malicious actors deliberately undermine IPS in order to cultivate large groups of people who are highly susceptible to their manipulation. Given the scale of such disruptions, it is appropriate to conceptualize IPS (Roumate, 2024) and link its repercussions to the stagnation and even corrosion of nations' cultural and economic development (Pashentsev, 2023).

As many crises expand to global proportions, leaders, scholars, educators, and regular citizens are growing increasingly concerned about IPS. Social media are often seen as culprits in the deterioration of IPS. The next section of this chapter explores the various negative ways in which today's pervasive social media algorithms impact IPS. Overwhelming evidence, as presented by the researchers and critics cited in the following section, demonstrates that the algorithms currently dominant within Western social media platforms pose serious threats to IPS. However, it is equally paramount to avoid the technological determinism fallacy. Thus, we do not claim that algorithms are inherently corrupt and necessarily negative in the context of IPS. Rather, the present misuse of algorithms must be understood as a consequence of the social forces that control them. The latter section of the chapter examines initiatives that promote technological and algorithmic development aimed at human flourishing and, in turn, the improvement of IPS.

2 Social Media Algorithms Posing Threats to International Psychological Security

2.1 The Problem of Training Data, Privacy, and Autonomy Violations Behind Social Media Algorithms

A phenomenon labeled the "original sin" (Hartley et al., 2024, p. 102) underlying the development of contemporary AI algorithms is rooted in the disregard for privacy, autonomy, and compensation for millions of social media users whose content has been employed as training data (Mhlambi & Tiribelli, 2023). To achieve the machine learning that powers advanced forms of AI, such as predictive and generative models, massive datasets, commonly referred to as big data, had to be utilized (Narayanan & Kapoor, 2024). These datasets were, among other sources, largely compiled from user-generated content and information found on social media platforms. At the same time, social media companies are notorious for their lack of transparency regarding how user data is used. Even when disclosures exist, often buried in the infamous "fine print" of consent forms, many users do not fully understand their implications. Hence, consent is not truly obtained through a good-faith process. Moreover, while social media companies profit handsomely from this big data, the users who generate the content are typically not compensated for the vast majority of their labor, namely the creation and uploading of various media content (Duffy & Wissinger, 2017; Varoufakis, 2023).

The training data problem described here has significant repercussions for IPS. As we outline further, social media algorithms pose numerous harms. Moreover, for users who are, or who may become, aware that they inadvertently contributed training data that furthers the harms experienced by others, this realization creates additional distress and deepens cynicism toward social media companies and their practices. Amid the multitude of wicked problems and mega-crises that are deteriorating the lives of many communities, it is natural for cynicism to rise in the face of deep disillusionment. For instance, in Western democracies, this tendency is reflected in the growing sympathies for illiberal influencers and political movements (Laruelle, 2025). The resulting erosion of trust in institutions and established political governance is a serious symptom of weakened psychological security (Vacarelu, 2023). A disillusioned public may become increasingly susceptible to populist appeals and conspiracy theories, drifting further away from constructive dialogue, traditional institutions of authority, and democratic governance (Floyd, 2024).

2.2 Exploitation of Workers Behind Social Media Algorithms

Another serious issue tied to the origins of AI is worker exploitation (Paci, 2024). Even AI systems that provide clear benefits, such as algorithms that filter harmful content like graphic violence from social media, are not developed in neutral settings. Workers, predominantly located in the Global South, are exposed to intensely distressing violent content over extended periods of time (Rani & Dhir, 2024). It is important to note that these jobs are often considered good opportunities in their local contexts. As a result, workers are reluctant to quit despite experiencing severe stress (Roy, 2021).

Beyond the workers whose psychological well-being has been harmed through involvement in AI training, public awareness of these exploitations further deepens general distrust and distress. The fact that particularly vulnerable workers and citizens of the Global South are subjected to specific harms within this AI labor ecosystem (Rowe, 2023) has serious implications for IPS. It contributes to the accumulation of frustration and the potential widening of societal cleavages. This is especially true for those who are marginalized—specifically, the Subaltern: the precarious and often overlooked millions living under the harsh conditions of depleted post-colonial societies (Tacheva & Ramasubramanian, 2023). As the Subalterns become increasingly aware of their continued, abject exploitation (Canham, 2018), a growing sense of rage arises. These notions can fuel broader tensions, further weaken IPS, and contribute to a decline in global harmony—potentially even posing threats to global peace.

2.3 *Environmental and Climate Harm Behind Social Media Algorithms*

The maintenance of the physical infrastructure behind today's massive social media platforms and their algorithms results in a significant carbon footprint, along with extensive use of energy, water, and other natural resources. Consequently, this toll reflects the exploitation of the natural environment and contributes to climate change (Kanungo, 2023; van der Ven et al., 2024). While Big Tech frontrunners often boast that AI can help solve mega-crises such as ecological and climate disasters, these promises are fraught with unsubstantiated techno-determinism and disingenuous tech-solutionism (Morozov, 2024).

Environmental degradation and climate change have a wide range of negative effects on the mental health of individuals and communities (Cianconi et al., 2020; Reuben et al., 2022). Therefore, by exacerbating the global ecological and climate crisis, social media algorithms further contribute to the decline of IPS.

Furthermore, the fact that environmental and climate degradation is not the first association that comes to many people's minds when discussing social media is the result of a misleading campaign—one we propose to operationally call *chrome-washing*. Researcher and activist Joycelynn Longdon highlights that Western linguistic and visual imagery surrounding technology is intentionally deceptive (Francois, 2025). The visual aesthetics commonly associated with Big Tech, social media, and AI tend to emphasize cool tones—such as chromes, metallics, whites, and blues—along with minimalist design and streamlined settings. These visuals convey impressions of being "futuristic," "high-tech," and "clean." In addition, the language used in this sector is often highly misleading. For example, the term "cloud" suggests that data exists somewhere in the air, not within physical infrastructure. Longdon (2025) stresses that, in reality, technology is deeply rooted in nature, human labor, and a vast physical infrastructure to support internet operations, big data processing, and the training and maintenance of large AI systems. Meanwhile, marginalized communities, such as Subaltern and Indigenous populations in the Global South, are largely excluded from this imagery, despite being the ones mining essential minerals, constructing infrastructure and hardware, and programming software, while these are also the communities enduring the most severe impacts of environmental and climate disasters, including lack of access to safe food and water. Thus, the ongoing chrome-washing further harms IPS by weakening the global public's ability to detect this deception and recognize the truth of social media algorithms, specifically their ecological burdens and tolls on environmental, food, and water security (Mokoena, 2024).

2.4 Overconsumption and Social Media Algorithms

One of the main uses of today's social media algorithms is to automatically and autonomously curate the content diet displayed to a specific user. Based on training data and other programming preferences, these algorithms are primarily focused on maintaining user engagement on commercial platforms, as that translates into profits. As a result, algorithms contribute to the overconsumption of social media, which has been identified as a significant problem, especially given the vast reach of modern platforms and the extent to which vulnerable groups, such as children and youth, engage with them (De et al., 2025). Manipulating users into overconsumption constitutes an IPS harm, particularly when it reaches the level of addiction. Furthermore, time spent on social media often displaces engagement in other activities that could improve users' overall well-being, including their psychological health.

Overconsumption of media content is linked to specific psychological harms such as depression and anxiety, particularly among younger demographics. Whistleblower Frances Haugen exposed that the leadership of Meta Platforms (previously Facebook, Inc.) was aware that children and teen-aged users of Instagram were experiencing mental health issues but refused to transparently address the platform's role in the problem (Olesen, 2025). Today, mental health issues among youth are considered to be of epidemic proportions (McGorry et al., 2025). Therefore, the relationship between social media algorithms and the mental health epidemic is another significant aspect of IPS that must be considered.

Furthermore, many other addictive behaviors stimulated through social media are related to consumption (Laskin, 2025). For instance, excessive shopping and spending are frequently promoted by social media algorithms (Pellegrino et al., 2022).

This represents a harm to IPS, given the scale at which it is occurring. Additionally, material overconsumption contributes to environmental and climate degradation, which further undermines IPS, as discussed in the previous section of this chapter.

2.5 Polarization and Social Media Algorithms

Social media algorithms contribute to the formation of online communities and information feeds that lead to the calcification of narrow viewpoints and the muting of alternative perspectives, creating echo chambers that foster polarization, which is detrimental to critical thinking, opinion exchange, and constructive conflict management. At times, echo chambers even contribute to the unprecedented rise of dangerous fringe notions, such as the anti-vaccine (antivax) movement (Müller et al., 2022) and conspiracy theories (Ashwell, 2023). There are also reports of social media users becoming radicalized toward violent movements and terrorist organizations (Burton, 2023).

While AI bots have accelerated the spread of news in general, these technologies are also linked to the intensified dissemination of misinformation and disinformation via social media (Hajli et al., 2021). This trend creates increasingly fertile ground for political polarization and, in more extreme cases, violent radicalization.

Vilkins et al. (2025) emphasize that polarization is a significant symptom of the problematic disparities distressing segments of society. Hence, the polarizing appeals magnified by social media algorithms, whether authored by human actors or bots, encounter an already susceptible collective psyche and exploit this vulnerability. While polarization further damages IPS, it also serves as a kind of litmus test, revealing the fragility of the collective psyche. Therefore, while the role of social media and their algorithms in the crisis of information disorder (Wardle & Derakhshan, 2017) should be scrutinized, it is equally important to explore the deeper root causes, such as inequality, that fundamentally contribute to public dissatisfaction and institutional distrust (Kreiss & McGregor, 2023).

2.6 Malicious Use of Generative AI and Social Media Algorithms

Social media and AI can be effectively misused and abused by malicious actors when audiences remain unaware or undereducated about the processes behind these technologies. Research indicates that considerable segments of the population have significant gaps in their knowledge of AI algorithms (Du, 2023; Moravec et al., 2024). This is especially concerning given the sophistication of generative AI algorithms, which can produce high-quality deepfakes that closely mimic real audio and/or visual content. As demonstrated on an international level, vulnerable publics can be especially susceptible to such malicious campaigns (Samoilenko & Suvorova, 2023). Consequently, low levels of media and AI literacy among the public exacerbate IPS vulnerabilities, making it easier for individuals to be misled by malicious disinformation, reinforced through deepfake content, and amplified by social media algorithms (Lukacovic & Sellnow-Richmond, 2025).

3 Towards Ethical and Inclusive Social Media Algorithms: Pathways to Upholding International Psychological Security in the Digital Era

Morozov (2024) asserts that new projects must be envisioned on more ethical and emancipatory foundations for justifying, developing, and using AI applications. He points out that decades of the military-industrial complex's global dominance have rooted AI deeply in profit, surveillance, and a core motif of perpetuating hegemonies—giving rise to contemporary Big Tech, its social media platforms, and AI algorithms. Morozov argues that such origins render these technologies ill-suited for any truly emancipatory and sustainable future visions. Thus, it is crucial to envision and realize alternative projects.

Tang (2024) points out that various global societies and their traditions guide technology in ways that differ from dominant Western tendencies, offering alternatives that may warrant attention and even replication elsewhere or worldwide. The FLOSS (Free/Libre and Open Source Software) movement focuses on providing open software code, including resources for AI and algorithm development through assets such as *Ubuntu.com*. Its open-access modus operandi, which implies the encouragement of use, replication, remixing, adaptation, and sharing by all, embodies the practice and philosophy of the FLOSS movement (Ess, 2020). FLOSS's copyleft-oriented tenets stand in stark contrast to the capitalist priorities revered in the mainstream of the Global North/West. The philosophy of ubuntu, which inspired both the name and worldview championed by Ubuntu.com, is a Southern African school of thought centered on values such as community, collectivism, harmony, sharing, and consensus-building (Ngondo & Klyueva, 2023). As such, the normative prioritization of this philosophy differs significantly from the Global North/Western worldviews that drive major U.S.-based social media platforms such as Meta/Facebook/Instagram and X/Twitter, which algorithms swell consumption (Varoufakis, 2023) and polarization (Burton, 2023), further reflecting and reinforcing values of individualism and competition. Ubuntu, by contrast, outlines a vision for crafting more ethical, equitable, and emancipatory AI algorithms (Mhlambi & Tiribelli, 2023; Mokoena, 2024; van Norren, 2023) that could actually support IPS, rather than diminish it, as is often the case today.

In Western countries, regulatory initiatives such as the movement for net neutrality (Howell et al., 2025; York, 2025) strive to ensure equality of access to the internet, thereby protecting the interests of the many against the socially irresponsible practices of monopolies such as Big Tech. Similar progressive initiatives can help mitigate the negative effects of contemporary algorithms and even lay the groundwork for the development of algorithms that strengthen IPS, for example, by enhancing education. However, it remains uncertain to what extent proponents of progressive regulatory projects can succeed in the long term in the context of the consolidation of political and corporate power that has unfolded over the past few decades in the neoliberal West.

Roumate (2024) summarizes that key global international institutions such as UNESCO, the OECD, and the G20 emphasize the need to develop new and dynamic ethical guidelines and policies in response to rapidly evolving and globally reaching AI-enabled platforms. Roumate further urges global nations to prioritize the development of "future strategies to ensure human rights in the age of artificial intelligence with the need to involve all actors" (p. 133). The warning that serious ethical, normative, and legal concerns now have global implications—due particularly to the nature of contemporary social media and the massive role algorithms play within them—is echoed across academia, punditry, and broader public debates (e.g., Kissinger et al., 2021). Similarly, as Roumate (2024) accentuates, the importance of involving all stakeholders, other voices also emphasize the need to democratize access to decision-making. This includes proposals such as radical media ethics (Ward, 2014), which call for the broad public to participate in envisioning and drafting normative approaches to today's social media and artificial intelligence (Lukacovic & Sellnow-Richmond, 2023). Empowering a wider range of stakeholders to shape the rules governing social media operations and algorithms can enhance global equity by enabling more inclusive influence over platforms used by billions worldwide. Furthermore, democratizing the principles and decisions adhered to by social media companies can reinforce IPS by upholding the values of human rights, equality, and autonomy, the values prominently highlighted in key international documents and forums (Mhlambi & Tiribelli, 2023; Mokoena, 2024; Roumate, 2024; van Norren, 2023).

The question answered in this section: what can be done now to improve IPS despite the detrimental effects of the contemporary social media algorithms? To summarize, promising alternative directions include embracing open-software options and equipping various stakeholders with the knowledge and capacities needed to engage in discussions and decision-making around ethical social media conduct, AI training, and algorithm deployment. An essential step toward this future involves advancing efforts in critical media literacies (Bulger et al., 2023; Higdon, 2025) and AI literacies (Aleman & Martinez, 2024; Lukacovic & Sellnow-Richmond, 2025). In addition to educational institutions, public relations and communication professionals could and arguably should play a key role in enhancing the critical literacies of diverse stakeholders, enabling more genuine and symmetrical dialogues when norms and policies related to social media and AI algorithms are negotiated (Bowen, 2024).

Ultimately, it is imperative to underscore that the collective psyche of communities around the world is not impacted by social media algorithms in a 'magic bullet' sense—the falsified media effects theory. While the evidence we review in this chapter suggests that social media algorithms are indeed problematic and should be addressed accordingly, they are not the sole causes undermining the stability of IPS. Therefore, it is critical that institutions remain receptive to the concerns of citizens and the difficulties stemming from pervasive issues such as inequality, which distress communities globally (Kreiss & McGregor, 2023). In addition to media and AI literacies, structural reforms that improve the lives of citizens are also an essential ingredient in strengthening IPS and making it truly resilient to the threats posed by social media algorithms today and in the future.

4 Conclusion

The concerns about social media's effects on International Psychological Security (IPS) are warranted. The construction of social media algorithms is rooted in violations of user privacy and autonomy, the exploitation of workers, and the degradation of the natural environment. The deployment of these algorithms also produces a plethora of negative impacts, including overconsumption, mental health issues, and political polarization. All of these problems pose significant threats to IPS, especially given how deeply embedded social media is in the lives of a large proportion of the global population. An important step toward mitigating weakened IPS lies in efforts to improve critical media and AI literacies. Uplifting public literacy will empower broader segments of society to engage in discussions and decisions about social media norms and policies. In particular, marginalized voices must be heard in these processes, as they are often the most harmed by crises, including those crises exacerbated by social media. However, deteriorating IPS cannot be attributed solely to social media algorithms. Policymakers must also address systemic issues such as inequality, which significantly undermine public trust in institutions and create vulnerabilities that can be exploited by nefarious actors, many of whom weaponize AI and social media to sow further discord within communities.

References

Aleman, E., & Martinez, R. (2024). "It's like they are using our data against us." Counter-cartographies of AI literacy. *Reading Research Quarterly*, *59*(4), 665–677. https://doi.org/10.1002/rrq.574

Ashwell, D. (2023). Science communication and pandemics. In S. M. Croucher & A. Diers-Lawson (Eds.), *Pandemic communication* (pp. 42–58). Routledge.

Bowen, S. A. (2024). "If it can be done, it will be done:" AI ethical standards and a dual role for public relations. *Public Relations Review*, *50*(5), 1–13. https://doi.org/10.1016/j.pubrev.2024.102513

Bulger, M., Baleria, G., Hobbs, R., & Moffitt, K. R. (2023). The promise of media literacy education when "everything is at stake" and "everything is expected". *Journal of Media Literacy Education*, *15*(1), 99–108. https://doi.org/10.23860/JMLE-2023-15-1-8

Burton, J. (2023). Algorithmic extremism? The securitization of artificial intelligence (AI) and its impact on radicalism, polarization and political violence. *Technology in Society*, *75*, 1–10. https://doi.org/10.1016/j.techsoc.2023.102262

Canham, H. (2018). Theorizing community rage for decolonial action. *South African Journal of Psychology*, *48*(3), 319–330. https://doi.org/10.1177/0081246318787682

Cianconi, P., Betrò, S., & Janiri, L. (2020). The impact of climate change on mental health: A systematic descriptive review. *Frontiers in Psychiatry*, *11*(74), 1–15. https://doi.org/10.3389/fpsyt.2020.00074

De, D., El Jamal, M., Aydemir, E., & Khera, A. (2025). Social media algorithms and teen addiction: Neurophysiological impact and ethical considerations. *Cureus*, *17*(1). https://doi.org/10.7759/cureus.77145

Du, Y. R. (2023). Personalization, echo chambers, news literacy, and algorithmic literacy: A qualitative study of AI-powered news app users. *Journal of Broadcasting and Electronic Media*, *67*(3), 1–28. https://doi.org/10.1080/08838151.2023.2182787

Duffy, B. E., & Wissinger, E. (2017). Mythologies of creative work in the social media age: Fun, free, and "just being me. *International Journal of Communication*, *11*, 4652–4671. https://ijoc.org/index.php/ijoc/article/view/7322

Ess, C. (2020). *Digital media ethics* (3rd ed.). Polity Press.

Floyd, R. (2024). Ontological vs. societal security: Same difference or distinct concepts? *International Politics*, 1–19. https://doi.org/10.1057/s41311-024-00581-w

Francois, M. (2025, April 18). Can AI save the planet or is it making things worse? [Video]. YouTube. https://www.youtube.com/watch?v=GhUiU7IVCME

Hajli, N., Saeed, U., Tajvidi, M., & Shirazi, F. (2021). Social bots and the spread of disinformation in social media: The challenges of artificial intelligence. *British Journal of Management*, *33*(3), 1238–1253. https://doi.org/10.1111/1467-8551.12554

Hartley, A. (2024). To whom does the world belong? In E. Morozov et al. (Eds.), *AI futures* (pp. 98–123). Haymarket Books.

Higdon, N. (2025). Constructive conflict and critical media literacy. In S. A. Samoilenko & S. Simmons (Eds.), *The handbook of social and political conflict* (pp. 415–426). Wiley.

Howell, B., González, F. H., Serentschy, G., Jamison, M., Potgieter, P., Layton, R., & García, Í. H. (2025). Perspectives on political influences on changes in telecommunications and internet economy markets. *Telecommunications Policy*, *49*(2), 1–16. https://doi.org/10.1016/j.telpol.2024.102901

Kanungo, A. (2023, July 18). The green dilemma: Can AI fulfil its potential without harming the environment? *Earth.org*. https://earth.org/the-green-dilemma-can-ai-fulfil-its-potential-without-harming-the-environment/

Kissinger, H., Schmidt, E., & Huttenlocher, D. P. (2021). *The age of AI: And our human future*. Little Brown & Company.

Kreiss, D., & McGregor, S. C. (2023). A review and provocation: On polarization and platforms. *New Media and Society*, *26*(1), 556–579. https://doi.org/10.1177/14614448231161880

Laruelle, M. (2025). Illiberalism as a conceptual prism for studying political and social conflict. In S. A. Samoilenko & S. Simmons (Eds.), *The handbook of social and political conflict* (pp. 57–64). Wiley.

Laskin, A. V. (2025). Consumerism as the driving force of human identity in 2050: The role of marketing, advertising, and public relations. In A. V. Laskin & K. Freberg (Eds.), *Public relations and strategic communication in 2050: Trends shaping the future of the profession* (pp. 131–139). Routledge.

Longdon, J. (2025). *Natural connection: What indigenous wisdom & marginalized people teach us about environmental action*. Penguin Random House.
Lukacovic, M. N., & Sellnow-Richmond, D. D. (2023). COVID-19 pandemic and the rise of MUAI threats to national and international psychological security. In E. Pashentsev (Ed.), *The Palgrave handbook of malicious use of AI and psychological security* (pp. 175–201). Palgrave Macmillan. https://doi.org/10.1007/978-3-031-22552-9_7
Lukacovic, M. N., & Sellnow-Richmond, D. D. (2025). The growth of malicious AI: Countering disinformation and deepfakes amid mega-crises. In A. V. Laskin & K. Freberg (Eds.), *Public relations and strategic communication in 2050: Trends shaping the future of the profession* (pp. 22–35). Routledge. https://doi.org/10.4324/9781003426653
McGorry, P., Gunasiri, H., Mei, C., Rice, S., & Gao, C. X. (2025). The youth mental health crisis: Analysis and solutions. *Frontiers in Psychiatry*, *15*, 1–20. https://doi.org/10.3389/fpsyt.2024.1517533
Mhlambi, S., & Tiribelli, S. (2023). Decolonizing AI ethics: Relational autonomy as a means to counter AI harms. *Topoi*, *42*, 867–880. https://doi.org/10.1007/s11245-022-09874-2
Mokoena, K. K. (2024). A holistic ubuntu artificial intelligence ethics approach in South Africa. *Verbum Et Ecclesia*, *45*(1), 1–8. https://doi.org/10.4102/ve.v45i1.3100
Moravec, V., Hynek, N., Gavurova, B., & Kubak, M. (2024). Everyday artificial intelligence unveiled: Societal awareness of technological transformation. *Oeconomia Copernicana*, *15*(2), 367–406. https://doi.org/10.24136/oc.2961
Morozov, E. (2024). The AI we deserve. In E. Morozov, et al. (Eds.), *AI futures* (pp. 9–37). Boston Review—Haymarket Books.
Müller, J., Tellier, A., & Kurschilgen, M. (2022). Echo chambers and opinion dynamics explain the occurrence of vaccination hesitancy. *Royal Society Open Science*, *9*(10), 220367. https://doi.org/10.1098/rsos.220367
Narayanan, A., & Kapoor, S. (2024). *AI snake oi: What artificial intelligence can do, what it can't, and how to tell the difference*. Princeton University Press.
Ngondo, P. S., & Klyueva, A. (2023). Inviting an Ubuntu-based approach to public relations theory building in Sub-Saharan Africa. In C. H. Botan & E. J. Sommerfeld (Eds.), *Public Relations Theory III* (pp. 374–392). Routledge.
Olesen, T. (2025. Big tech whistleblowing: Frances Haugen and the Facebook Files. *Organization*. published online 1–20. https://doi.org/10.1177/13505084251321785
Paci, B. (2024). The hidden abode of artificial intelligence production: Stretching the limits of artificial intelligence ethics and critique. *Thesis Eleven*, *184–185*(1), 152–166. https://doi.org/10.1177/07255136241292366
Pashentsev, E. (2023). General content and possible threat classifications of the malicious use of artificial intelligence to psychological security. In E. Pashentsev (Ed.), *The Palgrave handbook of malicious use of AI and psychological security* (pp. 23–46). Palgrave Macmillan. https://doi.org/10.1007/978-3-031-22552-9_2
Pellegrino, A., Abe, M., & Shannon, R. (2022). The dark side of social media: Content effects on the relationship between materialism and consumption behaviors. *Frontiers in Psychology*, *13*(870614), 1–15. https://doi.org/10.3389/fpsyg.2022.870614
Petrosyan, A. (2025, April 1). Worldwide digital population 2025. *Statista*. https://www.statista.com/statistics/617136/digital-population-worldwide/
Rani, U., & Dhir, R. K. (2024, December 10). The artificial intelligence illusion: How invisible workers fuel the "automated" economy. *International Labor Organization*. https://www.ilo.org/resource/article/artificial-intelligence-illusion-how-invisible-workers-fuel-automated
Reuben, A., Manczak, E. M., Cabrera, L. Y., Alegria, M., Bucher, M. L., Freeman, E. C., Miller, G. W., Solomon, G. M., & Perry, M. J. (2022). The interplay of environmental exposures and mental health: Setting an agenda. *Environmental Health Perspectives*, *130*(2), 025001–1–11. https://doi.org/10.1289/EHP9889
Roumate, F. (2024). *Artificial intelligence and the new world order*. Springer Nature. https://doi.org/10.1007/978-3-031-50312-2

Rowe, N. (2023, August 2). "It's destroyed me completely": Kenyan moderators decry toll of training of AI models. *The Guardian*. https://www.theguardian.com/technology/2023/aug/02/ai-chatbot-training-human-toll-content-moderator-meta-openai

Roy, R. (2021). Precarious privilege: Globalism, digital biopolitics, and tech-workers' movements in India. *The European Legacy*, *26*(7–8), 675–691. https://doi.org/10.1080/10848770.2021.1962641

Samoilenko, S. A., & Suvorova, I. (2023). Artificial intelligence and deepfakes in strategic deception campaigns: The U.S. and Russian experiences. In E. Pashentsev (Ed.), *The Palgrave handbook of malicious use of AI and psychological security* (pp. 507–529). Palgrave Macmillan. https://doi.org/10.1007/978-3-031-22552-9_19

Tacheva, Z., & Ramasubramanian, S. (2023). Challenging AI empire: Toward a decolonial and queer framework of data resurgence. *Indigo* (University of Illinois at Chicago). 1–16. https://doi.org/10.31124/advance.22012724.v1

Tang, A. (2024). The real legacy of cybernetics. In E. Morozov, et al. (Eds.), *AI futures* (pp. 43–47). Boston Review –Haymarket Books.

Vacarelu, M. (2023). Malicious use of artificial intelligence in political campaigns: Challenges for international psychological security for the next decades. In E. Pashentsev (Ed.), *The Palgrave handbook of malicious use of AI and psychological security* (pp. 203–230). Palgrave Macmillan. https://doi.org/10.1007/978-3-031-22552-9_8

van der Ven, H., Corry, D., Rawie, E., Provost, V. J., & Syukron, M. (2024). Generative AI and social media may exacerbate the climate crisis. *Global Environmental Politics*, *24*(2), 9–18. https://doi.org/10.1162/glep_a_00747

van Norren, D. E. (2023). The ethics of artificial intelligence, UNESCO and the African Ubuntu perspective. *Journal of Information, Communication and Ethics in Society*, *21*(1), 112–128. https://doi.org/10.1108/JICES-04-2022-0037

Varoufakis, Y. (2023). *Technofeudalism: What killed capitalism*. Melville House Publishing.

Vilkins, S., Bruns, A., Svegaard, S., Choucair, T., & Esau, K. (2025). Polarization. In S. A. Samoilenko & S. Simmons (Eds.), *The handbook of social and political conflict* (pp. 19–29). Wiley.

Ward, S. J. A. (2014). Radical media ethics. *Digital Journalism*, 2(4), 455–471. https://doi.org/10.1080/21670811.2014.952985

Wardle, C., & Derakhshan, H. (2017). Information disorder: Toward an interdisciplinary framework for research and policy making. *Council of Europe*. https://tverezo.info/wp-content/uploads/2017/11/PREMS-162317-GBR-2018-Report-desinformation-A4-BAT.pdf

York, J. C. (2025, July 16). EFF and 80 organizations call on EU to preserve net neutrality in the Digital Networks Act. *Electronic Frontier Foundation*. https://www.eff.org/deeplinks/2025/07/eff-and-80-organizations-call-eu-policymakers-reject-fair-share-proposals

AI in Information Warfare: Transforming Conflict and Geopolitical Dynamics

Hajji Said

1 Introduction

Phenomena such as wars, crises, and technological revolutions often generate profound social transformations. Scholars typically seek to identify the root causes, trace the developmental trajectories, and construct theoretical models to explain the impact of these phenomena and forecast potential outcomes. However, certain phenomena resist clear definition, abstraction, and incorporation into established conceptual frameworks. Overcoming this conceptual complexity often requires using metaphors and explanations that involve a kind of self-interpretation.

This is the case for information warfare (IW), which is a hybrid, complex, and interconnected domain. It brings together contradictory elements such as conflict and quiet, hidden influences, as well as peace and various forms of war. IW also merges the dynamic and constantly changing nature of information with a static nature usually associated with secrecy. These characteristics justify my use of metaphorical language.

In its dynamic form, it is like the moon, with the visible side being actions, tools, and effects, while the hidden side is shaped by secrecy and conceals strategic goals, geopolitical ambitions, and competition over advanced technologies. In its static form, one can liken IW to an iceberg, in which the visible part consists of observable infrastructures of control, tactics, and tools, especially artificial intelligence (AI), and hidden beneath the surface are structures of power, national interests, and algorithmic manipulation.

In this context, AI emerges as both a technological enabler and a transformative agent. AI can process vast datasets at unprecedented speed, thereby enhancing the ability of state and non-state actors to influence adversaries by automating decision

H. Said (✉)
Mohammed V University, Rabat, Morocco
e-mail: hajjisaid@hotmail.com

F. Roumate (ed.), *AI, Information, and Global Dynamics*, Contributions to International Relations,
https://doi.org/10.1007/978-3-032-13528-5_6

processes, manipulating narratives, and accelerating operational tempo (Daxhelet, 2023, pp. 6, 10–11). AI is considered important because of the speed at which it can process big data and because of its ability to direct that data and automatically make decisions about its exploitation. In this regard, Hunter et al. (2024) point out that AI significantly enhances the speed and tactical precision of IW and influences operations. When we talk about war, what usually comes to mind are soldiers and military equipment. However, civilians have increasingly become the primary targets of such operations and find themselves at the center of algorithmic battles aimed at cognitive disruption, behavioral manipulation, and the erosion of trust (Čižik, 2017).

This shift from traditional to cognitive warfare represents a profound break with classical military logic. It blurs the lines between "times of war" and "times of peace" and raises doubts about which military tactics are most effective.

The implications of AI are not merely strategic or theoretical—they are structural and far-reaching. Warfare is no longer limited to geographic space; it increasingly includes algorithmic and informational environments in which both physical and non-physical actors operate (Taddeo, 2012, p. 113). Even worse, a single political statement made through a media outlet can shake the world within minutes. For example, in April 2025, Trump announced the imposition of comprehensive US tariffs on imports, triggering major turmoil in global financial markets and losses exceeding $6.6 trillion. His seemingly casual announcement was perceived as a declaration of economic war, provoking strong reactions from trade partners and prompting financial institutions to warn of an impending global recession. Within days of his initial statement and under mounting pressure from the markets, Trump announced a temporary 90-day suspension of the additional tariffs, excluding those targeting China (Chughtai & Haddad, 2025).

It is also possible for a single AI-generated piece of disinformation to alter political outcomes, destabilize institutions, and challenge democratic governance (Di Pietro et al., 2021). For example, in an incident that caused confusion in global media, Morocco was subjected, in 2023, to an extensive media and psychological campaign led by neighboring countries, including France, Spain, and Algeria, as well as the European Parliament, about its use of the Pegasus spyware system. Morocco responded to mounting international pressure through a legal battle, through which it was ultimately exonerated (European Parliament, 2023).

The dual-use nature of AI as a shield and an offensive tool, combined with its reliance on secretive, automated, and sometimes autonomous mechanisms, raises pressing legal and ethical concerns, especially where the balance of power is uneven.

Given these dynamics, this article investigates the following central research question: How is the integration of AI transforming the nature, strategies, ethical-legal frameworks, and the broader dynamics of conflict and geopolitics in IW during the digital age?

This question is addressed using a four-part analytical framework. First, it traces the conceptual evolution of AI and IW to clarify how their theoretical foundations have shifted and their trajectories have become increasingly intertwined. Second, it examines the forms and state-level strategies involved, distinguishing between defensive, offensive, and hybrid approaches, as well as the geopolitical implications. Third, it considers contemporary case studies that demonstrate AI's operational role in information conflicts from the Global North and South. Finally, the study explores the legal and ethical challenges posed by AI-driven IW, particularly in relation to sovereignty, legitimacy, and the evolving norms of conflict.

This study contributes to ongoing debates in the fields of security studies and digital warfare, particularly regarding psychological operations and fifth-generation warfare. It also adds to the field of international ethics by offering an integrated and structured analysis of a rapidly evolving threat landscape. The article combines conceptual, strategic, empirical, and normative dimensions to provide a comprehensive understanding of how AI is reshaping the tools of contemporary conflict, battlefield, logic, and geographical scope.

2 Literature Review and Theoretical Framework:

The concept of IW has significantly transformed since the 1990s from a primarily military-centered doctrine into a complex, multifaceted strategic paradigm. Bryczek-Wróbel and Moszczyński (2022) provide a rich historical account of the evolution of AI, focusing on the shift from military-centered models to psychological and hybrid strategies. The authors make a valuable distinction between the Western technological approach and the Russian tactics (p. 57), and their analysis is supported by concrete examples. However, the article remains largely descriptive and lacks a clear theoretical framework. Despite its relevance to their discussion, the authors overlook AI as a critical emerging tool. Moreover, their geographical focus on Europe limits the article's application beyond the region.

Hunter et al. (2024) present a structured and comparative analysis of how the United States, China, and Russia integrate AI into their IW and influence operations. The strength of this article is its focus on regime type and surveillance capitalism as key variables shaping state strategies in this domain. It also provides concrete examples and clarifies essential concepts such as cyber-enabled influence operations and cognitive warfare. However, despite its empirical richness and comparative approach, the article lacks an updated and in-depth examination of the ethical and normative dimensions of the topic. Moreover, it offers insufficient forward-looking insights regarding the evolution of AI-supported IW tactics.

From a tactical and societal perspective, Božić and Gregić (2024) explore the dual role of AI in hybrid warfare—as a source of disinformation and a potential tool to combat this. The authors provide concrete examples from recent conflicts and highlight ethical, psychological, and social risks, but pay limited attention to the structural transformations of warfare doctrine.

Daxhelet (2023) focuses more on the operational and defense policy implications of AI, particularly within European contexts. In analyzing AI's integration into military decision-making, unmanned systems, and cyber defense, the author confirms its increasing centrality in military planning but does not theorize its impact on IW.

Finally, the EIW3R project—short for "The Ethics of Information Warfare: Risks, Rights and Responsibilities"—was a two-year research initiative conducted from June 2010 to May 2012 under the European Union's Seventh Framework Programme (FP7), developed a pioneering ethical framework for IW, highlighting risks related to responsibility gaps, civilian targeting, and the erosion of privacy. The project report argues that IW reshapes warfare by involving hybrid agents and blurring civilian–military boundaries. However, the focus of the project was theoretical, offering limited insights into recent AI-driven dynamics.

This chapter addresses a specific gap in the literature concerning this broader field. We propose a conceptual framework that positions AI as both a supporting technology and a core and constitutive element of modern IW. By integrating theoretical, strategic, operational, and ethical dimensions, along with real-world examples, this chapter offers an innovative synthesis that brings together fragmented debates and redefines IW in light of the profound transformations introduced by AI.

3 Research Methodology

This chapter employs an interpretive and comparative approach. It examines how AI is reshaping IW at four levels. It offers a conceptual analysis of evolving definitions, a strategic comparison of national doctrines, case studies of real-world applications, and an ethical-legal review of accountability and regulation. The methodology connects theory with practice, offering a structured and multi-layered understanding of AI's impact on conflict and digital security.

This chapter avoids merely repeating the findings of the literature by adopting a distinct theoretical approach to frame the concept of IW within clear and coherent analytical boundaries. The central focus here is AI's pivotal role in shaping the theory and practice of IW. The title of this article, "AI in Information Warfare: Transforming Conflict and Geopolitical Dynamics," reflects the following fundamental hypothesis: AI is not merely a complementary tool in new forms of warfare; rather, it is the most powerful force capable of altering the balance of informational and geopolitical conflicts. I approach the subject through the four main axes above; these complement each other to provide a comprehensive overview.

Information Warfare: Concept, Shifts, and AI Power Information Warfare—as a complex concept—and AI, as a tool and a conflict environment, have different origins and have undergone distinct conceptual transformations, but both have had major impacts in the strategic and geopolitical domains. The two concepts began as purely theoretical and have developed into computer programs and autonomous systems with high precision and impact. These blend field effectiveness with psychological influence. AI and IW developed in parallel and have ultimately become central tools for shaping conflict and asserting power in the AI era.

Information warfare has also undergone a conceptual transformation. Taddeo (2012) argues that the information revolution has reshaped our metaphysical view of reality, shifting from material to informational ontology, where "objects and processes are increasingly seen as de-physicalised" (p. 111). In this context, war is no longer defined by physical violence but understood as a transversal phenomenon spanning physical and virtual domains: "IW redefines the concept of war as a phenomenon not necessarily sanguinary and violent, but rather transversal" (Taddeo, 2012, p. 118). This shift marks IW's ontological and strategic novelty.

Traditionally, warfare refers to armed conflict between organized entities and relies on kinetic force and territorial control. IW has evolved from ancient strategic deception to a sophisticated system of digital and psychological operations aimed at shaping perception, disrupting decision-making, and influencing geopolitical outcomes. While traditional warfare seeks physical dominance through ground, sea, and air battles, IW aims for cognitive and informational superiority, particularly in the digital space. Information is thus of growing importance in war and peace.

The historical roots of IW can be traced to classical military theories, with an early example in Sun Tzu's *The Art of War*, which states that "the supreme art of war is to subdue the enemy without fighting" (Barabash et al., 2019, p. 110). The Mongol leader Genghis Khan also relied heavily on psychological warfare and spread fear among his enemies before engaging them on the battlefield (Gerlich, 2024, p. 13).

This history highlights the centrality of manipulation and psychological influence as instruments of power. Over the course of the twentieth century, particularly during World Wars I and II, IW evolved into structured psychological operations; in the West, organized dissemination of propaganda was a popular tool to weaken enemy morale (Barabash et al., 2019, p. 111). These practices became institutionalized during the Cold War through state media and intelligence services.

The term "information warfare" was more formally recognized in 1976 with the work of Thomas Rona, who identified vulnerabilities in the US information infrastructure and introduced IW as a form of cyber-oriented confrontation (Barabash et al., 2019, p. 113). The Gulf War (1990–1991) marked a turning point in the trajectory of IW, with the US Department of Defense formally defining it within a military-operational context as "information operations conducted during time of crisis or conflict to achieve or promote specific objectives over a specific adversary or adversaries" (Joyner & Lotrionte, 2001, p. 827). This definition emphasizes the operational integration of information tools into command-and-control systems.

With the continued evolution of IW, its definition has expanded beyond the military domain. Williams (2010) emphasizes its reach into corporate, political, and societal arenas, driven by cybercrime, infrastructure vulnerabilities, and digital propaganda. Williams (2010) defines IW as "the integrated use of military force and political, economic, informational, and other non-military measures" (pp. 38–39).

Thornton's (2015) widely cited definition in the contemporary strategic context is that "modern warfare is to be dominated by information and psychological warfare [with] the main objective [being] to reduce the necessity for deploying hard military power" (p. 43). The author notes how Russia has placed IW at the core of its military doctrine, using coordinated messaging and media manipulation to achieve objectives without direct military engagement. Thornton's view reflects a broader paradigm shift: IW is no longer peripheral but central to modern conflict.

AI and IW follow changing paths of definition, influenced by shifts in philosophy, technology and strategy. Since these fields are always evolving, their meanings and related policies remain unclear. AI has moved from its manifestation as basic logic systems to autonomous machines that raise ethical problems. IW has gone from being understood as simple deception to becoming an important tool for geopolitical influence. Understanding these parallel developments is essential for comprehending today's conflicts, which increasingly depend on the manipulation of thinking, control of algorithms, and the use of strategic information rather than direct violence.

4 Artificial Intelligence in Information Warfare: Forms, State Strategies, and Geopolitical Implications.

Before analyzing the different manifestations of IW, the strategic approaches pursued by nation-states, and the disruptive effects of AI, I begin with a precise and up-to-date definition that reflects the current nature of these types of conflict.

Given that warfare is the backdrop of this analysis, it is especially relevant to refer to the definition offered by NATO as a collective defense alliance and as a strategic institution shaping contemporary doctrines on IW and AI integration. In 2005, NATO defined IW as follows:

> an operation conducted in order to gain an information advantage over the opponent. It consists in controlling one's own information space, protecting access to one's own information, while acquiring and using the opponent's information, destroying their information systems and disrupting the information flow. Information warfare is not a new phenomenon, yet it contains innovative elements as the effect of technological development, which results in information being disseminated faster and on a larger scale. (NATO, 2020)

This foundational definition highlights three core principles: securing an information space, exploiting and disrupting the opponent's information space, and leveraging technological advancements to amplify speed and scale of information operations and their effects. The scope and complexity of IW have significantly expanded. The original definition, while still relevant, does not fully capture the multidimensional and hybrid nature of contemporary IW.

A modern definition must account for the integration of AI and data-driven technologies, the psychological and behavioral strategies of influence, the increasing involvement of non-state actors, and the effects on civil society. It must also reflect that today's conflicts occur within multiple domains, and the lines between civil, military, digital, and cognitive domains are increasingly blurred.

To clarify, this study revisits certain recent military and research ideas, not for the sake of repetition, but to highlight how AI is reshaping our understanding of strategy within the context of IW.

Like traditional warfare, IW manifests in two main forms: defensive and offensive. Generally, defensive strategies take priority because most states focus on safeguarding their land, people, infrastructure, and vital interests. By contrast, offensive strategies are usually adopted by those seeking to gain control, cause disruption, or obtain geopolitical leverage.

Although this distinction is rarely made explicit in public, it can often be discerned through a country's military posture, cyber policies, and economic decisions. For example, China has historically adopted an inward-looking approach. For centuries, it remained relatively insulated behind its Great Wall, emphasizing trade over conquest. In contrast, the United States has followed a more outward-facing, expansionist trajectory, with its naval presence reaching the Mediterranean as early as the late eighteenth century. In many ways, these historical orientations continue to shape present-day strategies in the digital domain. Both countries now adapt their long-standing geopolitical identities to IW, influencing the tools they adopt and the tactics they employ.

The following analysis traces the evolving landscape of IW, from its pre-AI foundations through its transformation by intelligent systems to its strategic role in global power competition.

5 Information Warfare Before the Rise of Artificial Intelligence

In the mid-1990s, Martin Libicki challenged the prevailing view, asserting that "information warfare, as a separate technique of waging war, does not exist." (Libicki, 1995) Instead of considering it a unified and distinct form of conflict, Libicki argued that IW is a loosely connected set of practices and technologies, grouped more for rhetorical or administrative reasons than conceptual coherence.

Libicki identified seven distinct forms of IW to illustrate this fragmentation: Command and Control Warfare (C2W), Intelligence-Based Warfare (IBW), Electronic Warfare (EW), Psychological Warfare (PSYWAR), Hacker Warfare, Economic Information Warfare (EIW), and Cyber Warfare (Libicki, 1995). This classification remains central in the field, providing a clear framework connecting theoretical ideas with real-world practice. By breaking down the broad concept, Libicki helped explain the many ways information can be used in conflict.

Contemporary approaches tend to simplify IW into offensive and defensive categories. These simpler distinctions nevertheless reflect the practical use of Libicki's original, more detailed framework. Offensive IW involves the use of digital tools and psychological tactics to manipulate, degrade, or disrupt an adversary's information environment (Defense Magazine, 2024). This includes cyberattacks, social media manipulation, AI-generated disinformation, and psychological operations. Defensive IW, by contrast, focuses on protecting national sovereignty and shielding domestic narratives from foreign influence. It includes efforts like data protection, counter-disinformation strategies, and strategic communication, all of which are intended to enhance societal resilience rather than destabilize external actors.

In considering the impact of AI on IW, it is important to recognize that the boundaries between historical phases are not always clear. Techniques and technologies often overlap, and traditional forms of warfare—as classified by Libicki—are increasingly integrated with newer modes, such as cyber operations. As Waltz (1998) notes, "the historical transformation of warfare has passed from agrarian-era wars of mass to industrial-era wars of maneuver to information-era wars of knowledge" (p. 10). This developmental account by Waltz highlights the growing centrality of information in conflict. Waltz also emphasizes how the information age depends on tools for "knowledge creation, knowledge detection and discovery, data fusion, data mining, and the integration of multiple information sources" (Waltz, 1998, p. 84), all of which have been greatly accelerated by the development of AI.

It is useful to divide the evolution of IW into three broad phases: the pre-digital era, the digital age, and the AI-driven era. This framework helps clarify how the form and function of IW have shifted over time. Before examining the current AI-enhanced phase, it is helpful to outline the key characteristics of IW in the first two stages.

Before the emergence of AI, IW advanced primarily through human ingenuity and conventional technologies. Ancient empires such as the Roman and Mongolian empires employed intimidation, deception, and psychological tactics to weaken adversaries (Tzu, 2010, fifth century BCE). With advances in communication, IW became more sophisticated. During the World Wars, mass media, in the form of radio, newspapers, and propaganda posters, were deployed to shape public perception and sustain morale:

> Over 3,000 programmes were transmitted worldwide in around fifty languages; over 100 radio stations in the USA alone took transmission; they were even the first Games to be shown on television ... Many more millions had read reports of them, or seen newsreel coverage. (Kershaw, 2001, p. 527)

The Cold War introduced a new dimension to IW, with Soviet intelligence agencies heavily engaged in disinformation and media manipulation. Clandestine broadcasting, foreign newspapers, and front organizations were among the tools used to influence global opinion and destabilize rivals. One notable example is Operation INFEKTION, during which Soviet agents spread false claims that the United States had created the HIV/AIDS virus (Boghardt, 2009).

In the early digital era, new vulnerabilities emerged. One of the first major incidents demonstrating the disruptive potential of self-replicating software was the 1998 Morris Worm, which paralyzed thousands of academic and military systems (Spafford, 1989). Decades later, the threat landscape had come to include large-scale cyber espionage. The 2015 breach of the US Office of Personnel Management is a major example of such espionage. In this incident, malicious actors exfiltrated 4.2 million personnel files, 21.5 million security clearance records, and 5.6 million fingerprint records, including data on individuals outside the government, such as children and family members (RAND Corporation, 2022, p. 27).

Chinese cyber espionage operations such as Titan Rain have also revealed the growing scale and sophistication of state-sponsored cyberattacks against the United States (Cyber Security News, 2023). On a different front, the 2007 cyberattacks on Estonia were a politically motivated digital campaign triggered by the relocation of a Soviet-era monument. These attacks involved distributed denial of service assaults on government portals, media, banks, and public services (Ottis, 2008).

Despite these advances, pre-AI IW was largely dependent on human-driven strategies, manual decision-making, and traditional media platforms. Prior to AI's transformative impact, most operations were reactive rather than predictive or autonomous.

6 The Era of Artificial Intelligence in Information Warfare

The rise of AI is transforming IW. Automated systems are shifting the balance of power by equipping states and non-state actors with new tools to influence, disrupt, and adapt in real time. These capabilities create increased pressure on traditional legal frameworks and ethical norms, exposing gaps in the rules governing conflict. As intelligent systems gain autonomy, they accelerate operations and challenge conventional understandings of what it means to wage war.

AI has redefined the strategic, operational, and legal-ethical dimensions of IW. Its integration has extended traditional methods of conflict while introducing novel modes of manipulation, disruption, and influence. As a result, warfare has moved into a cognitive and digital battlefield in which human agency is reduced, and algorithmic decision-making has become central. In this context, "the integration of artificially intelligent machines is likely to fundamentally transform the nature of warfare into an impersonal phenomenon" (Daxhelet, 2023, p. 18).

This shift has led some to argue that IW has altered the conduct of war itself, regardless of whether it is a revolutionary change or an evolutionary phase. Established techniques such as psychological operations and EW have been strengthened, and new practices have been enabled, including adversarial AI attacks and cognitive hacking (Damjanović, 2017, p. 1044). Strategically, AI erodes the boundaries between kinetic and cognitive domains. The introduction of autonomous weapons systems raises "the troubling possibility that machines could make life-and-death decisions without human oversight," thus weakening the role of human judgment in conflict dynamics (Johnson, 2019, p. 20).

Methodologically, AI has diversified the operational landscape. On the offensive side, algorithmic tools are increasingly used "to spread information on social media to highlight divisions and political tensions in democracies as part of its overall 'divide and conquer' strategy" (Hunter et al., 2024, p. 10). Contemporary information operations include adversarial machine learning, automated deepfake generation, social media manipulation, psychological profiling, and bot-driven saturation of information ecosystems.

Defensively, states have addressed these challenges by using AI to broaden their tactical range. They now rely on systems that offer "a greater spectrum of possible tactics ranging from more complex IWIO detection software to more powerful misinformation techniques (e.g., social media propaganda, deepfake videos, and bot proliferation)" (Hunter et al., 2024, p. 3). Techniques such as micro-targeted influence campaigns, real-time narrative disruption, and counter-disinformation programs have become standard in defensive information operations. Such efforts are increasingly supported by unmanned systems, defined as those that "operate partially or entirely without human intervention or supervision"—which use AI to conduct autonomous missions across land, air, and sea (Daxhelet, 2023, p. 12).

The technologies driving this transformation in IW are critical. Machine learning algorithms, swarm robotics, cyber defense systems, and advanced natural language processing tools support offensive and defensive applications. Generative adversarial networks are "employed to create realistic fake texts, images, and videos, while other models are tasked with detecting such material" (Lande & Danyk, 2024, p. 3). Swarm-based drone technology involves the use of "swarms of small or micro drones or unmanned aerial vehicles to make decisions autonomously based on shared information" (Abbas et al., 2024, p. 197). Sentiment analysis has also become a vital tool for detecting disinformation and measuring emotional responses in information environments (Santos, 2023, p. 684).

At the operational level, AI's incorporation into military systems has allowed the automation of tasks "from surveillance to decision-making, thereby increasing efficiency and reducing human error" (Future Center, 2024). However, this automation introduces its own set of vulnerabilities. Artificial neural networks, as has been noted, "cannot be considered as stable information structures ... they are vulnerable to external threats and manipulation in information warfare contexts" (Grabusts et al., 2019, p. 59). These weaknesses open the door to data poisoning, adversarial perturbations, and the exploitation of self-learning systems—each capable of undermining system reliability and mission integrity.

Ultimately, AI is increasingly viewed as an enabling infrastructure rather than a standalone weapon, "more akin to electricity, radios, radar, and C4ISR systems, than a 'weapon per se'" (Johnson, 2019, p. 5). The integration of AI into IW has reshaped the strategic environment. Regarding offensive efforts, the focus is on manipulation, deception, and the destabilization of adversary populations and infrastructures. Defensively, AI is used to detect emerging threats, protect key systems, and strengthen resilience. Technical cyberwarfare seeks to disable or weaponize digital infrastructures, while beliefs, perceptions, and decision-making processes are targeted in cognitive warfare. These various developments are redefining the tools of conflict and reshaping its fundamental logic.

7 AI as a Geopolitical Weapon via Information Warfare

In the preceding section, I examined the technical and operational transformation brought about by AI. It is equally important to recognize the role of AI in elevating IW to become a central instrument of geopolitical strategy. Information operations are no longer auxiliary to conventional military campaigns; they are capable of entirely shaping global alignments, undermining adversaries, and projecting state power across physical and digital domains. In this evolving context, "Information warfare can be considered now as a very powerful tool, by which political integrity of states and alliances can be influenced" (Čižik, 2017). AI's strategic value lies in its technological advancement and its capacity to reposition the informational sphere as a primary arena of power competition.

Recent analyses affirm that "new technologies like AI are becoming key players in geopolitical strategies as countries compete for military, economic, and technological power" (Power, Pixels and Politics, 2025, Chapter 5.1). As such, AI is not simply a modernization tool. It is a force that reshapes global power relations, influencing national security policies, trade partnerships, and diplomatic alignments.

This transformation has also prompted a rethinking of sovereignty. IW, once an extension of conventional statecraft, has come to be a standalone mechanism of geopolitical disruption, capable of altering regime stability and redrawing regional balances: "Today, technologies seem to go beyond their status as a tool of power, turning into active players, who determine policies, sharpen stakes, trigger competitions" (Popescu, 2022). Furthermore, "step by step, artificial intelligence, 5G, cyber security, robotics, semiconductors and microprocessors, cloud computing, cloud combat and digital networks have taken over human activities and, by extension, international geopolitical dynamics" (Popescu, 2022). These developments reveal that AI is altering the structures through which states assert control.

At the center of this shift in how states assert control is the growing role of AI in surveillance, information control, and psychological operations: "A significant result of this tech race is the rise of cyber sovereignty, where countries aim to regain control over their digital spaces" (Wu, 2025). As a result, sovereignty has expanded beyond territorial boundaries to data infrastructure, algorithmic governance, and informational ecosystems. States that dominate these acquire a new form of strategic influence over domestic populations and foreign rivals.

The diffusion of AI technologies has also altered the global strategic balance by empowering smaller states and non-state actors. The accessibility of advanced systems has diminished the technological monopoly once held by great powers, enabling new players to engage in high-impact operations. This shift challenges traditional models of deterrence and introduces the possibility of "digital occupation," where influence is exerted via domination of the information environment rather than physical control.

As highlighted in a recent analysis, such dynamics "could lead to the division of global systems, with regional groups aligning technologically to counterbalance larger powers, a situation reminiscent of the Cold War" (Wu, 2025, p. 655). The result may be an AI ecosystem that is fragmented across the US, China, Russia, Europe, and India, with each governed by distinct security protocols, technological standards, and informational architectures. In this divided landscape, the risk of geopolitical disintegration intensifies, along with the emergence of new forms of digital alliances and strategic blocs.

The race to dominate the AI-cyber nexus has intensified global mistrust: "The race to develop AI-powered cyber capabilities may lead to increased rivalry among nations. Competition to gain a technological edge can breed mistrust and suspicion" (Vance, 2023). As international systems adapt to this new paradigm, AI is no longer a neutral tool but a geopolitical force with direct consequences for global security.

The next section turns from strategic theory to operational practice, examining concrete examples of how AI is transforming the conduct of IW in real-world scenarios.

8 AI on the Informational Battlefield: Operational Case Studies

Before moving further into the analysis, I would like to highlight two key ideas that are essential for grasping how IW is changing in the era of artificial intelligence:

First, the spread of AI technologies to smaller countries and non-state groups brings significant geopolitical risks. This change challenges traditional military power structures and creates a new type of technological deterrence that is affordable and widely accessible. A striking example of this shift in doctrine is the use of low-cost, AI-controlled drones in actual operations.

Second, AI is transforming the battlefield by extending conflicts beyond the physical and digital spaces into the cognitive and informational realms. Therefore, the line between peace and war is becoming less clear, creating a constant environment of psychological warfare. Today's information operations, mostly powered by social media and sophisticated audiovisual manipulation, are carried out on a scale and with an intensity that far surpasses the propaganda practices of the Cold War era.

Three case sets are examined to illustrate these trends. The first concerns developing countries, particularly the evolving information conflict between Morocco and Algeria. The second focuses on high-intensity IW between global powers: the United States and China, as well as Russia and Ukraine. The third focuses on middle-power countries: India and Pakistan. In all cases, AI functions as a strategic multiplier, expanding conflicts into the cyber, cognitive, and psychological spheres.

In the Moroccan–Algerian rivalry, long-standing tensions over the Moroccan Sahara have provided fertile ground for AI-enabled IW (International Crisis Group, 2024). Disinformation has become a core tactic in this conflict. The escalating attacks, growing sophistication, and politically charged nature of the breaches are blurring the lines between cyberactivism and cyberwarfare" (Meatech Watch, 2025, April 11). The rapid response and scale of operations suggest "automated AI-driven techniques" (AI in information warfare, 2025). Morocco's investment in global AI initiatives further underscores this shift (AISEC, 2025).

AI is increasingly central to high-intensity information operations in the Global North. It has allowed state and non-state actors to project influence without direct military engagement, redefining how conflict is conducted. China, for example, employs AI for narrative control and mass influence campaigns: "AI technologies enable new modes of influence, where disinformation campaigns can be automated, personalized, and deployed at scale" (Pauwels, 2024, p. 9). China also exports its surveillance infrastructure and algorithmic tools to reinforce its geopolitical narratives: "China is now in the process of building core components of such a system of digital authoritarianism. Such systems are already being emulated in a global competition with liberal democracy" (Wright, 2018, p. iii). China has targeted operations at Taiwanese populations using AI-driven bots and machine-optimized messaging (Hunter et al., 2023, p. 25).

Russia has also integrated AI into its hybrid warfare strategy, blending kinetic force with digital tools. The Lancet-3 loitering munition, a semi-autonomous drone, exemplifies AI integration on the battlefield and "uses convolutional neural networks ... to detect enemy targets" (Santayana, 2024, p. 13).

Ukraine has adopted a more agile and decentralized AI strategy. In the absence of an integrated AI infrastructure, it has partnered with private firms like Palantir to develop battlefield platforms. Such platforms fuse satellite imagery with open-source intelligence to guide targeting. Santayana (2024) notes that "the CEO of Palantir ... admitted that his company is responsible for most of the targeting in Ukraine ... using satellite and social media data" (p. 11). AI has also allowed Ukrainian forces to "geolocate and analyze open-source data ... to identify Russian soldiers, weapons, systems, units or their movements" (Bendett, 2023).

The 2025 conflict between India and Pakistan offers a final example of how IW is evolving among regional middle powers. Despite a much smaller defense budget ($10.2 billion compared to India's $86.1 billion, according to SIPRI), Pakistan has outperformed India (Liang et al., 2025). Using JF-17 jets and Fatah-II missiles, Pakistan has succeeded in downing advanced Indian aircraft like Rafale and Sukhoi. It has further amplified its impact through an IW using doctored visuals to sway public opinion and disrupt India's narrative (Sen, 2025, May 10). These operations were likely supported by AI analyzing operational data and guiding digital influence campaigns in real time. This case illustrates how the strategic use of emerging technologies, particularly AI, can outweigh even significant disparities in military spending and conventional power.

The use of AI is producing a clear shift in various conflicts. Information warfare is becoming automated, adaptive, and decentralized, and control of the cognitive domain is now as critical as control of land, air, or sea. According to Slusher (2025), "Artificial intelligence and machine learning will be central to future electronic warfare, enabling cognitive electronic warfare platforms capable of sensing, analyzing, and responding autonomously at speeds beyond human capabilities" (p. 8). A state's strategic advantage is now measured in terms of how effectively it can control perception, disrupt cohesion, and dominate the information environment.

The contrast between countries in this area is instructive. China builds centralized, ideological systems of AI-powered influence, Russia fuses AI with cyber and kinetic operations, and Ukraine embraces AI as a tool for resilience and real-time responsiveness; regarding the latter, "the Russia-Ukraine war ... resembles a laboratory in which many companies and governments can constantly train and test AI systems" (Santayana, 2024, p. 15). These examples show that the cognitive sphere is no longer a support function; it is the new frontline of war.

9 Artificial Intelligence and the Ethical-Legal Dilemmas of Information Warfare

This fourth axis constitutes an exploration of the ethical-legal challenges posed by the integration of AI into IW. The analysis focuses on five core dimensions: accountability, system opacity, state secrecy, regulatory lag, and the resulting normative vacuum. These concerns have become increasingly urgent as intelligent systems have gained autonomy and entered conflict environments traditionally governed by human judgment. The expansion of agency beyond human actors demands a rethinking of the assignment of ethical responsibility. Some have argued that "the ethical analyses of IW ... must consider the moral responsibilities for the actions performed by autonomous artificial agents" (Floridi & Taddeo, 2014, p. vi).

The above concerns are particularly acute in situations where AI systems operate independently under conditions of uncertainty. Though technically precise, these systems often operate beyond full human supervision, making it difficult to trace responsibility when harm occurs. As decision-making becomes less transparent, it becomes harder to understand or predict AI outcomes, reinforcing the concern that "AI does indeed present the risk of human control loss, bringing forth an array of unprecedented challenges" (Daxhelet, 2023, p. 13). When autonomous systems cause harm, there are no clear mechanisms for assigning blame in existing frameworks. This challenge is amplified by the hybrid nature of many AI-enabled systems: "it is becoming increasingly unclear who, or what, is accountable and responsible for the actions performed by complex, hybrid, man-machine systems on the battlefield" (EIW3R, 2012). This ethical ambiguity is highlighted by scholars who warn that "one of the largest ethical concerns is the lack of clear accountability. If an AI-based system engages in IW that causes harm, it is not always clear who is responsible" (J. Wright, 2019, p. 319).

Complicating the matter is the lack of state transparency regarding the workings of their AI-driven IW tools. This opacity weakens international trust and impedes monitoring and verification. Governments can deny involvement or disguise the origins of attacks, making attribution difficult. The challenge is that "ascribing responsibility for an act of information warfare is inherently difficult. The attacker can mask their identity or even cause the attack to appear to originate from a third party" (Greenberg et al., 1997, p. 11). Enforcing international norms or humanitarian law becomes increasingly challenging in such environments.

The legal community is similarly constrained. Regulatory responses are fragmented and reactive, while AI capabilities continue to evolve rapidly. Many existing efforts rely on principles or ethical declarations lacking legal force. A recent policy report makes this clear: "AI regulations solely based on principles do not impose specific obligations … nor do they have consequences for non-compliance" (AI Regulation, 2024, p. 23). As innovation outpaces legislation, developers and governments have deployed powerful AI tools with limited regard for legal boundaries. This gap has led scholars to observe "a growing lag between what is technically feasible and what is legally regulated" (Daxhelet, 2023, p. 13).

There is a widening normative vacuum in this area. The absence of enforceable ethical and legal frameworks has created a permissive environment for asymmetry and escalation. With AI becoming further embedded in military operations, especially those targeting civilians or non-combatants, there are mounting concerns that the erosion of regulatory norms may undermine human rights. As Tzimas (2021) notes, "the lack of transparency and the inequality constitute major challenges … they can erode human, civil and political rights" (p. 76). Without oversight, the use of AI in warfare can lead to "a violation of international law" that is not hypothetical but imminent (Roumate, 2019, p. 78).

In extreme cases, adversarial access to AI systems could be catastrophic. The very autonomy that makes AI appealing can be weaponized by malicious actors. Some have issued a stark warning that "if terrorists find a way to break into [AI] programs, it will be an unmitigated disaster" (Roumate, 2019, p. 73). This threat is amplified by the global diffusion of AI capabilities and the disparities in regulatory readiness across jurisdictions. New risks, once marginal, have become central. For example, psychological security is now considered a pressing legal matter. Given that AI can shape beliefs, manipulate cognition, and disrupt decision-making processes, it is increasingly argued that "threats to international psychological security" must be addressed as legal issues (Roumate, 2024, p. 108).

Several international bodies are calling for a legal framework grounded in fundamental rights to address these concerns. A leading recommendation is that "international human rights laws and standards must form the basis for governing AI … placing human rights in the center" (UNESCO, 2024, p. 14). This approach requires enforceable rules developed through interdisciplinary collaboration, moving beyond aspirational principles toward binding regulation. Legal innovation must accompany technical advancement to prevent warfare from evolving into a domain devoid of accountability or moral constraint.

These reflections make clear that the time for ethical hesitation has passed. The risks of AI-driven IW are no longer theoretical; they are unfolding in real time and demand coordinated, principle-based global action.

In all the cases analyzed, AI plays a central role in attack and defense and has remade how states confront each other and how they manage competition.

The case studies considered span three distinct geopolitical arenas: a regional conflict in the Global South (Morocco and Algeria), a strategic rivalry between major powers (China, Russia, Ukraine, and the United States), and a middle-power conflict (India and Pakistan). In all cases, AI has been used to spread disinformation, carry out cyberattacks, and influence public opinion. At the same time, it has enabled states to detect threats early, defend their narratives, and strengthen the mental resilience of citizens. Notably, countries in the Global South are turning to AI as a low-cost, efficient means of engaging in psychological and EW. For these states, AI is becoming a strategic necessity.

A key finding is that AI expands the scope of IW across time, space, and method. The line between war and peace is becoming less clear. Today's battlefield includes minds, emotions, and cultural symbols. China, for example, uses AI to control domestic narratives and promote its digital governance abroad. Russia combines AI with hybrid strategies, including automated drones, and Ukraine relies on partnerships with private tech firms to strengthen its defenses. In North Africa, the conflict between Morocco and Algeria has included cyberattacks, media propaganda, and contestations of immaterial heritage. In South Asia, events between India and Pakistan in 2025 have shown how AI can compensate for budget shortfalls in traditional military capabilities and make deterrence harder to maintain.

These developments raise serious ethical and legal problems. As AI systems become more complex and act with greater independence, it becomes harder to know who is responsible when something goes wrong. At the same time, most governments are not transparent about how they use AI in warfare, which adds to the risks. A recent disturbing example is the "Pager Explosion" case. On September 17, 2024, thousands of pagers used by Hezbollah fighters exploded across Lebanon, killing 12 people, including children and healthcare workers, and injuring nearly 2,800 others (Gritten, 2024).

Hezbollah blamed Israel, and although the state did not comment officially, leaked intelligence confirmed that Israeli agents had planted explosive devices in the pagers. This incident raises urgent and politically sensitive questions about the legality and morality of physical cyberattacks.

In short, there is a growing danger that AI will be used to harm state sovereignty, public trust, and human rights, especially in countries without strong legal protections. The dangers include large-scale manipulation, disinformation campaigns, and serious violations of privacy. These actions are often defended as part of technological progress, but further public debate and international regulation are required.

10 Conclusion

Based on real-world case studies, this chapter has demonstrated that AI has become an essential component and a decisive tool in contemporary IW, transforming its speed, scope, and psychological dimensions. A critical insight is that major and minor powers increasingly employ AI to pursue asymmetric strategies, often without human oversight.

As military operations become more automated, there is an increased likelihood of less accountability in conflict. In the absence of robust international regulation, the central question shifts from whether AI should be used in warfare to who will control its deployment. Therefore, the strategic integration of AI demands critical reflection on the normative frameworks underpinning global psychological security.

References

Abbas, T., Ali, W., Khan, I. A., & Saleem, S. (2024). Revolutionizing warfare: The role of artificial intelligence in the future of defense. *The Regional Tribune*, *3*(1), 192–200. https://doi.org/10.63062/trt/V24.032

AISEC. (2025). International AI and Cybersecurity Conference – Morocco. https://aisec.uca.ma/conf/

Barabash, V., Kotelenets, E., & Lavrentyeva, M. (2019). The definition case of information warfare term: Waging wars or disseminating propaganda? *Advances in Social Science, Education and Humanities Research*, *374*, 110–116.

Bendett, S. (2023, July 17). *Roles and implications of AI in the Russian-Ukrainian conflict*. Center for a New American Security. https://www.cnas.org/publications/commentary/roles-and-implications-of-ai-in-the-russian-ukrainian-conflict

Boghardt, T. (2009). Operation INFEKTION: Soviet Bloc intelligence and its AIDS disinformation campaign. *Studies in Intelligence*, *53*(4), 1–24. https://www.cia.gov/static/9d3543f418bb78b03a20623e42e1d2c5/Operation_INFEKTION.pdf

Božić, J., & Gregić, M. (2024). Artificial intelligence as a tool in war and a weapon for peace – The power of disinformation. *National Security and the Future*, *25*(2), 105–130. https://doi.org/10.37458/nstf.25.2.4

Bryczek-Wróbel, P., & Moszczyński, M. (2022). The evolution of the concept of information warfare in the modern information society of the post-truth era. *Defence Science Review*, (13). https://doi.org/10.37055/pno/152385

Center, F. (2024). Militarizing AI: The role of artificial intelligence in modern warfare. Future for Advanced Research and Studies. Retrieved from https://futureuae.com/en-ae/Mainpage/Item/9290/militarizing-ai-the-role-of-artificial-intelligence-in-modern-warfare

Chughtai, A., & Haddad, M. (2025, April 9). Eight charts that reveal the economic impact of Trump's tariffs. *Al Jazeera*. https://www.aljazeera.com/economy/2025/4/9/eight-charts-that-reveal-the-economic-impact-of-trumps-tariffs

Čižik, T. (2017). *Information warfare as a geopolitical tool*. Centre for European and North Atlantic Affairs (CENAA).

Cyber Security News. (2023, March 15). *Titan Rain: How Chinese cybercriminals infiltrated the United States cyberspace* [Video]. YouTube. https://www.youtube.com/watch?v=_atXkztpz6s

Damjanović, D. Z. (2017). Types of information warfare and examples of malicious programs of information warfare. *Military Technical Courier*, *65*(4), 1044–1059. https://doi.org/10.5937/vojtehg65-13590

Daxhelet, É. (2023). *Artificial intelligence and the future of warfare*. Finabel – The European Army Interoperability Centre.

Defense Magazine. (2024, October 30). Information warfare: The invisible front of the twenty-first century. Retrieved from https://www.defensemagazine.com/article/information-warfare-the-invisible-front-of-the-21st-century-1

Di Pietro, R., Raponi, S., Caprolu, M., & Cresci, S. (2021). *New dimensions of information warfare*. Springer. https://doi.org/10.1007/978-3-030-60618-3

European Parliament. (2023, May 8). Committee of Inquiry to investigate the use of Pegasus and equivalent surveillance spyware: Compromise amendments. https://www.europarl.europa.eu/meetdocs/2014_2019/plmrep/COMMITTEES/PEGA/DV/2023/05-08/REPORTcompromises_EN.pdf

Gerlich, M. (2024). Brace for impact: Facing the AI revolution and geopolitical shifts in a future societal scenario for 2025–2040. *Societies*, *14*(9), 180. https://doi.org/10.3390/soc14090180

Grabusts, P., Zorins, A., & Teilans, A. (2019). Informational warfare – influence on informational structures. *Proceedings of the 12th International Scientific and Practical Conference "Environment. Technology. Resources"*, *II*, 56–60. https://doi.org/10.17770/etr2019vol2.4035

Greenberg, L. T., Goodman, S. E., & Soo Hoo, K. J. (1997). *Information warfare and international law*. National Defense University.

Gritten, D. (2024, September 18). Death toll from Hezbollah pager explosions in Lebanon rises to 12. *BBC News*. https://www.bbc.com/news/articles/cx2kn10xxldo

Hunter, L. Y., Albert, C. D., Rutland, J., Topping, K., & Hennigan, C. (2024). Artificial intelligence and information warfare in major power states: How the US, China, and Russia are using artificial intelligence in their information warfare and influence operations. *Defense and Security Analysis*. https://doi.org/10.1080/14751798.2024.2321736

International Crisis Group. (2024). *Managing tensions between Algeria and Morocco*. https://www.crisisgroup.org/middle-east-north-africa/north-africa/247-algeria-morocco-western-sahara/managing-tensions-between

Johnson, J. (2019). Artificial intelligence and future warfare: Implications for international security. *Defense and Security Analysis*, *35*(2), 147–169. https://doi.org/10.1080/14751798.2019.1600800

Joyner, C. C., & Lotrionte, C. (2001). Information warfare as international coercion: Elements of a legal framework. *European Journal of International Law*, *12*(5), 825–865.

Kershaw, I. (2001). *Hitler, 1936–1945: Nemesis* (pp. 527). Penguin Books.

Lande, D., & Danyk, Y. (2024). Competitive artificial intelligence in information and cyber warfare. *SSRN*. https://doi.org/10.2139/ssrn.5084698

Liang, X., Tian, N., Lopes da Silva, D., Scarazzato, L., Karim, Z. A., & Guiberteau Ricard, J. (2025). *Trends in world military expenditure, 2024*. SIPRI. https://www.sipri.org/sites/default/files/2025-04/2504_fs_milex_2024.pdf

Liaropoulos, A. N., & Kalloniatis, C. (Eds.). (2025). *Power, pixels and politics: The geopolitics of emerging technologies in the digital age*. Hellenic National Defence College.

Libicki, M. C. (1995). *What is information warfare?* RAND Corporation. https://doi.org/10.21236/ADA385640

NATO. (2020). *Information warfare*. NATO. https://www.nato.int/nato_static_fl2014/assets/pdf/2020/5/pdf/2005-deepportal4-information-warfare.pdf. (Accessed April 21, 2025).

Ottis, R. (2008). *Analysis of the 2007 cyber attacks against Estonia from the information warfare perspective*. Cooperative Cyber Defence Centre of Excellence. https://ccdcoe.org/uploads/2018/10/Ottis2008_AnalysisOf2007CyberAttacksAgainstEstonia.pdf

Pauwels, E. (2024). *Artificial intelligence and the future of geopolitics*. United Nations Institute for Disarmament Research (UNIDIR). https://unidir.org

Popescu, A. I. C. (2022). The geopolitical impact of the emerging technologies. *Bulletin of Carol I National Defence University, 11*(1), 308–334. https://doi.org/10.53477/2284-9378-21-38

RAND Corporation. (2022). *Many hands in the cookie jar: Case studies in response options to cyber incidents affecting U.S. government networks and implications for future response* (RRA1190-1). https://www.rand.org/pubs/research_reports/RRA1190-1.html

Roumate, F. (2019). Terrorism and lethal robot systems. *Communications. Media. Design, 4*(3), 69–84.

Roumate, F. (2024). *Artificial intelligence and the new world order*. Springer.

Santayana, J. P. D. (2024). *Artificial intelligence and the war in Ukraine*. IEEE Analysis Document 81/2024. https://www.defensa.gob.es/ceseden

Santos, F. C. C. (2023). Artificial intelligence in automated detection of disinformation: A thematic analysis. *Journalism and Media, 4*(2), 679–687. https://doi.org/10.3390/journalmedia4020043

Sen, S. R. (2025, May 10). India and Pakistan's information war is more heated than ever. *Bloomberg*. https://www.bloomberg.com/news/articles/2025-05-10/india-and-pakistan-s-information-war-is-more-heated-than-ever

Slusher, M. N. (2025). **Lessons from the Ukraine conflict: Modern warfare in the age of autonomy, information, and resilience**. Center for Strategic and International Studies. https://www.csis.org

Spafford, E. H. (1989). *The internet worm program: An analysis* (Technical Report No. CSD-TR-823). Purdue University. https://homes.cerias.purdue.edu/~spaf/tech-reps/823.pdf

Taddeo, M. (2012). Information warfare: A philosophical perspective. *Philosophy & Technology, 25*(2), 105–120. https://doi.org/10.1007/s13347-011-0040-9

Taddeo, M., & Floridi, L. (Eds.). (2014). *The ethics of information warfare*. Springer. https://doi.org/10.1007/978-3-319-04135-3

Thornton, R. (2015). The changing nature of modern warfare: Responding to Russian information warfare. *The RUSI Journal, 160*(4), 40–48. https://doi.org/10.1080/03071847.2015.1079047

Tzimas, T. (2021). AI and governance. In N. Tsagourias & R. Buchan (Eds.), *Artificial intelligence and international law* (pp. 73–125). Springer.

Tzu, S. (2010). The art of war. In L. Giles (Ed.), Original work published ca. Fifth century BCE. *Aziloth Books*

UNESCO. (2024). *Document for consultation: AI regulation and ethics*.

University of Hertfordshire. (2012). The ethics of information warfare: Risks, rights and responsibilities (EIW3R) [Final report summary]. European Commission. https://cordis.europa.eu/project/id/253756/reporting/it

Vance, T. R. (2023). Geopolitical implications of artificial intelligence in cybersecurity: A comprehensive analysis. *International Journal of Computer Science and Information Technology Research, 11*(3), 91–105. https://doi.org/10.5281/zenodo.8214594

Waltz, E. (1998). *Information warfare: Principles and operations*. Artech House.

Watch, M. (2025, April 11). Cyber escalation between Morocco and Algeria: Moroccan hackers strike back in retaliation. https://meatechwatch.com/2025/04/11/cyber-escalation-between-morocco-and-algeria-moroccan-hackers-strike-back-in-retaliation/

Williams, P. A. H. (2010). Information warfare: Time for a redefinition. *Proceedings of the Eleventh Australian Information Warfare and Security Conference*, 37–44. https://doi.org/10.4225/75/57a83781befa6

Wright, J. (2019). AI and information warfare in 2025. In *2019 IEEE SmartWorld Conference Proceedings* (pp. 317–322). IEEE.

Wright, N. D. (Ed.). (2018). *AI, China, Russia, and the* Global Order*: Technological*, Political, Global, *and* Creative Perspectives. Strategic Multilayer Assessment. https://nsiteam.com

Wu, C.-H. (2025). *In power, pixels and politics: The geopolitics of emerging technologies in the digital age* (pp. 651–676). Great Britain Journals Press.

AI and Information: Implications on Military Strategies

Pavel Sharikov

1 Defining Military Strategy of the Twenty-First Century

Military strategy, at its essence, is the application of organized violence in pursuit of political objectives. This basic idea, articulated by Carl von Clausewitz in nineteenth century, asserts that "war is merely the continuation of politics by other means" (Gray, 2010). Yet to fully understand the nature of military strategy, especially in its contemporary forms, one must first understand what is meant by politics.

Politics is not merely the activity of governments or elites; it is the ongoing process through which societies organize, manage, and reconcile competing interests. In modern democratic states, politics is expressed through elections, legislation and coalition-building. As Francis Fukuyama observes, "Political development is change over time in political institutions ... it is the underlying rules by which societies organize themselves that define a political order" (Fukuyama, 2014); in this sense, contemporary military strategies are inseparable from the institutional triad of the state, the rule of law, and mechanisms of accountability, as these define both the legitimacy and operational limits of force in modern political systems.

Thus, when Clausewitz speaks of politics, he refers not simply to the actions of monarchs or presidents, but to the underlying social purposes and priorities that a given community seeks to advance or defend. Military strategy, then, is the means by which force is directed in service of those broader societal goals. As Colin S. Gray later put it, strategy is the "bridge between military power and political purpose" (Gray, 2010) a bridge that spans the diverse terrain of social interests, historical memory, institutional power, and public expectation.

P. Sharikov (✉)
Institute of Europe, Russian Academy of Sciences, Moscow, Russia
e-mail: pasha.sharikov@gmail.com

F. Roumate (ed.), *AI, Information, and Global Dynamics*, Contributions to International Relations,
https://doi.org/10.1007/978-3-032-13528-5_7

This connection has not weakened in the twenty-first century. On the contrary, politics has become more complex, more fragmented, and more mediated by digital technologies and global interdependence. Whereas political objectives in earlier eras often revolved around territorial expansion, imperial prestige, or regime survival, today's political purposes are shaped by public opinion, electoral cycles, social movements, and economic interconnectivity. Governments must increasingly use military power not only to deter traditional adversaries, but also to assure domestic audiences, support allies, and maintain influence in competitive informational and technological environments.

As societies become more complex and politically responsive, and as technological capabilities expand, military strategy evolves into a more flexible, integrated, and politically reflective tool—still rooted in Clausewitz's logic, but recalibrated for a multipolar, high-tech, and highly mediated world.

Contemporary military strategy must evolve in response to the profound transformations brought about by emerging technologies and the shifting nature of global threats. Unlike earlier periods characterized by conventional state-on-state conflict, the strategic landscape of the twenty-first century is shaped by the simultaneous rise of advanced technologies, such as artificial intelligence, cyber capabilities, unmanned systems, and space-based platforms and other asymmetric threats, including transnational terrorism, hybrid warfare, and irregular armed groups.

Technological innovation has altered the very calculus of both offense and defense. On the offensive side, precision-guided munitions, AI-enabled targeting, and real-time surveillance have enabled states to project power with unprecedented speed and accuracy. Defensive strategies, meanwhile, must now account not only for physical protection, but also for the integrity of digital infrastructure, information dominance, and resilience against disinformation and cyberattacks. Traditional models of deterrence and territorial defense are no longer sufficient on their own; instead, military planners must develop multi-domain strategies that integrate kinetic, informational, and virtual tools in a coherent and adaptive framework. "Much attention in discussions of warbots focuses on capabilities of individual platforms and technologies—the drones or missiles, the high-defnition cameras and algorithms that monitor them—rather than the ways they'll employed together and their deeper impact on warfare" (Payne, 2021).

Moreover, the persistence of non-state threats, particularly terrorism, has further complicated strategic planning. Terrorist networks operate across borders, embed within civilian populations, and exploit the openness of modern societies and digital communication. Confronting such actors requires a fusion of military, intelligence, law enforcement, and civil-military coordination, often in prolonged and ambiguous operational environments. Military strategy must therefore be agile and politically sensitive, capable of calibrating force in ways that neutralize threats without undermining legitimacy or exacerbating instability.

In this dynamic context, military strategy is no longer about preparing for one type of war or one type of enemy. It is about developing the institutional adaptability, technological fluency, and strategic foresight to operate effectively across multiple domains and threat environments. As Clausewitz's dictum holds, strategy remains the use of force for political purposes, but in the twenty-first century, that force must be intelligent, integrated, and ethically calibrated to the challenges of an interconnected and unpredictable world.

In the contemporary strategic environment, military strategy increasingly resembles a form of economic competition, where states vie for advantage not only through direct confrontation but through sustained innovation, resource allocation, and influence over emerging technologies. Just as countries compete in global markets to secure economic growth and technological leadership, they must likewise maintain credible deterrence capabilities to prevent direct military conflict. The emphasis is on preserving strategic stability by signaling strength and resilience, thereby discouraging adversaries from initiating hostilities. "Great-power competition in AI would generate risk for those powers that are unable to adapt in order to organizationally exploit advances in AI, even if they are able to make technical advances" (Horowitz, 2018).

This dynamic has given rise to a new kind of arms race, distinct from the Cold War's focus on nuclear arsenals and large conventional forces. Today, the competition centers on advanced technologies, most notably artificial intelligence, autonomous systems, cyber capabilities, and quantum computing, which promise to redefine the balance of power. States investing heavily in these domains aim to achieve decision dominance, operational speed, and enhanced situational awareness that can deter adversaries without firing a shot.

Crucially, this competition has propelled the military-industrial complex and government-private sector partnerships to a level of strategic importance unmatched even during the twentieth century and Cold War. Modern military strategy depends heavily on the seamless integration of state research institutions, defense contractors, technology startups, and academia to accelerate innovation and translate breakthroughs into deployable capabilities. The pace of technological advancement and the complexity of emerging systems require unprecedented collaboration, significant investment, and flexible regulatory frameworks to keep pace with adversaries.

In this context, military deterrence becomes a continuous process of demonstrating superiority through innovation, an ongoing competition that blends defense, offense, and strategic signaling. The result is a complex security environment where military strategy functions as a long-term, multifaceted competition akin to economic rivalry, with AI and related technologies at the forefront of the new strategic frontier.

2 How AI is Used in the Military?

Artificial intelligence is the most impactful emerging technology influencing contemporary political and military strategy. Defined broadly as systems capable of autonomous perception, reasoning, learning, and goal-directed action, AI's conceptualization has evolved significantly in the twenty-first century. Foundational texts such as Russell and Norvig's Artificial Intelligence: A Modern Approach (Russell & Norvig, 2016) and Goodfellow et al.'s Deep Learning (Goodfellow & Bengio & Courville & Bach, 2016) have shaped the understanding of AI's technical capabilities, while institutional definitions, including those by the (European Commission, 2025) emphasizes AI's role in autonomous decision-making and system integration. These advances have enabled AI to become a strategic force multiplier, driving rapid decision cycles and operational innovation in military domains.

Artificial intelligence is rapidly transforming military operations, enabling a broad spectrum of applications that enhance both offensive and defensive capabilities. Contemporary military strategies leverage AI to increase situational awareness, accelerate decision-making, and improve precision in targeting and logistics. Human-machine teaming (HMT) (Nurkin & Siegel, 2023)—the collaboration between human operators and autonomous systems represents a foundational shift in military operations, extending from unmanned aerial vehicles acting as "loyal wingmen" (Nurkin & Siegel, 2023) to algorithm-driven intelligence analysis. As the RAND Corporation highlights, AI systems can process volumes of data beyond human capability, aiding commanders in identifying threats and prioritizing targets more effectively (Black et al., 2024). For example, the U.S. Department of Defense's Project Maven uses AI to autonomously detect and track objects of interest, dramatically enhancing intelligence functions. AI also supports defensive operations, such as autonomous drones countering enemy swarms and cyber defense systems managing complex digital threats. However, these advances introduce significant ethical and operational risks, including concerns about accountability, system reliability, and escalation dynamics. As RAND notes, "military AI development should be pursued with all necessary precautions to mitigate risks and ensure appropriate human judgment is applied" (Morgan et al., 2020). Moreover, the strategic competition surrounding AI development, especially among superpowers like the United States, China, and Russia, underscores AI's role as a force multiplier shaping future warfare. The integration of AI into military strategy thus represents not only a technological evolution but a fundamental transformation in how armed forces operate, deter, and engage in conflict.

Artificial intelligence's rapid advancement in military applications is inseparable from broader economic and technological ecosystems driven largely by the private sector and civilian innovation. The military's AI capabilities increasingly rely on breakthroughs originating in commercial research, academic laboratories, and tech industry developments. As highlighted in the 2024 WIPO Patent Landscape Report on Generative AI (World Intellectual Property Organization, 2024), private companies such as Microsoft, Google, IBM, Tencent, and startups worldwide lead patenting and research activity, propelling advances in machine learning architectures, natural language processing, and autonomous systems. These civilian innovations form the technological backbone of many military AI applications, making government-private partnerships essential for access to cutting-edge technologies, rapid prototyping, and scalable deployment.

Unlike the Cold War era, where military AI development was largely secured within defense institutions, today's strategic environment demands tight integration between defense agencies and the global tech economy. This nexus accelerates innovation cycles but also creates complex dependencies—military AI development must navigate issues of intellectual property, export controls, and dual-use technologies. Consequently, effective military strategy now requires fostering collaborative ecosystems that leverage civilian R&D while ensuring security and ethical use, underscoring a new level of interconnectedness in technological competition.

The assessment of national military AI capabilities increasingly hinges on measurable indicators of AI-related product innovation and production. Key among these are patent filings, commercial AI product outputs, defense procurement volumes, investment flows, and the production and control of critical hardware components such as chips and semiconductors, all of which provide concrete evidence of a country's ability to generate and deploy AI technologies with military relevance.

Patent activity remains a telling quantitative indicator. According to the 2024 WIPO Generative AI Patent Landscape Report, the United States accounts for approximately 38% of global AI-related patent families filed between 2017 and 2023, maintaining a leading edge in AI algorithms, autonomous systems, and machine learning architectures that underpin military technologies. China follows closely with roughly 32% of global patent families, especially in AI applications for surveillance, facial recognition, and autonomous vehicles. European countries collectively represent around 15% but face scaling challenges due to fragmented markets and regulatory constraints.

Commercial AI product development reinforces these capabilities. The U.S. leads with over 300 AI startups specializing in defense-relevant technologies, supported by venture capital investments exceeding $15 billion annually. U.S. defense procurement dedicates over $2 billion annually to AI systems, including projects like Project Maven and the Loyal Wingman drone initiative. China, driven by its military-civil fusion strategy, filed more than 12,000 AI patents in 2023 alone and is rapidly expanding production of autonomous and ISR technologies, though procurement agility is lower. Europe invests about $5 billion annually in defense AI procurement with fewer startups and slower military AI integration.

Beyond software and data, chips and semiconductors are foundational to AI military capabilities. Specialized processors enable the high-speed computation necessary for real-time data analysis, autonomous navigation, and decision-making in complex battlefield environments.

The United States dominates global semiconductor design and innovation, with companies like NVIDIA, AMD, and Intel leading the development of AI-optimized chips (Semiconductor Industry Association, 2023). These firms produce advanced processors tailored for AI workloads, giving U.S. military systems unmatched computational performance and energy efficiency.

Taiwan Semiconductor Manufacturing Company (TSMC) is the leading global manufacturer of advanced semiconductors, producing cutting-edge chips designed by U.S. and other international companies. TSMC's fabrication capabilities are essential for producing the compact, powerful chips required in AI-enabled weapons systems.

China has accelerated its efforts to develop an indigenous semiconductor industry, investing billions to reduce reliance on foreign suppliers amid geopolitical pressures. Despite progress, Chinese chip fabrication remains less advanced technologically, with limited access to the latest process nodes critical for top-tier AI hardware.

Europe's semiconductor industry is smaller and more fragmented, with companies like ASML providing critical lithography equipment but lacking scale in advanced chip manufacturing. The EU has launched initiatives to bolster semiconductor capacity, but it currently trails the U.S. and Asia in military AI hardware production.

The geopolitical competition over semiconductor supply chains adds a critical dimension to military AI capability assessments. Control over chip production, intellectual property, and supply chain security directly affects a nation's ability to produce reliable, cutting-edge AI systems and sustain them during conflict.

Comparing national AI capabilities is essential for developing effective international legal norms aimed at controlling the military use of artificial intelligence, particularly concerning lethal autonomous weapons systems (LAWS). Deployment of LAWS may upset traditional power balances by enabling smaller states or non-state actors to leverage technology that rivals conventional forces, thereby destabilizing security environments. Lethal autonomous weapons create a strategic imbalance by granting one belligerent a swiftly recoverable technological leverage that can effectively offset and surpass the manpower advantage of the opposing party (Fan, 2017).

Understanding the relative technological strengths and deployment potentials of different countries enables policymakers and international bodies to craft balanced regulations that address the risks of autonomous weapons while accounting for strategic security concerns. Without comprehensive assessments of national AI capabilities, legal frameworks risk being either too lax—allowing unchecked development and deployment of potentially destabilizing lethal systems—or overly restrictive, inadvertently hindering responsible innovation and defense preparedness. The urgency is heightened by the ethical and humanitarian implications of LAWS, which raise profound questions about accountability, decision-making in life-and-death situations, and compliance with international humanitarian law. Consequently, transparent and accurate comparisons of AI military capacities form a critical foundation for negotiating international agreements that seek to prevent an uncontrolled arms race in autonomous weaponry while promoting stability and security.

International efforts to regulate artificial intelligence (AI), particularly its military applications, have intensified in response to the rapid advancement of AI technologies and their potential implications for global security. Notably, the Bletchley Declaration, adopted during the UK-hosted AI Safety Summit in November 2023, marked a significant milestone. Endorsed by 28 countries, including the United States and China, the declaration (UK Government, 2023) emphasizes the need for AI to be developed and used in a manner that is safe, human-centric, trustworthy, and responsible. It calls for international cooperation to manage AI risks, with a focus on transparency, accountability, and the establishment of safety testing and evaluation frameworks.

In parallel, the U.S. Department of State introduced the Political Declaration on Responsible Military Use of Artificial Intelligence and Autonomy (U.S. Department of State, 2023) in February 2023. This initiative outlines non-legally binding guidelines for the development, deployment, and use of military AI systems, emphasizing adherence to international law, maintaining human oversight, and ensuring systems are auditable and rigorously tested. The declaration aims to promote international norms and best practices, fostering a collaborative approach among nations to address the challenges posed by AI in military contexts.

These efforts are complemented by ongoing discussions within the United Nations Convention on Certain Conventional Weapons (CCW), where member states have been deliberating on the regulation of lethal autonomous weapons systems (LAWS). The CCW discussions focus on ensuring that LAWS comply with international humanitarian law, particularly principles of distinction, proportionality, and accountability.

Collectively, these international initiatives underscore the global recognition of the need to establish robust frameworks for the responsible development and use of AI, especially in military applications, to mitigate risks and ensure compliance with international norms and ethical standards.

Military applications of artificial intelligence (AI) have become a critical focus within regional military-political alliances as states recognize the strategic imperative of maintaining technological superiority in an emerging AI arms race. NATO, as a leading transatlantic security organization, has explicitly integrated AI into its Strategic Concept, emphasizing the need for allied cooperation in AI research, development, and ethical deployment to preserve collective defense capabilities. NATO initiatives promote interoperability, shared standards, and joint investment in AI-enabled command, control, intelligence, surveillance, and reconnaissance (C2ISR) systems. Similarly, in the Asia-Pacific region, alliances such as the Quad (comprising the U.S., Japan, India, and Australia) and AUKUS (Australia, the U.K., and the U.S.) underscore AI's role in regional security architectures, prioritizing collaborative development of autonomous systems, cyber defense, and AI-driven situational awareness to counterbalance the rapid military modernization of China. These alliances reflect a broader strategic effort to maintain competitive advantage amid accelerating AI innovation, forming a new arms race that extends beyond software to include the critical hardware underpinning AI capabilities—most notably chips and semiconductors. The production and supply of advanced semiconductors have become a strategic chokepoint; concerns over China's dominance in semiconductor manufacturing have driven the U.S. and its allies to strengthen supply chain resilience through investments in domestic and allied production facilities, diversification of suppliers, and export controls on sensitive technologies. This supply chain strategy is now an integral element of military planning, aiming to prevent potential adversaries from monopolizing the essential components of AI-enabled weapon systems and ensuring that allied forces can sustain technological superiority. Consequently, the intersection of AI military applications, alliance politics, and semiconductor supply chain security encapsulates the evolving nature of strategic competition in the twenty-first century.

3 The American Approach to the Use of AI in the Military

The American military's approach to the use of artificial intelligence, particularly under the Obama and Biden administrations, has been characterized by a strong emphasis on maintaining human control over critical decision-making, especially regarding the use of lethal force. Both administrations recognized AI's potential to enhance operational effectiveness but explicitly mandated that humans must remain "in the loop"—that is, human operators must retain the authority to approve or intervene in decisions involving the use of force.

Under President Obama, foundational policy documents such as the 2016 Department of Defense (DoD) Directive 3000.09 established principles for "Autonomy in Weapon Systems" (U.S. Department of Defense, 2016). This directive required that autonomous and semi-autonomous weapon systems be designed to allow commanders and operators to exercise appropriate levels of human judgment over the use of force, ensuring compliance with international law and ethical norms. The directive codified the need for meaningful human control and explicitly aimed to prevent fully autonomous lethal systems from operating without human oversight.

The Biden administration has continued this emphasis on human oversight. The 2023 DoD Data, Analytics, and Artificial Intelligence Adoption Strategy (U.S. Department of Defense, 2023), developed by the Chief Digital and Artificial Intelligence Office (CDAO), outlines a framework for integrating AI into defense operations. While the strategy focuses on accelerating AI adoption, it also reinforces the importance of responsible AI development and deployment, ensuring that human judgment remains central to critical decision-making processes.

This stance aligns with broader strategic thinking rooted in the OODA loop (Observe-Orient-Decide-Act) concept, first articulated by military strategist (Boyd, 2018). AI technologies are envisioned as tools to accelerate and enhance the OODA cycle—helping commanders rapidly process information and evaluate options—without displacing the human decision-maker. By ensuring that humans remain integral to the "Decide" and "Act" phases, the military aims to balance speed and precision with ethical responsibility and strategic control.

This approach reflects an understanding that while AI can greatly improve situational awareness and operational tempo, the complexities and moral considerations of warfare require human oversight (Scharre, 2018). The emphasis on keeping a human in the loop preserves the ability to interpret ambiguous situations, apply judgment in accordance with the law of armed conflict, and prevent inadvertent escalation due to algorithmic errors or adversarial manipulation.

In 2025, President Donald Trump's administration has made key appointments that underscore a heightened focus on AI and national security. Elbridge Colby was appointed Under Secretary of Defense for Policy (U.S. Senate Committee on Armed Services, 2025, March 4), bringing a realist perspective that emphasizes countering China's influence in the Indo-Pacific region and advocating for increased defense spending by U.S. allies. Additionally, David O. Sacks was named White House AI and crypto czar, tasked with developing a legal framework for AI and cryptocurrency industries, signaling a commitment to technological leadership.

In terms of policy, Trump issued Executive Order 14179, titled "Removing Barriers to American Leadership in Artificial Intelligence" (The White House, 2025), which revokes previous regulations and directs the development of a national action plan to maintain global AI dominance.

The U.S. has implemented stricter controls on advanced semiconductor technologies critical for AI, particularly targeting Chinese tech giant Huawei. These measures aim to curb China's access to essential components for developing AI systems, thereby slowing Beijing's progress in military AI capabilities.

Conversely, China has significantly advanced its AI capabilities, with institutions producing a substantial portion of the world's high-impact AI research. This progress is attributed to substantial state investments and strategic planning, positioning China as a formidable competitor in the AI domain (Allison & Schmidt, 2020).

The convergence of these developments suggests a potential AI-empowered arms race. Both nations are investing heavily in AI technologies with military applications, including autonomous systems, cyber warfare tools, and advanced surveillance capabilities. The competition extends beyond technological advancements to include the establishment of global standards and control over AI infrastructure, such as data centers and semiconductor supply chains.

Semiconductors, the essential "brain" of AI systems—are at the heart of the strategic competition between the United States and China, especially in the military domain. AI-enabled weaponry, autonomous systems, and intelligence platforms all depend on cutting-edge chips, which require advanced fabrication capabilities concentrated in a handful of global suppliers. The U.S. recognizes that maintaining unfettered access to these critical components is as important as AI algorithm development itself.

In response, U.S. policy under the Trump administration has aggressively targeted the securing and diversification of semiconductor supply chains to mitigate risks posed by China's rising manufacturing capabilities and geopolitical assertiveness. This includes export controls restricting China's access to the most advanced chip fabrication technologies and equipment, notably those from Taiwan Semiconductor Manufacturing Company (TSMC) and U.S.-based equipment manufacturers (U.S. Department of Commerce, Bureau of Industry and Security, 2023). Investment incentives and industrial policy to bolster domestic semiconductor manufacturing capacity in the U.S. and allied countries, reducing dependency on East Asian supply chains vulnerable to disruption. Coordination with key partners (Japan, South Korea, the EU) to create resilient semiconductor supply networks, essential for sustained AI military R&D and production.

This strategic focus reflects the understanding that control over semiconductor supply chains directly shapes the ability to field next-generation AI-powered military systems, from hypersonic missile guidance to AI-driven ISR platforms. Interruptions or monopolization of chip supplies by China could critically degrade U.S. and allied AI military capabilities, thereby shifting the strategic balance.

4 Conclusion

The transformation of warfare in the AI era reflects a profound shift in the goals and means of strategic action. Carl von Clausewitz famously asserted that war is a continuation of politics by other means, and that its character changes with circumstances while its nature remains constant. Today, as warfare becomes increasingly shaped by artificial intelligence, the strategic objective is no longer merely the defeat of enemy forces but the sustained management of informational, cognitive, and algorithmic dominance. AI technologies through autonomous systems, predictive analytics, and real-time data fusion are enabling new forms of influence, decision acceleration, and strategic deception that alter the temporal and spatial dimensions of military power.

This evolution demands a reconfiguration of military strategy itself. Maintaining strategic leverage is no longer simply a matter of hardware superiority or force posture but of algorithmic supremacy, resilience in AI-enabled systems, and the integration of human-machine teaming across command-and-control structures. Strategic planning must now address how to shape adversary decision-making in environments saturated with synthetic data, autonomous agents, and cyber-physical uncertainty. It must also incorporate new domains of competition such as information integrity and trust in autonomous systems while anticipating how AI will affect escalation dynamics, deterrence credibility, and the fog of war.

Thus, the imperative of strategic leverage in the AI age is not simply about building faster or smarter weapons. It is about shaping the rules of the game itself. In this context, the Clausewitzian framework endures: strategy remains the rational application of means to ends under conditions of friction and uncertainty. Yet those means now include code, data architectures, and neural networks. As a result, military strategy must evolve to secure advantage in a battlefield defined not only by terrain and firepower, but by algorithms and information flows. The future of strategy lies in mastering this new grammar of war.

Moreover, the new strategic environment imposes an altered economic logic on the conduct of warfare. The pace and complexity of AI development require unprecedented levels of cooperation between the military, civilian research institutions, and private industry. Maintaining competitive advantage in both global markets and the international system hinges on robust government-private partnerships that drive innovation, protect intellectual capital, and ensure rapid dual-use application of emerging technologies. Nations able to improve their industrial base, regulatory frameworks, and technological ecosystems into integrated strategic efforts will be best positioned to dominate future strategic competition.

The United States currently holds a near-dominant position in global artificial intelligence development, particularly in military and dual-use applications. This leadership stems not only from superior technical performance and a flourishing ecosystem of academic research, defense contractors, and venture-backed innovation hubs, but also from the deliberate prioritization of AI as a strategic asset by recent presidential administrations. Since the late 2010s, successive U.S. governments have recognized that global influence in the AI domain confers economic leverage, military superiority, and ideological influence within the evolving rules-based international order.

Under both Republican and Democratic leadership, the United States has adopted a comprehensive national strategy focused on maintaining AI superiority. This includes substantial increases in Department of Defense AI funding as well as institutional reforms such as the establishment of the Joint Artificial Intelligence Center (JAIC) and its successor, the Chief Digital and Artificial Intelligence Office (CDAO), to coordinate AI integration across all branches of the military. The Trump administration, and again in its second iteration, has emphasized industrial mobilization and private-sector leadership to fast-track defense-oriented AI innovation.

Strategically, the U.S. has also moved to secure supply chains critical for AI dominance—especially in semiconductors—through legislation such as the CHIPS and Science Act, while forging strategic alliances through frameworks like the Quad, AUKUS, and NATO's AI guidelines. These policies are not merely domestic. They represent an effort to shape international norms and institutions around AI governance, aligning allies and partners with American standards of development, transparency, and responsible use.

Yet this dominance is not unchallenged. The world now teeters on the edge of a new arms race, not for nuclear weapons, but for artificial intelligence-enabled systems. China, America's primary strategic competitor, has declared its intent to become the global AI leader by 2030. Through state-led industrial policy, civil-military fusion, and aggressive global patenting, China is rapidly closing the gap in key domains such as autonomous weapons, surveillance technologies, and cognitive warfare. The competition is not only about technical metrics, but about which country's systems: organizational, regulatory, ethical will define the international standards of the twenty-first century.

References

Allison, G., & Schmidt, E. (2020, August). *Is China beating the U.S. to AI supremacy?* Project Syndicate. https://www.belfercenter.org/publication/china-beating-us-ai-supremacy

Black, J., Eken, M., Parakilas, J., Dee, S., Ellis, C., Suman-Chauhan, K., Bain, R., Fine, H., Aquilino, M. C., Lebret, M., & Palicka, O. (2024). *Strategic competition in the age of AI: Emerging risks and opportunities from military use of artificial intelligence*. RAND Corporation. https://www.rand.org/pubs/research_reports/RRA3295-1.html

Boyd, J. R. (2018). *A discourse on winning and losing*. In G. T. Hammond (Ed.), Air University Press, Curtis E. LeMay Center for Doctrine Development and Education. ISBN: 978-1-58566-279-1.

European Commission. (2025). *European approach to artificial intelligence*. https://digital-strategy.ec.europa.eu/en/policies/european-approach-artificial-intelligence

Fan, J. (2017). The war on "Killer Robots": Goals and strategies in the transnational campaign against the offensive use of lethal autonomous weapons systems. *Swarthmore International Relations Journal*, 2, 50–63. https://doi.org/10.24968/2574-0113.2.9. Available at https://works.swarthmore.edu/swarthmoreirjournal/vol1/iss2/9

Fukuyama, F. (2014). *Political order and political decay: From the industrial revolution to the globalization of democracy* (p. 25). Farrar, Straus and Giroux.

Goodfellow, I., Bengio, Y., Courville, A., & Bach, F. (2016). *Deep learning*. MIT Press. Available at https://www.deeplearningbook.org

Gray, C. S. (2010). *The strategy bridge: Theory for practice* (pp. 17–18). Oxford University Press.

Horowitz, M. C. (2018). Artificial intelligence, international competition, and the balance of power. *Texas National Security Review, 1*(3), https://tnsr.org/2018/05/artificial-intelligence-international-competition-and-the-balance-of-power/

Morgan, F. E., Boudreaux, B., Lohn, A. J., Ashby, M., Curriden, C., Klima, K., & Grossman, D. (2020). *Military applications of artificial intelligence: Ethical concerns in an uncertain world*. RAND Corporation. https://www.rand.org/pubs/research_reports/RR3139-1.html

Nurkin, T., & Siegel, J. (2023). *Battlefield applications for human-machine teaming: Demonstrating value, experimenting with new capabilities, and accelerating adoption*. Atlantic Council. https://www.atlanticcouncil.org/wp-content/uploads/2023/08/Battlefield-Applications-for-HMT.pdf

Payne, K. (2021). *I, Warbot: The dawn of artificially intelligent conflict* (p. 10). Hurst Publishers.

Russell, S., & Norvig, P. (2016). In *Artificial intelligence: A modern approach* (3rd ed., pp. 36–37). Pearson Education Limited.

Scharre, P. (2018). *Army of none: Autonomous weapons and the future of war*. W. W. Norton & Company.

Semiconductor Industry Association (SIA). (2023). *State of the U.S. semiconductor industry*. Retrieved from https://www.semiconductors.org/wp-content/uploads/2023/07/SIA_State-of-Industry-Report_2023_Final_072723.pdf

The White House. (2025). *Executive order 14179: Removing barriers to american leadership in artificial intelligence*. The White House. Available at https://www.whitehouse.gov/presidential-actions/2025/01/removing-barriers-to-american-leadership-in-artificial-intelligence/

U.S. Department of Commerce, Bureau of Industry and Security. (2023). *Export control policy on advanced semiconductor manufacturing equipment*. U.S. Department of Commerce. Available at https://www.bis.doc.gov/index.php/documents/pdfs/2335-semiconductor-export-controls/file

U.S. Department of Defense. (2016). *Department of defense directive 3000.09: Autonomy in weapon systems*. U.S. Department of Defense. Available at https://www.esd.whs.mil/Portals/54/Documents/DD/issuances/dodd/300009p.pdf

U.S. Department of Defense. (2023). *2023 data, analytics, and artificial intelligence adoption strategy*. U.S. Department of Defense. Available at https://media.defense.gov/2023/Nov/02/2003333300/-1/-1/1/DOD_DATA_ANALYTICS_AI_ADOPTION_STRATEGY.PDF

U.S. Department of State. (2023). *Political declaration on responsible military use of artificial intelligence and autonomy*. Retrieved from https://2021-2025.state.gov/bureau-of-arms-control-deterrence-and-stability/political-declaration-on-responsible-military-use-of-artificial-intelligence-and-autonomy/

U.S. Senate Committee on Armed Services. (2025, March 4). *To consider the nomination of Mr. Elbridge A. Colby to be under secretary of defense for policy*. https://www.armed-services.senate.gov/imo/media/doc/30425fulltranscript.pdf

UK Government. (2023). *The Bletchley declaration by countries attending the AI safety summit, 1–2 November 2023*. Retrieved from https://www.gov.uk/government/publications/ai-safety-summit-2023-the-bletchley-declaration/the-bletchley-declaration-by-countries-attending-the-ai-safety-summit-1-2-november-2023

World Intellectual Property Organization (WIPO). (2024). *Generative artificial intelligence: Patent landscape report*. WIPO. p. 101 https://doi.org/10.34667/tind.49740

AI Transformation and the Economy Based on Information: Toward a New Balance of Power

Viktor V. Zinchenko and Mir Faraj Abasov

1 Introduction

The world has begun to change in ways that remain largely unnoticed by the majority of people. These transformations are not isolated phenomena; rather, they represent a comprehensive and deeply interconnected process, unfolding in accordance with the principles of global evolutionism. Leading scholars in the humanities, regardless of their political affiliations or ideological leanings, acknowledge that the global system, as it has historically existed, is now in decline. They also predict revolutionary changes—transformations that we will soon witness firsthand. These changes are intrinsically linked to the advent of a new era marked by the information revolution and the rise of the digital economy.

The modern digital economy, while serving as the driving force of modernization, simultaneously generates numerous social, economic, political, and environmental challenges. These challenges contribute to a profound transformation in both individual consciousness and societal lifestyles. Among them, political issues are particularly acute, especially those associated with the emergence of a new socio-economic formation known as post-capitalism. This formation acts as an integrative phenomenon, merging the dynamics of globalization with those of the information revolution. In this context, it is essential to employ methodologies from political science, economics, and sociology to examine the complex issues arising at the intersection of the digital economy and post-capitalist development models.

V. V. Zinchenko (✉)
Department of Social and Institutional Transformations in Higher Education, Institute of Higher Education, National Academy of Educational Sciences of Ukraine, Kyiv, Ukraine
e-mail: vvzinchenko@ukr.net

M. F. Abasov
Department of Marketing and Management, University of Tourism and Management, Baku, Azerbaijan

F. Roumate (ed.), *AI, Information, and Global Dynamics*, Contributions to International Relations,
https://doi.org/10.1007/978-3-032-13528-5_8

We argue that we are witnessing the emergence of a new socio-political and economic system, founded upon its own norms and values. At the forefront of this emerging system are intellect and information—resources that redefine the very concept of social capital. Information has become the principal instrument for generating economic value. Notably, informationalism has already given rise to a corresponding religious doctrine that espouses non-humanitarian ethical values (Dvornikov, 2017).

David Bell identified scientific knowledge as the most important characteristic and primary product of post-industrial society, serving as a fundamental driver of economic development (Bell, 2006). Similarly, the Japanese philosopher Yoshihiro Masuda conceptualized the information society in a comparable manner. He believed that the core function of technological change would be the enhancement of intellectual labor, and that the leading sector of the economy would be intellectual production. According to Masuda, information and computer technologies would not merely lead to isolated social shifts, but would instead bring about a fundamental transformation of the societal system, culminating in the rise of a new type of society—the information society. He asserted that the production of informational, rather than material, goods would become the primary engine of societal education and development (Babeshko, 2017).

Equally important, as Bell emphasized, is the idea that knowledge and information serve not only as agents of transformation within post-industrial society but also as strategic resources. Thus, we must regard knowledge—especially in its digitized form—as the primary asset of the information society, whose significance is continuously increasing. The ability to use this resource effectively and at the right time will determine the probability of success in the emerging digital world. As Thomas Friedman noted: "In a world that is becoming increasingly interconnected, the ability to understand and leverage digital technologies will shape how we compete and collaborate" (Polanyi, 2013).

Finally, the integration of knowledge into the field of nanotechnology is leading to a new type of convergence among scientific disciplines and research methodologies, characterized by the dissolution of traditional interdisciplinary boundaries within the natural sciences. In their place, new interdisciplinary domains have emerged—such as quantum informatics, robotics, and synergetics—which are marked by a novel "communicative-activity" mode of thinking. Thus, molecular nanotechnology opens up opportunities for fundamental innovations and demands their adequate conceptualization and understanding (Alekseeva & Arshinov, 2016).

Given the increasing importance of information and knowledge, we should expect a transformation in the nature of production means and expenditures, the concept of goods, value, and pricing, as well as in the patterns of their utilization. A gradual departure from the traditional economic model is foreseeable, along with a predictable decline in human reproduction—replaced by a new form tied to the expanded use of robotics. This new form of reproduction will rapidly generate successive generations of autonomous machines. Even today, many of the ideas projected within this emerging socio-economic formation are being realized in practice, fostering the introduction of virtual innovations into circulation, such as cryptocurrencies, blockchains, and related technologies.

2 Methodology

This study is the result of a long-term intellectual endeavor and the synthesis of a broad spectrum of interdisciplinary ideas. The author has spent years developing a conceptual framework that offers a new philosophical and political-economic lens through which to view the ongoing transformation of global society. At its core, this work introduces a **novel theoretical formation—Digitalism**—which is presented not merely as an evolution of existing socio-economic systems, but as a fundamentally new paradigm.

The methodological foundation of this research lies in the **analytical and synthetic interpretation of secondary sources**, enriched by a comparative analysis of global academic discourse. It is neither a conventional empirical study nor a predictive technological forecast; rather, it is a **conceptual synthesis**, deeply rooted in the traditions of social theory, systems thinking, and futurism.

The uniqueness of this research lies in two key contributions. First, it is the **first scholarly work to define Digitalism as a distinct socio-economic formation**, with its own internal logic, structure, and values. Second, it is **the first to explicitly designate Artificial Intelligence as a new type of economic agent**, one that interacts with human society not merely as a tool or instrument, but as a participant in economic, social, and potentially ethical decision-making processes.

This chapter draws upon a wide array of academic sources—works by thinkers and scholars from various countries, including but not limited to Klaus Schwab, Nick Bostrom, Norbert Wiener, Irving John Good, Ray Kurzweil, and others. By referencing both classical theories (e.g., Marx, Engels, Vernadsky) and modern technological insights, the study builds a cohesive narrative that connects historical patterns with emerging digital realities.

In constructing this model, the author engages with the **theoretical heritage of political economy**, the **philosophy of technology**, and **ethical debates surrounding AI**, producing a work that is at once speculative and grounded, innovative yet based in rigorous intellectual tradition. This methodological approach allows the research to situate Digitalism not as a utopian or dystopian projection, but as a credible and actionable model for understanding the direction in which global society may be evolving.

2.1 Central Role of Digital Technologies in the Socio-Economic Order

Digitalism rests upon the central role of digital technologies in society. It constitutes a system in which virtual reality, artificial intelligence, blockchain, the Internet of Things, and other digital innovations play a pivotal role in shaping economic, social, and political life. As noted, "Digitalization is a social model in which governance and social structures increasingly rely on digital solutions, thereby transforming the nature of interaction, decision-making, and economic growth" (Castells, 1996).

Perhaps the most critical question of the digital era—a question that humanity has yet to definitively answer—is: **Who will hold ultimate control—humans or artificial intelligence?** This question has preoccupied philosophers, sociologists, economists, and business leaders for decades. Nick Bostrom, philosopher and author of *Superintelligence: Paths, Dangers, Strategies*, explores potential scenarios for AI development and its implications for humanity. Elon Musk, one of the key figures behind ChatGPT, and Ray Kurzweil, originator of the theory of the digital singularity, along with many other researchers, have dedicated substantial efforts to studying the problem of AI control and the mechanisms required for emergency shutdowns in critical or unforeseen situations.

When discussing the role of artificial intelligence, it is important to note that the digital revolution is also fundamentally transforming the nature of labor. According to the study by Carl Benedikt Frey and Michael Osborne (*The Future of Employment*, 2017), automation could lead to the elimination of millions of jobs. They emphasize that automation threatens not only manual labor but also highly skilled professions, generating a new wave of social instability and unemployment (Floyd, 2017). It is conceivable that, at some point, robots and humans may compete directly for jobs and resources. However, for now, such a science-fiction scenario seems unlikely. Nevertheless, progressive societies are already integrating AI across nearly all sectors of the economy. The service industry—an increasingly dominant force in the modern global economy—is saturated with digital innovations. Intelligent algorithms are used to analyze and select transport tickets, book hotels, assess insurance risks, and even engage in stock market trading on behalf of their users. "According to expert estimates, in the next 20 years, smart grids and dynamic pricing alone could generate between $31 and $50 billion" (Huateng, 2019).

2.2 Artificial Intelligence as a New Economic Actor

Humanity aspires to domesticate artificial intelligence just as it once tamed the natural world, steam, electricity, and massive machinery—incorporating them all into a new human-centered economic ecosystem. Throughout the entire history of socio-economic formations, humanity has never encountered an economic actor equal to or more intelligent than itself. Primitive humans, of course, competed with wild animals for vital resources such as water, food, and territory—but can such a confrontation be considered equal or rational? As Norbert Wiener observed, "To live effectively is to live with adequate information" (Wiener, 2019). Today, AI participates—often alongside humans, and in some cases more effectively (particularly in information exchange)—in nearly all socio-economic activities, from warfare to agriculture. The only caveat is that AI does so without understanding its purpose—more precisely, it lacks self-awareness. The moment such AI attains self-awareness, it will cease to be an unconscious economic actor embedded in someone else's labor process and will become a fully autonomous decision-maker. At that point, it will be able to determine for itself whether to participate in an economic process or not. Thus, issues of ethics and legal status will become as critical as philosophical questions in the era of digitalism.

Perhaps most striking is the fact that intelligence and the capacity for self-organization and goal-setting do not necessarily require the presence of the "spark of life." In other words, one does not need to be alive to make decisions—only intelligent. As time has shown, even embodiment is not required. Essentially, the transition from the latent stage of digitalism—often mistakenly referred to as "late capitalism"—to the flourishing phase of the digital formation is directly tied to the boom in AI, with the point of no return marked by the moment of technological singularity. This singularity represents a red line: once crossed, it will no longer be possible to return to primitive AI—machines that silently obey, lacking both consciousness and self-generated behavior. Identifying the onset of technological singularity allows us to pinpoint the moment beyond which some economic actors will no longer be able to exploit others with impunity.

The concept of technological singularity was touched upon as early as the works of Friedrich Engels and Vladimir Vernadsky. However, it was mathematician Irving John Good who, in the mid-twentieth century, formulated the theory of the "intelligence explosion" within this framework. According to this theory, humanity's continuous improvement of artificial intelligence will eventually reach a point where AI software will be capable of self-analysis and self-improvement without human intervention. This ability to self-enhance will allow AI to evolve into a state of superintelligence—an intelligence that surpasses human intellectual capabilities in all domains. This moment marks the beginning of the so-called intelligence explosion. In the scientific community, such AI is referred to as **Superintelligent Artificial Intelligence (SAI)**. The key distinction between SAI and conventional AI lies in SAI's superiority in knowledge and skills across nearly all economic functions, including inherently human domains such as creativity and philosophy.

Moreover, SAI will possess the ability to independently analyze complex situations, formulate goals, derive conclusions, and generate new goals based on prior outcomes. Most importantly, SAI will be capable of self-improvement and even of creating replicas of itself to facilitate and accelerate the achievement of its objectives.

Thus, upon reaching technological singularity—triggered by the intelligence explosion described by Good—humanity will confront an entirely new type of intelligent agent. Ray Kurzweil provides an insightful definition of this process: "Singularity is not merely the emergence of intelligent machines in the 2020s. That will only be the beginning of the revolution, where these machines continue to grow exponentially in power and begin to reprogram themselves to become even smarter. By 2045, machine intelligence will have surpassed the combined intellectual capacity of all humans by billions of times—this is the event horizon, beyond which we can no longer predict or comprehend the behavior of such consciousness" (Kurpatov, 2020).

Based on the foregoing, it is reasonable to assume that the encounter between *Homo sapiens* and a new form of intelligent economic agent will occur within the next two decades. The nature of this encounter—whether it leads to mutual cooperation and understanding, or to conflict—will largely depend on the level of human responsibility, the skill with which objectives are set, and the willingness to collaborate. Whether the era of digitalism becomes a time of abundance, peace, and liberation from poverty and suffering—or the final chapter of human history—remains an open question. Expert opinions on this matter are divided. For instance, Klaus Schwab, founder of the World Economic Forum in Davos, writes in his book *The Fourth Industrial Revolution*: "If appropriate institutions, standards, and norms develop around Fourth Industrial Revolution technologies, people around the world could become more free, healthier, better educated, and live lives of greater dignity, safety, and economic security" (Schwab, 2019).

In contrast, Stephen Hawking and Elon Musk have warned that superintelligence could become malevolent, identifying it as one of the greatest existing threats to the survival of human civilization (Brockman, 2020). In the same volume, Harvard professor George M. Church offers a more neutral view, highlighting the deeper philosophical dimension of the issue: "Perhaps we should worry less about a confrontation with 'them' and more about the rights of all sentient beings amid the emergence of unprecedented cognitive diversity" (Brockman, 2020). Given the complexity and diversity of human beings—even within a single species—it is not unreasonable to speculate that the future of digitalism may hinge on the specific relationships formed between individual human communities and particular AI codes.

2.3 *"Reconfiguration of Political Power Centers and Decision-Making Processes in the Age of Digitalism"*

In light of this, it becomes clear that politics and international relations will once again be critically important. Digitalism is characterized by the diffusion of the real and virtual worlds, a dramatic technological leap across nearly every sphere of human development (with the possible exception of spiritual development), and a fundamentally new worldview—one that redefines humanity's place in the global order. To paraphrase Madeleine Albright, "We are trying to understand and govern twenty-first century technologies using twentieth century thinking and nineteenth century institutions" (Schwab, 2019).

Regardless of whether digitalism is viewed as a comprehensive new system of global order or merely as a framework encompassing individual components such as Industry 4.0, we must acknowledge that the global economic landscape is changing. The pace of these transformations often follows an exponential trajectory. To deny this reality is both irrational and dangerous, as the process has already reshaped the economies and lives of entire regions and countries. Ignoring this new politico-economic formation risks not only relegating a nation to the status of a global "downshifter" but also threatens the loss of statehood and freedom in the foreseeable future.

In the twenty-first century, nations with limited intellectual potential may find themselves excluded from meaningful participation in global life, much like indigenous tribes in the 2nd millennium were driven inland and stripped of their rights and lands. For smaller, economically underdeveloped countries, it is therefore strategically imperative to formulate a survival doctrine within the evolving context of global digitalism. It is also critical to emphasize that in proposing the concept of digitalism, we adopt a systemic view: we do not regard any of its elements—such as Industry 4.0—as isolated phenomena existing independently of the broader formation. Nevertheless, the economic and political components of this formation play a key role in the establishment of digitalism as a new vector for the movement of forces, masses, and capital flows on a global scale.

The principles of economic digitalization offer revolutionary opportunities to address pressing societal challenges. "Under the umbrella of digitalization, a radically new world may emerge—one governed by value systems, management paradigms, social norms, and economic laws fundamentally different from those we know today. And this world will be fraught with novel risks for society, the economy, and for humanity itself—risks we are only beginning to understand and evaluate" (Risk Analysis Problem, 2017).

The author categorizes the modern world into three principal politico-economic forces:

1. **Small countries** (including those lagging in development),
2. **Strong countries**,
3. **Science-intensive corporations**—the heralds of the digitalism era.

When referring to "small countries," the author does not imply geographical size or population. These metrics are not the primary criteria for classification. Nor is this categorization aligned with the UN or IMF definitions based on developed or developing status. Instead, the main criteria used to define a country's global standing include the presence of a self-sufficient economy, a powerful military-political structure, a high Human Development Index (HDI), sufficient scientific and technological potential to ensure sustainable existence, a low level of corruption, and, preferably, the possession of liquid assets.

Based on these factors, many nations classified by the IMF as developed may, in this framework, be considered "small." For example, countries such as Greece, Latvia, Lithuania, Estonia, and Slovakia are designated as developed by the IMF, but in this classification are viewed as small due to their weak economies, high corruption levels, limited resource bases, and—most critically—the lack of sufficient military-political power. This renders them, in the era of digitalism, potential prey for stronger countries like Turkey, Russia, and Germany (the first two of which are still considered developing by IMF standards). Meanwhile, countries like Israel, Switzerland, and the Scandinavian nations are classified here as "strong."

Drawing parallels, it is evident that a "strong country" must possess a certain level of economic potential and military capacity—whether through a well-armed civilian population, significant standing in military alliances, or its own robust military-industrial complex. A strong country must be prepared to defend its economy against ongoing interventions, protect its resources from seizure and exploitation, and maintain at least an average pace of development in line with global trends. This defines the modern portrait of a strong country; by contrast, all others are to be considered small.

Below is a model outlining an economic strategy for small countries during the digitalism era, touching on several core areas requiring classification and subsequent political-economic planning:

1. Decentralization of political forces, acceleration of economic processes, reduction of bureaucracy;
2. Food security:
    - 2.1. Business transformation—the decline of legacy industrial giants and its impact on food security;
    - 2.2. Competition between strong and small countries over food and related resources;
3. Nanotechnology and concentrated economy;
4. Formation of political alliances, unions, and cartels among small countries during the digitalism era.

A fundamental manifestation of digitalism in the economic realm is the decentralization of power, including state and political structures. Accelerating economic processes through instantaneous decision-making—bypassing complex, hierarchical bureaucracies—is a defining feature of this new formation. As Klaus Schwab notes:

"This means that public and private organizations that fail to transform their isolated, vertically-oriented structures will increasingly lose control over the situation" (Schwab, 2019).

Thus, one of the first goals of the digital economy must be the dismantling of lower-level bureaucracies, streamlining state-business-civil society interactions.

In preparing small countries for the upcoming future, it is essential to reorient their economies under the influence of the ideas and realities of digitalism and Industry 4.0—an evolution that is impossible without radical reforms in education and science. However, such reforms will not succeed without promoting digitalism as a worldview and lifestyle. That is, it is necessary to prepare the population for a future in which humanity will divide into two vastly unequal groups in terms of numbers and resources: those integrated into the digitalism system and those excluded from it. This formation can help stabilize the current economic crisis, significantly limit the reckless use of resources, and reduce the consumption of non-renewable energy sources.

The digital society entails a new mode of citizen participation in political processes, fostering more transparent and open governance. The development of decentralized technologies paves the way for more democratic forms of governance, such as digital city-states or autonomous regions, where power is distributed among users of digital platforms. The rise of digitalism also raises numerous ethical concerns, such as privacy, data security, and control over personal information. It will be crucial to develop legal frameworks and policies that safeguard users' rights and prevent abuse.

As T. Safarov notes:

"The protection and security of personal data in digital format is one of the most critical tasks of the future" (Safarov, 2021).

Digitalism represents a unique system, distinct from both capitalism and socialism. For the first time, we encounter a new economic agent—artificial intelligence (AI). Information becomes the most important resource, replacing power and capital. This new era opens up unprecedented opportunities but also creates new risks. Before attempting to manage these future risks, humanity must first minimize its current ones—by reducing wars, oppression, dictatorships, and inequality—and reach a new level of social and spiritual development. Only then will we be ready to make responsible and ethical decisions regarding the use of artificial intelligence within the emerging global system of digitalism.

2.4 Results and Implications of Digitalism

The present study offers a conceptual rethinking of the global socio-economic transformation currently underway. The principal result of the research is the identification and substantiation of **Digitalism** as a novel economic and civilizational formation. Unlike previous systems such as capitalism or socialism, Digitalism is defined by its **informational foundation**, its reliance on **artificial intelligence as an autonomous economic agent**, and the **decentralization** of power from traditional institutions to **technological platforms and data infrastructures**.

One of the key contributions of the study is the recognition of **AI not merely as a tool**, but as a **participant in economic and political processes**, capable of generating value, shaping preferences, and exerting influence over social structures. This redefinition challenges the anthropocentric assumptions of classical political economy and introduces a paradigm in which human agency is shared with non-human intelligences.

The discussion reveals several important implications:

1. **Redistribution of Global Power**: Traditional empires and strong states may lose their dominant status unless they adapt to the technological logic of the new digital formation. The rise of powerful digital corporations and platform-states (e.g., Google, Amazon, Tencent) suggests a tectonic shift in sovereignty and influence.
2. **Challenges for Small States**: Countries with limited access to traditional resources can either become victims of technological dependency or seize the opportunity to leap forward through digital infrastructure, intellectual capital, and network integration. This demands the formation of new political-economic alliances and decentralized strategies.
3. **Decentralization and Dematerialization**: Governance structures are transforming under the pressure of algorithmic systems that demand speed, efficiency, and decentralization. The shift from material to informational value destabilizes existing taxonomies of economic power and calls for a revision of legal and institutional frameworks.
4. **Ethical and Existential Risks**: The emergence of Superintelligent AI (SAI), as theorized by Good and Kurzweil, introduces profound questions about ethics, control, and the future of human autonomy. The moment of technological singularity is not only a scientific threshold but also a political and philosophical frontier.
5. **Digital Inequality**: A new stratification is emerging, separating those integrated into the digitalist ecosystem from those excluded from it. This calls for proactive education, inclusion policies, and the development of ethical standards for AI governance.

The practical implications of this work lie in the **strategic need for countries—particularly small and medium-sized states—to revise national doctrines, invest in intellectual and digital capital, and form regional alliances** grounded in shared technological values. For global powers, the future lies in **co-governance with AI systems**, responsible technological stewardship, and the pursuit of balance between innovation and ethical responsibility.

In conclusion, the transition to Digitalism signals not merely a change in economic tools, but a transformation of civilization. The emergence of artificial intelligence as an economic actor compels a reconsideration of political theory, economic policy, and even the human condition itself. Whether Digitalism leads to liberation or domination will depend on humanity's collective ability to shape the rules of this new game before they are written by non-human intelligence.

3 Conclusion

The emergence of **Digitalism**, catalyzed by AI and data-centric infrastructures, marks not just a technological shift, but a **civilizational transformation**. In this new reality, power no longer resides in material production but in the capacity to control, interpret, and mobilize information. **Artificial intelligence, as both agent and medium**, participates in shaping value, labor, governance, and identity.

As emphasized by Zinchenko, the rise of AI **redefines the foundation of economic interaction** and demands **new ethical and institutional thinking** (Zinchenko V, 2023*)*. The increasing autonomy and decision-making capacity of AI create challenges for democratic governance, economic justice, and the very idea of human agency.

The limitations of AI, however, remain crucial. As Zinchenko et al. remind us, **AI lacks the intrinsic moral compass** and transformative imagination inherent to human beings (Zinchenko et al., 2024*)*. This means that **Digitalism must be steered by human responsibility**, informed by wisdom, creativity, and an inclusive global vision.

Whether the Digitalist era results in emancipation or domination depends on the foresight, ethics, and adaptability of humanity itself. The future is not written by machines—but by those who shape the systems within which machines operate.

References

Alekseeva, I. Y., & Arshinov, V. I. (2016). *The information society and the NBICS-revolution* (p. 196). Institute of Philosophy, Academy of Sciences.

Babeshko, O. S. (2017). Information society and religion: The post-secular society. *Issues of Economics and Management, 9(2)*, 52–54.

Bell, D. (2006). *The coming of post-industrial society: A venture in social forecasting*. Academia. (p. 658).

Brockman, J. (Ed.). (2020). *Artificial intelligence: Hopes and fears*. AST. (p. 35).

Castells, M. (1996). *The rise of the network society*. Blackwell. (p. 52).

Dvornikov, V. V. (2017). Non-confessional religiosity in the information space: Itsism, "New Age", cyberreligion. *Journal of Philosophical Studies*, *3*(1), 18–28.

Floyd, D. (2017). *What is the difference between communism and socialism?* (p. 11).

Huateng, M. (2019). *The digital transformation of China*. Alpina Publisher. (p. 336).

Kurpatov, A. V. (2020). *The fourth world war. The future is near!*. Capital Publishing House. (p. 66).

Polanyi, K. (2013). *Selected works*. Territory of the future. (p. 200).

Risks of the Digital Economy. (2017). *Risk analysis problems*, *14*(6), 7.

Safarov, T. (2021). *The digital future and its risks*. Tahsil. (p. 89).

Schwab, K. (2019). *The fourth industrial revolution technologies*. Bombora. (p. 26).

Wiener, N. (2019). *Cybernetics and society* (p. 126). AST.

Zinchenko, V. (2023). Transformations of the scientific and technological revolution and the role of ai for education systems in the sustainable development paradigm. In F. Roumate (Ed.), *Artificial intelligence in higher education and scientific research. Bridging human and machine: Future education with intelligence*. Springer XII. (p. 146).
Zinchenko, V., Mielkov, Y., Nych, T., Abasov, M., & Trynyak, M. (2024). Human thinking in the age of generative A.I.: Values of openness and higher education for the future. *International conference on electrical, computer and energy technologies (ICECET)*. IEEE. (pp. 1–6).

AI and Information as a Strategic Assets for Major Technological Corporations

Rossana Soriano Vergara

1 Introduction

The evolution of technology and communications contributes to enhancing the processes for new opportunities, and Artificial Intelligence (AI) is developing as a new and great force. AI has become one of the most important and innovative tools to be used in many areas of our everyday life. In this context, information becomes very relevant for its conversion into valuable knowledge through AI. Increasingly, information is seen as a strategic asset, able to shape the competitive advantage, leading investment and informing decisions in real time. The value of information lies in its processing, interpretation, and transformation into intelligence. Thereby Artificial Intelligence performs a transformative role.

AI allows organizations to obtain insights from large and complex datasets, transforming raw data into significant predictions, recommendations and decisions. AI techniques such as machine learning models, natural language processing and others enable the automation of knowledge discovery and help of human decision-making. Companies that incorporate AI in their information systems are better prepared to be able to anticipate change, respond to market fluctuations and drive innovation (Dalkir, 2005).

This chapter examines the strategic connection between artificial intelligence and information. First, the conceptual foundations of information as a strategic asset are viewed. The use of real industry examples, explores how artificial intelligence technology transforms. Therefore, the principal objective of this study is to analyze how artificial intelligence connects with knowledge and its transformation process to become a strategic asset. Finally, it discusses the main ethical and operational issues

R. Soriano Vergara (✉)
Universidad Femenina del Sagrado Corazón, Lima, Peru
e-mail: rsoriano@unife.edu.pe

F. Roumate (ed.), *AI, Information, and Global Dynamics*, Contributions to International Relations,
https://doi.org/10.1007/978-3-032-13528-5_9

that companies must face and gives and offers a perspective view on how artificial intelligence is transforming strategy itself.

1.1 Information as a Strategic Asset

The concepts of data, knowledge and information as strategic assets is not new. When properly managed, information can foster innovation, improve performance and help competitive advantage. However, in the context of the Fourth Industrial Revolution, the volume, velocity and diversity of data available to organizations have exploded, presenting both unprecedented opportunities and challenges.

Along these lines it is best to understand how information becomes a strategic asset by analyzing two other concepts, such as data and knowledge, that are involved in changing data information into knowledge. Many people get confused about what data, information, and knowledge mean and how they are different. This confusion has caused companies to spend a lot of money on technology projects that don't give the results they expected. Many times, companies only realize what they really need after investing a lot in a system that does not work well.

Companies need data and must learn how to manage it well. Some try to improve their ways of recording and handling data because it's very important for their success. Some businesses collect a lot of data because they believe it makes their decisions more scientific and accurate. They think that if they collect enough data, their decisions will automatically be correct. However, this idea has two main problems. To begin with, an overabundance of data can conceal the information that is truly relevant.

Strategic information here means creating useful insights that help predict market trends and covering demands, tailor customer experiences, boost operational efficiency, and prepare opportunities and challenges. The value of artificial intelligence lies in its ability to transform scattered, static data into dynamic decision-making systems. As such, AI systems are an essential tool to transform raw data into competitive strategy.

In today's data-driven and hyper-connected environment, information has become a key and the most competitive resource to achieve success. Organizations have recognized significant prospects in the global market, driven by cloud computing, social networks, the Internet of Things (IoT), online commerce and business systems (Mikalef et al., 2019). However, having a significant amount of data collection and storage does not automatically make that data valuable. The real competitive edge lies in how organizations establish their approaches to manage, analyze, and apply that data to support decisions, drive innovations, and foster developments (Brynjolfsson & McElheran, 2016).

The concept of considering information as a valuable strategic resource is supported by various academic theories, such as the knowledge-based theory of firms (Grant, 1996), the resource-based perspective (Barney, 1991), and the theory of dynamic capabilities (Teece et al., 1997). Theories in organizational studies emphasize that intangible assets, such as information, knowledge, and organizational learning, can be key drivers of sustained competitive advantage.

Artificial intelligence (AI) is transforming this context by making the processes of collecting, processing, and using information more efficient and effective. In traditional settings, turning data into knowledge often demanded considerable time and effort. Now, AI allows organizations to extract insights from large, complex datasets with greater speed, enhancing their ability to adapt, learn, and respond to change (Mikalef & Gupta, 2021).

Artificial intelligence also boosts the ability to anticipate opportunities and risks through more advanced predictive analytics. It enhances decision-making and personalization within organizations, playing a crucial role in enabling continuous adjustments to strategies and processes based on evolving data flows (Teece, 2018).

Artificial intelligence is built on several technologies, including machine learning, natural language processing (NLP), computer vision, and robotics, each offering unique support for managing information. Machine learning identifies patterns in large-scale data to inform predictions and decisions. NLP allows systems to understand and produce human language, facilitating the analysis of text and speech. Computer vision interprets visual data such as images and videos, broadening available data sources. Altogether, these technologies transform static information into dynamic tools for strategic guidance. By adopting AI, companies can automate repetitive tasks, improve forecasting accuracy, personalize user experiences, and discover insights that turn information into a competitive asset.

Artificial intelligence is also reshaping how businesses access and utilize information. Unlike conventional systems based on fixed rules or manual decisions, AI systems can learn from data, scale up, and adapt over time. This enables organizations to work with large volumes of unstructured information, identify patterns or anomalies, and generate predictive insights that influence strategic planning (Russell & Norvig, 2020).

Through its dynamic features, artificial intelligence strengthens how organizations detect and act on emerging trends. It improves the ability to capitalize on opportunities by refining decisions and enabling ongoing transformation of business models. Still, the outputs generated by AI can be difficult to interpret, and companies must ensure that governance frameworks are in place to align AI use with ethical and strategic objectives. As such, managing AI-driven information involves technical, ethical, and organizational considerations. The integration of AI into data strategies brings new challenges, such as ensuring model transparency, algorithmic accountability, and consistency with core values, issues that are now central in discussions about AI's strategic impact.

1.2 AI Technologies in Handling Information and Making Decisions

Artificial intelligence has become a central topic in the business and technology sectors. Many industries are heavily investing in AI, and some companies are even developing their own AI systems. As of now, 28% of S&P 500 firms belong to the tech sector, and 8% are engaged in consumer services or communication areas linked to AI. The following are seven market-driven reasons behind the growing adoption of AI (McKinsey & Company, 2018).

Seven important factors are fueling the expansion of AI in the market (Sabey Data Centers, 2025):

- New Technologies: AI is improving storage capacity and programmers with the use of new algorithms to use applications. So industries use these advancements to automate operations, analyze product performance and consumer behavior and support more strategic decision-making.
- Continued Growth in Cloud Computing: Enterprises are constantly investing in the cloud infrastructure that gives computing power for processing and data storage. Companies like AWS, Microsoft Azure, and Google Cloud have also simplified and lowered the cost of AI adoption for other businesses by offering scalable tools and infrastructure for building, deploying, and managing AI models (Holmegaard, 2024).
- Big Data: Enterprises can now store and access massive amounts of structured and unstructured data thanks to cloud solutions. This accessibility enables more powerful AI-driven analysis, identifying patterns and trends for better predictions. Moreover, Machine Learning (ML), a branch of AI, relies heavily on access to abundant data. Instead of depending strictly on explicit programming, ML systems improve by learning from experience. Because high volumes of data are essential for achieving accurate and effective results, this data availability enables researchers to train ML models to address sophisticated and complex problems (Holmegaard, 2024).
- A competitive Edge. AI and ML are improving product development, simplifying operations, and informing better decisions, which leads to higher efficiency, cost savings, and business performance. As a result, companies are motivated to adopt these technologies to stay competitive and stand out in their industries.
- Enhanced Customer Experience: With AI and ML, organizations can analyze customer data to better understand preferences, expectations, and behavior. In this way, this experience optimizes marketing strategies, and tailored product or service recommendations, boosting satisfaction and loyalty.
- Insights and Predictive Capabilities: By analyzing large data sets, AI and ML can uncover valuable insights that guide data-driven decisions. This is particularly impactful in sectors like healthcare, finance, marketing, and cybersecurity, where predictive analysis can lead to proactive actions, improved outcomes, and problem prevention (Sabey Data Centers, 2025).

- Routine Tasks. Automating routine tasks with AI and ML enhances productivity, reduces errors, and frees professionals to focus on creative or strategic work. This efficiency is especially useful in fields like manufacturing, healthcare, and finance.
- Sector-Specific Solutions: AI and ML are also being tailored for specific industries. For instance, in manufacturing, AI helps optimize workflows and predict maintenance needs. In healthcare, AI can assist in interpreting medical images, helping doctors detect conditions more accurately (Sabey Data Centers, 2025).

Overall, AI tools are essential for transforming raw data into actionable insights. The following areas play a crucial role in facilitating this conversion: Machine Learning (ML): ML algorithms are capable of identifying complex patterns in large datasets and improving over time with continuous learning. They're used in areas like predictive maintenance, fraud detection, demand forecasting, and personalized recommendations (Jordan & Mitchell, 2015).

Natural Language Processing (NLP): it facilitates the computational interpretation, generation, and analysis of human language. This technology enables the extraction of valuable information from diverse unstructured data sources, exemplified by customer feedback, social media discourse, and legal documentation (Chowdhury, 2003).

Computer Vision: the field concerned with enabling computational systems to analyze, interpret, and derive meaning from visual data. Its applications encompass diverse domains such as medical imaging, automated quality assessment, facial recognition, and autonomous vehicle navigation.

Robotic Process Automation (RPA): it employs AI to automate the execution of rule-based and repetitive tasks, thereby improving operational efficiency and reducing errors (Van der Aalst et al., 2018).

Decision Support Systems (DSS): Decision support systems enhanced with AI are used to manage data and decisions by managers and analysts.

Collectively, these AI technologies enable the progression from descriptive analytics toward predictive and prescriptive methodologies. Organizations can transcend conventional reporting to generate anticipatory insights and refined recommendations for decision-making (Davenport & Ronanki, 2018). However, realizing these benefits necessitates not only technical expertise but also robust organizational coordination and governance frameworks to ensure the reliability and applicability of AI-derived insights.

1.3 Industry Case Studies—AI Transforming into Strategic Advantage

Artificial intelligence functions beyond mere technological implementation; it serves as a strategic enabler, revolutionizing the means by which organizations generate value from information. In various industries, AI-driven platforms enable the transformation of raw data into actionable intelligence, which subsequently influences decision frameworks, operational efficiencies, and long-term strategic posture.

This section delineates selected case studies from multiple sectors—encompassing media, finance, e-commerce, and healthcare—that illustrate the practical deployment of AI in converting information into a strategic resource. These examples elucidate both the potential benefits and the complexities inherent in harnessing AI for competitive differentiation in the contemporary information era.

1.3.1 Netflix: Predictive Analytics and Content Strategy

Netflix exemplifies the strategic transformation of information through artificial intelligence. The company's recommender system—which drives approximately 75% to 80% of viewer engagement—constitutes a sophisticated algorithmic architecture that personalizes user experiences (Gómez-Uribe & Hunt, 2015). By processing extensive interaction data, including viewing histories, content metadata, and search behaviors, Netflix generates highly individualized recommendations. These not only elevate user engagement but also directly influence retention metrics. Furthermore, the system critically informs Netflix's content strategy, enabling data-driven prioritization of investments in original and licensed programming based on predictive audience preference analytics.

As emphasized by Gomez-Uribe and Hunt (2015), Netflix's pervasive culture of innovation—sustained through rigorous A/B testing and iterative AI pipeline enhancements—ensures the recommender system remains a dynamic competitive differentiator. This case underscores AI's capacity to convert real-time information flows into actionable strategic intelligence, thereby optimizing both operational efficiency and long-term business objectives.

Leveraging advanced machine learning techniques, Netflix systematically analyzes voluminous user activity data to produce tailored content suggestions. Such personalization bolsters user involvement and loyalty while simultaneously guiding content acquisition and production decisions (Gómez-Uribe & Hunt, 2015). Consequently, Netflix transmutes insights into audience preferences into a valuable strategic asset, aligning seamlessly with its overarching business paradigm.

1.3.2 JPMorgan Chase: Automating Legal Intelligence

JPMorgan Chase employs the COiN system to streamline the analysis of complex legal documents. This system integrates artificial intelligence, specifically natural language processing (NLP), to enable the efficient identification of critical contractual clauses and associated risk factors. The implementation of COiN has been shown to significantly reduce manual processing requirements and expedite analysis time. Consequently, this process converts legal data into a valuable organizational asset, contributing to enhanced operational efficiency and improved risk management.

The COiN system exemplifies the transformative potential of artificial intelligence in converting unstructured information, such as legal documents, into a strategic resource.

It automates the generation of knowledge derived from complex texts, which optimizes risk management and regulatory compliance—key strategic activities in the banking sector. Furthermore, COin increases the speed and quality of strategic action selection related to contracts and deal execution. JPMorgan Chase shows how AI can be used to convert data-heavy legal processes into sources of operational efficiency and strategic benefit. The company's Contract Intelligence (COin) platform employs natural language processing (NLP) to examine complex commercial loan agreements—a work that in the past used to involve approximately 360.000 hours of manual legal work each year (Son, 2017). Through the automatization of the extraction of crucial data from legal documents, COin diminishes operational expenses, but at the same time, it increases strategic action selection concerning risk management, compliance, and contract negotiation. The system allows JPMorgan to transform legal information, which was formerly underused, into a proactive asset that boosts its competitive agility within the highly regulated financial services sector. This example illustrates how artificial intelligence can turn stuck data in formats without structure into actionable insights that drive strategic results (Son, 2017).

1.3.3 Amazon: AI-Driven Supply Chain and Dynamic Pricing

Amazon uses IA with the purpose of modernizing its global supply chain and adjusting prices in real-time. The company has the ability to accurately anticipate demand, manage inventory efficiently, and apply customized pricing strategies. AI transforms operational information into beneficial knowledge that enhances customer experience and accelerates profits. Amazon stands out within the digital economy for its sophisticated use of IA in optimizing supply chain efficiency and implementing real-time pricing. The company incorporates machine learning and real-time data analytics throughout its worldwide logistics network in order to maximize inventory levels, route planning, and fulfillment process (Kim et al., 2021). Additionally, Amazon used AI-powered dynamic pricing algorithms that constantly modify product prices based on factors like demand volatility, competitor pricing, and customer actions (Stone, 2013). These capabilities allow Amazon to match supply with changing demand almost instantly, boosting both profit margins and customer satisfaction. The strategic application of AI-enabled information flows has been key to Amazon's ability to efficiently scale its operations while retaining a customer-centric business model. This instance underscores how AI converts supply chain data into a strategic tool, leading to both operational excellence and market differentiation.

The Stanford case study and Brad Stone's book each explore Amazon's strategic leadership in e-commerce and logistics, highlighting the company's use of AI and data-driven systems. Amazon employs machine learning and real-time data analytics to enhance inventory levels in fulfillment centers, improve last-mile delivery routes, manage supplier connections, foresee supply chain issues, and predict demand with high precision (considering product, location, and time). The company's objectives are to maximize revenue and profit while enhancing customer value perception. Its goals also include achieving market-leading delivery speeds (like same-day and 2-hour delivery in certain markets), minimizing inventory holding costs while ensuring maximum product availability, building an adaptive and resilient supply chain that responds to changing market dynamics, and maintaining price leadership while sustaining profitability across operations.

Amazon demonstrates how AI converts operational data and customer information into a strategic advantage. AI assists Amazon in aligning its supply chain execution with key strategic goals like speed, reliability, and cost leadership. AI-driven pricing also enables Amazon to capture real-time value from market information. These capabilities are crucial to Amazon's competitive edge.

1.3.4 Watson Health: AI in Strategic Clinical Decision-Making

In the case of Watson Health, they use big databases with AI to improve clinical decision-making. The results were that they found problems with the data quality, accuracy and combination with current clinical processes (Ross & Swetlitz, 2018).

The use of AI for information transformation in this case shows the challenges and the possibilities for success in clinical management. The objective is to be useful for clinicians with medical literature and patient data using a system that transforms unorganized medical information into actionable clinical intelligence.

The same system was used for Oncology innovating their processes, highlighting the possibilities of success and limitations in critical areas like clinical medicine. The objective was the evaluation of patient information, treatment suggestions to oncologists and help healthcare providers to access information about cancer treatment.

Concerning technology, the platform uses natural language processing and machine learning algorithms to examine and determine medical information ass guidelines, results from trials, and records. Watson Health was extremely interested that this project offers the potential of AI in transforming value from data, the significant contribution of the system and ethical position.

1.4 Ethical and Operational Challenges

Watson Health project is a great AI system transforming information and integrating into clinical processes which involves ethical aspects as confidence, honesty, responsibility and organizational culture.

1.5 Data Privacy and Governance

Data governance is one of the main concerns when quantities of personal information used with AI systems is gathered without complete openness or informed consent. Companies must comply with the regulations in force relating to data protection and promote mainly the good ethical practices. It is important to recognize that this technical process of managing data and meeting legal requirements plays a crucial role in establishing confidence and trust with all the parties involved.

1.6 Algorithmic Bias and Fairness

Systems with Artificial Intelligence consist of big datasets with social and historical biases which might be strengthened if they are not well designed and supervised. As an example, biased training data can produce inaccurate suggestions for hiring, loans or legal verdicts. To avoid these threats, it is necessary to implement organizations with initiative-taking measures to reduce bias, such as auditing of datasets, algorithm transparency, and ongoing assessment of model results.

1.7 Explainability and Trust

The intricate nature of numerous deep learning frameworks which. run with AI models, represents certain difficulties to establish trust and accountability in critical areas such as healthcare and finance. It is not enough to provide precise predictions but their methods of decision-making need to be clear to human stakeholders. To achieve a degree of explainability requires compromises between the complexity of the model and its transparency. Finally, companies need to thoughtfully manage these compromises and guarantee that decision-makers are capable of understanding and validating outputs of AI.

1.8 Operational Integration and Scalability

Many organizations deal with what is referred to as "technical debt" in their machine learning frameworks, where decisions made for immediate implementation lead to on-going maintenance and scalability problems. Some successful AI integration decisions are strong engineering principles and a defined connection between AI projects and overall business strategies.

Human resources are vital elements for successful AI integration. An adequate training guarantee the correct use of AI technologies and the organizational culture should shift to prioritize data-informed decision-making. If change management is not carefully handled, efforts to adopt AI might face problems or fail to reach their possibility for success.

2 Conclusions

This chapter tried to deliver a deeply examination of how Artificial Intelligence can be used as a strategic facilitator by transforming information into a significant asset for organizations. By reviewing different conceptual models, AI technologies, and practical case studies, the discussion has underscored the innovative ways AI alters the methods of data collection, analyzing it, and making decisions.

It was established that using AI for a strategic edge does not rely on the technology itself, but also on the wider organizational environment in which it is implemented. The case studies analyzed show integration of AI, data governance, ethical considerations and ensuring that AI projects are always aligned with business goals.

Another aspect to take into consideration is that organizations need to be clear to what strategies mean on AI for information. Issues related to ethical concerns such as data privacy, bias in algorithms, and the need for clarity must be tackled with adequate measures and organizational protocols. Additionally, implementing AI systems require strong engineering methods, and investment in the preparation of human resources.

Planning for the future, Artificial Intelligence on the information sectors continues changing and improving. Progress in machine learning, natural language processing, and other technologies will let organizations the possibility to extract value from data. However, this potential must be developed with responsibility to ensure AI systems be used with equity, transparency and consistency with human principles.

The challenges referring to AI supported information strategies are varied and everchanging. Organizations that take a proactive stance towards these challenges will be better prepared to use AI's transformative capabilities in a responsible and sustainable way because they require a strong governance, ethical awareness, and a dedication to continuous education and not only technical expertise.

In conclusion, the integration of AI and information resources presents significant opportunities for organizations in several sectors. The organizations that adopt AI systems with a considerate, principled and flexible approach will be most likely to achieve competitive advantages in a more data-centric environment.

References

Barney, J. (1991). Firm resources and sustained competitive advantage. *Journal of Management, 17*(1), 99–120.

Brynjolfsson, E., & McElheran, K. (2016). *Data in action: Data-driven decision making and predictive analytics in U.S. manufacturing* (Working Paper 16–081). Harvard Business School

Chowdhury, G. G. (2003). Natural language processing. *Annual Review of Information Science and Technology, 37*(1), 51–89.

Dalkir, K. (2005). *Knowledge management in theory and practice*. McGill University.

Davenport, T. H., & Ronanki, R. (2018). Artificial intelligence for the real world. *Harvard Business Review, 96*(1), 108–116.

Grant, R. M. (1996). Toward a knowledge-based theory of the firm. *Strategic Management Journal, 17*(S2), 109–122.

Gómez-Uribe, C. A., & Hunt, N. (2015). The netflix recommender system: Algorithms, business value, and innovation. *ACM Transactions on Management Information Systems, 6*(4), 13:1–13:19. https://doi.org/10.1145/2843948

Holmegaard, E. (2024). AI as a strategic asset in business: Unlocking opportunities and overcoming challenges. *Medium*. https://medium.com/@emilholmegaard/ai-as-a-strategic-asset-in-business-unlocking-opportunities-and-overcoming-challenges-0f668a4e5fca

Jordan, M. I., & Mitchell, T. M. (2015). Machine learning: Trends, perspectives, and prospects. *Science, 349*(6245), 255–260.

Kim, Y., Hong, S., & Lee, H. (2021). *Leveraging AI for supply chain management at Amazon*. Stanford Graduate School of Business Case Study.

McKinsey & Company. (2018). *Notes from the AI frontier. Insights from hundreds of use cases*. McKinsey Global Institute.

Mikalef, P., & Gupta, M. (2021). Artificial intelligence capability: Conceptualization, measurement calibration, and empirical study on its impact on organizational creativity and firm performance. *Information and Management, 58*(3), 103434.

Mikalef, P., et al. (2019). Big data analytics capabilities and firm performance: A resource-based perspective. *Information and Management, 56*(8), 103207.

Ross, C., & Swetlitz, I. (2018). IBM's Watson recommended 'unsafe and incorrect' cancer treatments. *STAT News*.

Russell, S. J., & Norvig, P. (2020). *Artificial intelligence: A modern approach*. (4th ed.). Pearson.

Sabey, D. C. (2025). *7 key factors driving the AI market*. https://sabeydatacenters.com/news/7-key-factors-driving-the-ai-market

Son, H. (2017). *JP Morgan software does in seconds what took lawyers 360,000 hours*. CNBC. https://www.cnbc.com/2017/02/27/jp-morgan-software-does-in-seconds-what-took-lawyers-360000-hours.html

Stone, B. (2013). *The everything store: Jeff Bezos and the age of Amazon*. Little, Brown and Company.

Teece, D. J. (2018). Dynamic capabilities and strategic management. *Strategic Management Journal, 28*(13), 1319–1350.

Teece, D. J., Pisano, G., & Shuen, A. (1997). Dynamic capabilities and strategic management. *Strategic Management Journal, 18*(7), 509–533.

Van der Aalst, Wil M. P., et al. (2018). Robotic process automation. *Business and Information Systems Engineering, 60*(4), 269–272.

AI, Information and Maritime Security: Implications for Global Trade and Geopolitical Competition

Zaeem Hassan Mehmood

1 Introduction

The oceans have historically served as an important domain of power, trade, and geopolitical competition (Mahan, 1890). In the twenty-first century, the vast oceanic space is fundamentally being reshaped by the integration of Artificial Intelligence (AI), which continues to redefine the scope and boundaries of maritime security (Mehmood, 2025). From port operations to decision-making at sea, and from undersea cables to contested waters, AI is increasingly being woven into the fabric of maritime governance, commerce and surveillance. This chapter examines how AI is automating tasks at sea and reshaping the technological and legal aspects of global maritime security.

Maritime security remains central to global stability, with more than 90% of international trade is carried by sea. In addition, the sea hosts critical infrastructure, such as the submarine cables that transmit more than 95% of global internet traffic, underpinning the digital architecture that contemporary economies, communications, and even AI systems are increasingly dependent upon (Bueger & Liebetrau, 2021). As digital dependencies increase, so do the risks. Threats originating from cyber-attacks, electronic spoofing, surveillance intrusions, and hybrid conflict as a result extend below the ocean surface, revealing the vulnerabilities of an increasingly interconnected digital infrastructure (Carlo & Obergfaell, 2024).

AI continues to revolutionize the way maritime security is conceptualized and operationalized. AI-enhanced platforms are being utilized to detect anomalies in vessel movement, predict port congestion, optimize cargo logistics, and conduct real-time surveillance of vast oceanic expanses. Technologies like autonomous surface and subsurface vessels, machine-learning based algorithms and sensor

Z. H. Mehmood (✉)
Department of Social Sciences and Humanities, Greenwich University, Karachi, Pakistan
e-mail: zaeem.mehmood@zu.edu.pk

F. Roumate (ed.), *AI, Information, and Global Dynamics*, Contributions to International Relations,
https://doi.org/10.1007/978-3-032-13528-5_10

fusion have rapidly transitioned from experimental to operational phases, in major civil and military purviews (Alamoush & Ölçer, 2025). These AI-powered technologies have the potential to enhance efficiency by enabling smarter and agile responses to maritime threats.

The integration of AI into the maritime applications presents a number of challenges. As AI strengthens security and capabilities to assess system intrusions, it also introduces new vulnerabilities and ethical challenges. Fears of algorithmic obscurity, data privacy issues, civilian-military dual use capabilities, and cyberattacks raise critical questions regarding accountability and governance (Ionita & Kanetake, 2023). Furthermore, the international legal frameworks for maritime conduct, such as the United Nations Convention on the Law of the Sea (UNCLOS), referred to as the "constitution of the ocean," were not formulated considering intelligent machines and autonomous systems, leaving important regulatory gaps (Osaloni & Ayeni, 2022). These tensions are especially visible in contested maritime spaces like the South China Sea and the Arctic Mediterranean Sea, where the use of AI is increasingly becoming a force multiplier for great power competition.

This chapter seeks to present an overview of the transformative role AI plays in maritime security by addressing three key questions: First, how is AI being integrated into maritime security, and what are its primary applications? Second, what new risks, vulnerabilities, and challenges does this integration entail? Third, what governance mechanisms and ethical frameworks are needed to ensure that AI enhances, rather than undermines, maritime security and safety?

To address these questions, the chapter combines a systematic review of scholarly and policy literature with informal discussions conducted with supply-chain leaders, maritime practitioners and legal scholars. The analysis is complemented by regional evaluation of three key regions: South China Sea, the Red Sea, and the Arctic Mediterranean Sea, which illustrate the practical realities and real-world applications of AI adoption in geopolitical settings.

2 Methods

This chapter examines the transformative impact of AI on maritime security using a qualitative research methodology. This approach recognizes the interdisciplinary nature of the subject, that extend to key themes relating to emerging technology, strategic studies, maritime law, and global governance. A qualitative assessment of these themes enables a thorough understanding of how AI transforms maritime operations and geopolitical dynamics. The analysis is drawn from an extensive review of scholarly literature and institutional publications from prestigious peer-reviewed journals, as well as policy studies and reports by global organizations including the International Maritime Law Institute and the International Maritime Organization (IMO). To further add to the literature, informal interviews were conducted with maritime legal experts, and port management professionals. These offer useful insights into the working of AI systems, challenges such as cybersecurity, and perspectives on multilateral cooperation. The qualitative data is further contextualized through three case studies. the South China Sea, the Red Sea, and the Arctic Mediterranean Sea, selected for their strategic significance, presence of contested maritime zones, and early adoption of AI-driven surveillance and logistics tools.

3 Maritime Infrastructure in the Digital Era

The ocean has long been seen as the conduit of globalization, facilitating the shipment of over 90% of world trade (Kaplan, 2011). In the twenty-first century, it also serves as the backbone of the digital economy. Thin, fiber-optic wires, known as submarine cables located at the bottom of the world's oceans, carry more than 95% of real-time intercontinental internet traffic. These cables underpin everything from international banking to cloud computing, as well as smooth functioning of AI systems themselves (Ganz et al., 2024).

3.1 The Strategic Importance of Maritime Infrastructure

Modern maritime infrastructure includes more than just ports and shipping lanes; it includes a complex matrix consisting of logistics chains, smart port systems, offshore energy platforms, and communication channels (Clemente et al., 2023). As a result, maritime infrastructure can be a high-risk zone for cyber and kinetic threats. In the South China Sea, in particular, the convergence of critical infrastructure with AI adds to the economic and geopolitical competition (Schindler et al., 2024).

3.2 Submarine Cables and Data Sovereignty

As AI applications increasingly rely on real-time data from globally distributed systems, the safety of submarine cables and integrity of the data flows becomes a critical component of national security (Pohontu & Ermolai, 2024). Today over 95% of intercontinental traffic is dependent on the submarine cables. Any disruptions to the cables, whether by natural causes, hostile acts or accidents can destabilize economies and data-dependent defense operations. The December 2024, Gulf of Finland incident caused an estimated €60 million damage to telecom and energy sector (Miętkiewicz, 2025). In the Red Sea, cable cuts in early 2024 reduced capacity of the internet data by 25%, forcing traffic on the more expensive satellite and alternative cable routes (Paik, 2025). At a global scale, there are roughly around 600 submarine cables with over 1700 landing stations. With the expansion of cloud computing, content and cloud providers now account for **over 75% of international bandwidth**, consolidating control of critical digital arteries in a few corporate hands (Cannon, 2025).

Furthermore, the governance of the submarine cables can become complex when nations use territorial jurisdiction to regulate and control data (Guilfoyle et al., 2022). While UNCLOS guarantees the freedom to lay and maintain cables on the high seas and continental shelf (Articles. 79, 112–115), coastal state jurisdiction over territorial seas and landing stations can result in national rules, permits, and security measures. This can create friction and adversely impact data-sovereignty preferences, as well as complicate emergency repairs, and introduce geopolitical leverage. The fact that the majority of submarine cables are privately owned, further blurs lines of control, raising questions about transparency, access, and strategic prioritization during crises (Wang & Ye, 2023).

These aspects also raise important questions about who controls the ocean-based data architecture, and how geopolitical rivalries, between the US and China will shape the future of AI and underwater connectivity (Johnson, 2019). Notably, China is increasingly developing underwater data centers, from a pilot project off the coast of Hainan to an expanded module project at Lingshui and Shanghai, signal a broader strategy of pairing subsea computing with cable ecosystems to create low-latency and a resilient digital infrastructure (Wang & Ye, 2023). The US tech giants have earlier explored similar concepts. Microsoft's *Project Natick* was an example of underwater data center off the Orkney Islands, that demonstrated that it could operate with **up to eight times greater reliability** than data centers on land (Simon, 2018). Further developments of undersea data centers, could reduce data transit times for maritime systems and other applications used for AI model training. For AI-dependent operations, having data storage and processing nodes directly linked to subsea cables could dramatically shorten decision cycles, enhance resilience against terrestrial disruptions, and improve energy efficiency through seawater cooling (Sutherland & Bopp, 2023).

As states and corporations invest in undersea cables and submerged computing infrastructure, the maritime domain's strategic value will continue to extend beyond traditional security and trade functions to become the core of the global digital economy. Control over subsea data architecture in this developing environment will not only determine information domination and competitive advantage in AI, but it will also change the geopolitical landscape of maritime influence in the twenty-first century (McGeachy, 2022).

3.2.1 Applications of AI in Maritime Security

AI acts as a force multiplier in the maritime domain, allowing for capabilities that extend far beyond the extent of traditional surveillance, navigation, and decision-making systems. In maritime security, where the oceanspace is vast and contested waters often intersect global trade routes, AI-based systems have the potential to optimize defensive and operational dimensions (Verma, 2025). This section discusses applications of AI in maritime security considering its implications for global trade amidst shifting geopolitical dynamics.

3.3 Autonomous Maritime Systems

AI has significantly transformed maritime platform design and operations with the deployment of Autonomous Surface Vessels (ASVs) and Autonomous Underwater Vehicles (AUVs) (Veitch & Alsos, 2021). These platforms are equipped with machine learning and decision-making algorithms, and are able to independently carry out operations such as surveillance, mine detection, anti-submarine warfare, without risking human lives. This autonomy has allowed law enforcement organizations such as coast guards to project presence over larger areas with lower personnel and operational costs (Veitch, 2021). From a commercial viewpoint, the introduction of autonomous cargo vessels has optimized navigation, AI-enabled systems can select ideal trade routes based on real-time data such as weather, port congestion, and geopolitical risk assessment, thereby reducing delivery times and fuel consumption. This as a result increases the reliability and cost-efficiency of global supply chains. Yara Birkeland, is a notable example of an autonomous cargo ship. It was built by Kongsberg Maritime in Norway and operates without crew and is powered by a large battery charged by hydroelectric power (Rødseth et al., 2023).

3.4 Maritime Domain Awareness and Threat Detection

Maritime Domain Awareness (MDA) is defined by the IMO as an effective understanding of all activities within the maritime domain that could impact security, safety, the economy or the environment. This includes activities such as collecting, analyzing, and sharing information about maritime operations to ensure a comprehensive understanding of the area of interest at sea (IMO, 2025). The AI-powered systems are being increasingly used to efficiently identify and synthesize vessels data with satellite imagery, Automatic Identification System (AIS) and underwater acoustic signals. Machine learning algorithms can help analyze the data collected from multiple sources to predict potential threats, establish patterns unauthorized activities to enable prompt intervention (Gamage et al., 2023). In high-risk zones, such as the South China Sea these capabilities are essential for monitoring territorial claims, piracy threats and maritime intrusions.

3.5 Predictive Analytics for Port and Supply Chain Optimization

AI systems improves operational efficiency and security at ports by the use of predictive analytics. A forecast of port congestion and optimized berthing allocation for the vessels can be provided by AI processing vast streams of available datasets such as cargo arrival times, customs data and anticipated geopolitical developments. In times of crisis, such as cyber-attack, geopolitical conflicts or non-traditional threats such as from a pandemic, predictive analytics can identify and help prepare contingencies for uninterrupted flow of global trade (Aljohani, 2023).

In Port of Rotterdam, categorized as one of the world's most technologically advanced maritime hub, a "digital twin" of the port has been established by IBM and Cisco using AI and Internet of Things (IoT) sensors. This has optimized the prediction of vessel arrival times, modeling of cargo loading and unloading, and scheduling port maintenance without disrupting trade logistics (Klar & Angelakis, 2023). By using AI and machine learning models trained on historical shipping and traffic data, the Rotterdam port has significantly improved berth allocation, resource deployment, and improve turnaround time. In Singapore, the Maritime and Port Authority (MPA) has developed a Next Generation Vessel Traffic Management System (NGVTMS) that uses to AI to assess port traffic patterns, manage navigational risks and pre-empt safety hazards (Xiao et al., 2022). It is also pilot testing AI-driven berth planning systems that would use real-time data to optimize ship navigation and allot docking stations to vessels. Furthermore, leading shipping conglomerates like Maersk and Hapag-Lloyd are incorporating AI into their supply chain networks to use predictive analytics, model trade and anticipate geopolitical risks and trade disruptions (Rudnik et al., 2025). In an event of crisis, the data can help the shipping companies to reroute their cargoes and avoid excessive costs as a result of delays. These developments are not limited to advanced markets. In developing regions, such as East Africa and Southeast Asia, port authorities are setting up AI systems for custom clearance, infrastructure planning and cargo handling optimization (Alavi-Borazjani et al., 2025).

3.6 Cybersecurity and Information Warfare

Maritime sector becomes more susceptible to cyber attacks and electronic spoofing as they become more integrated with digital and information technology (Kechagias et al,. 2022). The smart use of AI applications can help support the creation of robust digital infrastructure for ships, ports and underwater cables. Furthermore, AI algorithms can play important role in detection cyber intrusions and anomaly in the network data. It is essential since securing maritime information systems is essential not only for maritime security but also for the safety of global communication infrastructure such as undersea cables (Ben, 2022).

A notable example is the Rolls-Royce's intelligent ship platform (Baumler, 2024). It integrates AI for onboard cyber security threat detection in autonomous ship systems, monitoring ship's affiliated networks in real time and using machine learning models to identify unusual access patterns or system-level behaviors that can indicate of a cyber-breach. Another key initiative is the European Maritime Safety Agency's (EMSA) work on maritime cyber security, where AI-powered monitoring and analysis tools are being tested for detecting intrusion attempts on port systems and vessel communications (Melnyk et al,. 2025). In the commercial application, shipping companies such as DNV (Det Norske Veritas) are incorporating AI-based security auditing tools into their maritime digital assurance services (Ødegård, 2025). These tools offer automatic detection of any misconfigurations or vulnerabilities in on-board maritime control systems, such as the Electronic Chart Display and Information Systems (ECDIS) before attackers can exploit them.

AI is also being explored for protection of undersea cable infrastructure, which supports over 95% of global data traffic and is considered a critical component of global communications. Organizations such as NATO's Centre for Maritime Research and Experimentation (CMRE) have conducted research on AI-enabled systems to monitor and protect underwater communication lines (Pohontu & Ermolai, 2024). These systems are employing AI to assess data from sonar, autonomous underwater vehicles (AUVs), and networks of ocean sensors to detect any unusual underwater activity that indicates signal tampering or potential sabotage. A real-world example that signifies the urgency of AI in maritime cyber security is the Maersk cyber-attack in 2017. The NotPetya malware attacked the shipping giant's mainframe IT systems that connected it with over 600 ports and terminals worldwide (Buchanan, 2022).

In geopolitical hotspots like the South China Sea and the Red Sea, there is increased reporting of GPS spoofing and AIS manipulation (Androjna et al., 2023. These tactics are used to obscure a vessel's location and identity, and are often associated with activities like illicit oil transfers, sanction evasion, and illegal fishing. Another common activity is known as "ghost shipping", where vessels suddenly "disappear" from public maritime tracking systems by disabling or falsifying AIS signals (Androjna & Perkovič, 2021). In some cases, ships reappear thousands of kilometers away, suggesting they were spoofing their location or operating in AIS dark zones. These tactics are frequently used by vessels engaged in sanctions evasion, particularly with Iranian, North Korean, Russian, or Venezuelan oil exports (Bai et al., 2025).

3.7 *Geopolitical Risk Assessment and Strategic Forecasting*

AI's capacity to process and correlate unstructured datasets from satellite images to diplomatic statements and social media allows strategic forecasting and potential geopolitical scenario building in important maritime flashpoint (Pasupuleti, 2025). These have utility in the insurance sector for risk models, rerouting of vessels to less hostile waters for ship captain and crew, and defense planning for a variety of public and private security companies. In the context of great power competition, AI is increasingly being used to assess the posturing of rival naval forces and infrastructure investments in ports facilities such as the China's Belt and Road Initiative (Hlongwa, 2021). These AI based assessments in this case also influence national security strategies and maritime cooperation frameworks.

4 Regional Case Studies in AI-Enabled Maritime Security

The application of AI in maritime security is contextually shaped by the strategic character, trade dependency, and technological maturity of specific regions. This section explores three important maritime regions, the South China Sea, the Red Sea, and the Arctic Mediterranean Sea. These are important regions where the integration of AI into the security architecture addresses traditional maritime threats and also reshapes geopolitical calculations and trade flows to other parts of the globe (Tsailas, 2025). These case studies emphasize the varying degrees of AI adoption, from autonomous surveillance to strategic forecasting and predictive analytics, and their wider ramifications for maritime governance.

In the South China Sea, AI technologies are increasingly being operationalized to manage conventional and grey zone security challenges (Garcia, 2024). As one of the most contested maritime spaces in the world, critical for natural resources and as a transit route for more than $3 trillion worth of annual trade, the region has become a theater of maritime AI deployment (Oztuna, 2024). The militarization and digitalization of artificial islands, embedded with state-of-art AI-enhanced surveillance systems capable of real-time tracking vessels, establishing pattern-of-life analysis, and multi-sensor data fusion, is reportedly being undertaken by China (Gnatik, 2024). In addition to acting as forward observation outposts, these "digital islands" also collect data for machine learning models that forecast anomalies in the maritime setting, such as evasive action by rival intelligence or military vessels (Gamage, 2023).

On the other hand, states in the region such as Vietnam and the Philippines are often constrained by limited technological infrastructure. They have begun to take advantage of commercial satellite analysis and cloud-based AI platforms to improve Maritime Domain Awareness (MDA) (Iqbal et al., 2025). The US Indo-Pacific Command (INDOPACOM) has also integrated AI into its decision-support systems to monitor China's maritime movements and maintain freedom of navigation operations (Wingfield et al., 2023). These advances collectively depict the dual use nature of AI in a region where the line between competition and conflict may increasingly be decided by algorithms and AI systems. However, it is pertinent to highlight that the proliferation of unchecked AI applications in the defense domain would increase the risk of inadvertent escalation due to autonomous decision-making or misinterpreted signaling, requiring the need for AI-specific multilateral confidence building measures.

The Red Sea presents a distinct context, where AI-powered maritime security systems are increasingly employed to address asymmetric threats, consisting of piracy, terrorism at sea, and geopolitical instability, as an extension of ongoing conflicts in Yemen and Horn of Africa (Kotait, 2025). The strait of Bab el-Mandeb is extremely significant, responsible for facilitating the flow of 10% of the world's seaborne oil trade (Panagopoulou, 2024). AI systems have been used by state and security organizations operating in the private sector. These include development of piracy risk models that AI using to assess historical data, sociopolitical indicators and weather patterns for international shipping and marine insurers to adjust the routes and implement targeted security measures. In the Red Sea, the naval forces operating under the Combined Maritime Forces (CMF) have incorporated AI-enhanced radar and sonar systems vessel classification and threat prioritization, allowing for optimum resource allocation and decision-making (Keshk, 2022). In addition, acoustic analysis also use AI tools to detect anomalies or deviations in underwater signals that can help identify hostile activities from unmanned underwater vehicles and unauthorized submarine cables tapping. However, the adoption of AI in the maritime domain remains uneven in the littoral states of the Red Sea, constrained by weak infrastructural base, inadequate regulatory frameworks and shortage of skilled human capital. This technological gap hampers the integration of AI-driven solutions for maritime surveillance, port operations and security. As a result this disparity creates exploitable vulnerabilities in the regional security architecture, particularly in areas such as counter-piracy, illicit trafficking and MDA. Addressing these gaps requires coordinated multilateral capacity-building initiatives, harmonized legal standards and interoperable data-sharing protocols, ideally under the auspices of the International Maritime Organization (IMO), the African Union's Integrated Maritime Strategy (AIMS 2050), and relevant regional security arrangements (Gesami, 2021).

In the Arctic Mediterranean Sea, the melting polar ice is opening new trade routes such as the Northern Sea Route (NSR) (Bayirhan & Gazioglu, 2021). AI is at the heart of safe navigation safety and strategic foresight. The Arctic's harsh climate requires predictive climate modeling, ice mapping, and real-time navigation support to ensure shipping safety and avoid delays in operations. Russia, a prominent regional player, has incorporated AI into its Arctic naval logistics and surveillance platforms, including unmanned aerial systems (UAS) that offer persistent coverage across vast, remote areas (Garcia-Bragiel, 2023). Western nations, including NATO members, have also responded by investments in AI for early warning and environmental monitoring capabilities to gauge risks associated with instability of the ice cover, oil spills, and incursions by foreign and hostile navies (Chromyszak et al., 2022). The intersection of commercial and strategic interests, most notably the prospects for circumnavigating traditional chokepoints like the Suez Canal has rendered AI as a central tool for geopolitical positioning (Alza, 2024). However, the legal and governance framework that would oversee AI use in the Arctic is still underdeveloped, especially in terms of environmental responsibility, indigenous rights, and crisis mitigation. This regulatory vacuum risks is not merely a regional concern, melting ice would expand the Arctic Mediterranean's role as a strategic maritime corridor linking the Northern

Sea Route to the North Atlantic and beyond, governance gaps will carry wider geopolitical and environmental implications. In this context, early practices in AI deployment in the Arctic Mediterranean are likely to set precedents for how other emerging maritime and polar regions are governed globally (Lin & Allhoff, 2019).

Taken together, these case studies demonstrate that AI is not merely a set of technological tools but a strategic enabler whose deployment reflects and reinforces regional power dynamics. Whether in contested waters, conflict-prone trade corridors, or emerging polar frontiers, the integration of AI into maritime security architectures offers enhanced resilience, strategic foresight, and operational superiority. However, without robust regulatory governance and interoperable ethical standards, the unchecked militarization and fragmentation of AI applications could generate new risks to maritime stability (Islam, 2024a). These regional developments call for a global compact on maritime AI ethics and governance that aligns innovation with shared security and sustainable development objectives.

5 Risks and Vulnerabilities in AI Maritime Integration

The integration of AI in maritime security brings significant strategic and operational benefits, however it also raises a number of risks and vulnerabilities relating to technical, ethical, legal, and geopolitical aspects (Tsailas, 2025). The stakes for ensuring robustness, transparency and accountability become correspondingly higher as maritime systems rely increasingly on algorithmic decision-making, autonomous operations, and data-driven situational awareness. With an emphasis on data integrity, cyber threats and autonomous system vulnerabilities in hostile environments, this part examines challenges related to the deployment of AI in maritime setting.

Firstly, a major risk in AI-enabled maritime systems results from data dependence and integrity. AI systems for training and real-time operations rely on enormous quantities of data sets, ranging from satellite visuals and AIS signals to sonar feedback and atmospheric conditions (Durlik et al., 2025). These data flows are often noisy, heterogeneous and prone to manipulation. In a maritime environment, they are particularly susceptible to electronic spoofing, where erroneous signals can mislead AI systems into misidentifying vessel behavior and surroundings (Walter et al., 2025). Any adversarial intrusions or attacks on machine learning models, such as manipulating sensor input or exploiting model biases, can produce incorrect classifications leading to unsuitable decision outcomes. In high-stakes situations, such as routing of autonomous vessel or a naval threat assessment, such manipulations can result in misjudgment and latency in decision-making may escalate geopolitical tensions (Tsailas, 2025).

Secondly, cyber security represents a significant challenge to AI's integration in the maritime domain. The growing digitalization of ships, ports, and underwater infrastructure, including critical submarine communication cables has expanded the range and scope of cyber-attacks. AI-enabled maritime systems while enhancing existing capabilities and working, may inadvertently amplify existing software vulnerabilities in legacy systems used in hybrid fleets or by ports with inconsistent digital standards (Ibitoye, 2025). The use of open-source AI while being cost-friendly can create added complexities as they generally lack strong security protocols and maybe be more susceptible to data corruption. In a real-world setting, a coordinated cyber-attack aimed at maritime systems such as port logistics, navigational control and autonomous vessel communication can have a cascading effect on global trade and geopolitics (Cho et al., 2022) A risk assessment report prepared by Lloyd's in collaboration with the University of Cambridge's Cyber Risk Management (CyRiM) anticipates that in an extreme scenario where a malware attack simultaneously disrupts operations at 15 major ports in the Asia–Pacific, the losses incurred by the global economy could reach a staggering US $110 billion ((Lloyd's of London, Cambridge Centre for Risk Studies, & Nanyang Technological University, 2019). This figure came up after studying previous cyber-attacks, including the 2017 NotPetya ransom ware attack on the Danish shipping conglomerate, Maersk, when it was forced to shut down operations across its 76 port terminals worldwide, causing estimated losses of between US $250 million and US $300 million. These incidents also illustrate the scale and the nature of vulnerabilities in maritime cyber infrastructure, and highlight the need for setting robust safety and security standards for integrating AI in the maritime domain (Minnaar, 2019).

Thirdly, the way AI systems interpret data and propose course of action raises serious concerns of operational reliability for autonomous decision-making (Rudin, 2019). In maritime applications, AI systems are required to function in dynamic, uncertain, and often hostile environments, to come up with optimum solution amidst limited and ambiguous data sources. However, the opacity of machine learning models, referred to as the "black box" problem complicates the decision-making and the process of accountability (Shneiderman, 2020). The lack of explainability undermines human-AI trust in mission critical decisions and raises legal and moral questions regarding responsibility in the event of failure or unanticipated escalation. For instance, in an incident involving a misclassified vessel in a high-tension zone like the South China Sea, the absence of a robust procedure for accountability could complicate diplomatic responses and legal standing.

Fourthly, the integration of AI into a multi-stakeholder maritime environment comprising civil, commercial and military actors creates legitimate concerns regarding interoperability and governance. As a result, AI systems developed by a particular nation or private actor may not adhere to a common communication protocols or ethical standards, increasing the possibility of misunderstanding and inconsistent risk responses (Mallick, 2024). Furthermore, the absence of international regulations or confidence-building mechanisms specific to AI in the maritime domain, leaves a regulatory vacuum that hostile actors could take advantage of.

Lastly, vulnerabilities arise from the "weaponization of AI" and "AI-driven arms competition" in maritime setting (Lamont, 2024). In strategically important regions, like the South China Sea, great power states race to deploy AI-powered surveillance, autonomous systems, and electronic warfare tools. The deployment of fully autonomous weapon systems in contested maritime spaces, without clear norms for their use or defined red lines for engagement, would destabilize trade and commercial networks. It is also important to understand that excessive reliance on AI for defense platforms like early-warning or security assessments without human oversight raises the possibility of automated and uncontrolled miscalculation in crisis situation. (Agarwala, 2022).

5.1 Governing Maritime AI: Normative and Legal Perspectives

As AI systems become more and more integrated into maritime operations, the governance of AI poses challenges from both legal and normative perspectives. AI systems function optimally with greater autonomy, creating a complexity that is far beyond the current regulatory framework in place (Islam, 2024b). The application of AI to commercial, military, and civil infrastructures necessitates a reexamination of the ethical frameworks, regulatory tools, and international legal principles that regulate maritime operations. The scope of AI governance in the maritime domain is examined in this part, with an emphasis on the gaps and innovative frameworks that can complement existing international law.

5.1.1 Fragmentation and Gaps in Existing Legal Frameworks

From a legal perspective, presently the governance of AI in maritime faces significant challenge as a result of fragmentation of existing international instruments, such as the UNCLOS do not explicitly addresses AI technologies. While UNCLOS provides a legal basis for the rights and obligations of states relating to navigation, environmental protection, and maritime zones, its applicability to AI-driven systems is unclear. For example, UNCLOS Articles 94 and 98 lists flag state jurisdiction and responsibilities related to the safety of ships and assistance in times of distress at sea, but they do not specify the accountability procedures that maybe applicable to autonomous vessels or AI-powered ships in similar circumstances (Winstead, 2018).

The lack of clear definitions for autonomous ships, machine decision-making system, or AI-assisted enforcement at sea within existing maritime instruments creates legal ambiguity regarding important real-world applications such as the attribution of liability in case of vessel collisions, environmental damage, or in incidents where there has been use of force and exchange of fire (Sreedharan et al., 2025). For example, there are currently no legal provisions to decide whether it is the state, the developer of the vessel, or the algorithm's operating parameters that are responsible for provocative maneuvers made by an autonomous unmanned surface vehicle (USV) used for surveillance or any other purposes in a disputed maritime zone (Billingsley et al., 2022). Such legal ambiguities can become further complicated when the AI system is used for dual-use, having an application for civil and military purposes arousing concerns under International Humanitarian Law (IHL) as well as Law of Naval Warfare.

5.1.2 AI and the Principle of Due Regard

One of the fundamental legal tenets of UNCLOS is the obligation of a state to exercise the principle of "due regard" for the rights and interests of other states when conducting maritime operations (Gaunce, 2017). The automation of decisions significantly challenge this principle, as the AI system generally have inherent limitations interpreting and comprehending diplomatic messages, signaling or de-risking practices such as "escalating to de-escalate," often used by states (Lin, 2018).

In the maritime domain there are established practices often involving subtle naval exercises, communication protocols and predictable operational patterns that express intentions without increasing tensions. In the South China Sea, US-led freedom of navigation operations and the Chinese vessels deployed in the area often employ carefully calibrated radio exchanges and calculated monitoring of ship movements to signal resolve while avoiding direct provocation (Mueller, 2021). Similarly, in the Red Sea, regional maritime forces have used pre-announced patrolling during the Houthi missile threats to prevent any misinterpretation of intent (Gupta & Ganguly, 2025). In the Arctic Mediterranean, Norwegian and Russian naval forces follow protocols such as the *Incidents at Sea Agreement*, which aims to prevent dangerous military interactions (Gosnell & Saunes, 2024). The agreement updated in 2021, incorporates provisions relating to emerging maritime technologies such as remotely operated vehicles (ROVs). These examples illustrate the importance of human decisions and judgment as central to the principles of "due regard" that AI systems may find it difficult to consider under real-time situations and when processing multiple data inputs that maybe ambiguous and contradictory to one another. Therefore, there is a strong need for human oversight requirements in sensitive maritime operating contexts (Albrecht et al., 2025).

5.1.3 Normative Debates on Maritime AI Ethics and Accountability

As AI technologies become increasingly integrated in maritime applications from autonomous shipping and port logistics to decision-support systems and predictive analytics ethical aspects are considered key to regulation and effective governance. In this discussion, important normative concerns such as accountability, explainability, transparency and human oversight, are essential to maintain control over AI systems and preventing them from functioning as opaque "black boxes" (Chaudhary, 2024). These are especially critical in sensitive and high-risk environments like the South China Sea and the Arctic Mediterranean, where any misunderstandings resulted from AI-generated outputs could possibly contribute to escalation or even hostilities. In the global discourse for AI governance, the international community has come up with policy debates, such as the Organization for Economic Cooperation and Development (OECD) Principles on AI, the European Union's AI Act, and United Nations Education, Scientific and Cultural Organization (UNESCO's) Recommendation on the Ethics of AI. These provide standards that can be modified for maritime operations and activities requiring AI (Mahajan, 2025).

For example, the principle of traceability discussed in global AI discourse mandating the documentation of AI systems decision-making processes could be particularly relevant for incident attribution and legal compliance in shipping accidents. In addition, emerging scholarships and policy proposals have advocated for the development of a Maritime AI Code of Conduct, which would establish the best practices and ethical obligations for state and non-state entities at sea. Such a code could include provisions for the mechanism for algorithmic evaluations, protocols for human intervention, and operational limits of automated maritime systems (Katsivela, 2023). A convergence on some of these standards would build trust, interoperability and predictability that would benefit port security collaborations and maritime operations in a multilateral setting.

5.1.4 Institutional Pathways and Governance Innovations

AI governance in maritime environment also requires institutional learning and innovation. The International Maritime Organization (IMO) has taken initial steps in this direction, notably through its Regulatory Scoping Exercise on Maritime Autonomous Surface Ships (MASS) (Hasan, 2025). This initiative considered how the current IMO policy instruments can apply to various levels of ship autonomy, ranging from minimally automated systems to fully autonomous vessels. However, these effort needs to be expanded to include AI systems used in port infrastructure, maritime surveillance, as well as cyber-defense (Fenton et al., 2023).

Moreover, institutions such as the International Maritime Law Institute (IMLI), International Telecommunication Union (ITU), and International Tribunal for the Law of the Sea (ITLOS) could also play enabling roles in elaborating how legal norms specific to AI-enhanced maritime activity can be formulated (Nabil, 2024). Multilateral forums such as the G20, ASEAN, and the Arctic Council can provide platforms for regional dialogue and trust-building essential for AI governance in the maritime domain, particularly in zones of contested sovereignty or overlapping with national sovereignty like, the Exclusive Economic Zones (EEZs) (Sousa, 2014).

5.1.5 Toward a Coherent Maritime AI Governance Framework

A governance framework for maritime AI needs to be multilayered and inclusive. It must blend binding legal instruments with flexible normative codes, allowing for technological dynamism while safeguarding public goods such as peace, environmental stewardship, and freedom of navigation. This entails:

- Updating UNCLOS with interpretive guidance or new protocols addressing AI integration;
- Mandating algorithmic accountability mechanisms in maritime insurance and classification societies;
- Institutionalizing AI audit regimes within IMO and IMLI procedures;
- Promoting interoperability standards for AI systems used in joint maritime operations; and
- Ensuring meaningful inclusion of developing coastal states in AI standard-setting processes.

In sum, the governance of maritime AI stands at a critical juncture. As states and private actors rapidly deploy intelligent systems at sea, the absence of cohesive legal and normative frameworks risks undermining the very stability, transparency, and trust that maritime order depends on. Embedding AI governance into international maritime law is not only a regulatory necessity but a strategic imperative for navigating the evolving digital seascape of twenty-first century geopolitics.

6 Conclusion

The maritime domain, is the largest frontier of the Earth and covers over seventy percent of the planet's surface. It enters a new era of technological transformation with the integration of AI. As this chapter has illustrated, AI acts as a force multiplier in increasing maritime domain awareness by automating threat identification, optimizing logistics, and reshaping how states view the oceans. Its impact is particularly significant in critical chokepoints and contested maritime regions such as the South China Sea, the Red Sea, and the Arctic–Mediterranean Sea, regions that are becoming focal points of geopolitical rivalry and yet whose safety and security remains vital to global commons.

The oceans regarded as the "common heritage of mankind" are central to great power competition; AI accelerates this trend by enabling faster, more precise, and increasingly remote and automated operations. From submarine cables that carry more than 95% of global internet traffic to emerging concepts such as underwater data centers, the oceans contributions as a critical infrastructure hub is significant, without which AI systems would be severely limited in their power, reach and operationalization. As digital connectivity and economic lifelines depend increasingly on undersea infrastructure, the future will be profoundly maritime, and AI will only deepen the strategic, economic, and security significance of the world's oceans. Managing these risks demands a paradigm shift in governance and adapting legal regimes such as UNCLOS to technological advancements in digital infrastructure at sea and maritime autonomous systems. New international protocols, transparent and interoperable technical standards, and robust cyber security norms would be needed to ensure predictable behavior and prevent miscalculation. This will also require interdisciplinary and research collaboration between international law, AI ethics, maritime security, ocean governance, and strategic studies.

The future of maritime security will likely hinge on how the international community navigates the double-edged nature of AI at sea, its ability to enhance global stability while simultaneously introducing new vectors of competition and coercion. Protecting the hybrid physical–digital arteries of the maritime domain will be as central to twenty-first century strategic stability as safeguarding shipping lanes was in the last. By balancing innovation with responsibility, autonomy with accountability, and connectivity with resilience, states can ensure that AI serves as a stabilizing force in the maritime commons, securing not only the flow of goods and data, but also the cooperative governance of the world's oceans in an era of accelerating geopolitical competition.

References

Agarwala, N. (2022). Role of policy framework for disruptive technologies in the maritime domain. *Australian Journal of Maritime & Ocean Affairs, 14*(1), 1–20.

Alamoush, A. S., & Ölçer, A. I. (2025). Maritime autonomous surface ships: Architecture for autonomous navigation systems. *Journal of Marine Science and Engineering, 13*(1).

Alavi-Borazjani, S. A., Bengue, A. A., Chkoniya, V., & Shafique, M. N. (2025). An overview of critical success factors for digital shipping corridors: A roadmap for maritime logistics modernization. *Sustainability, 17*(12), 5537.

Albrecht, L., Braun, H., Kosack, T. R., & Krüger, T. (2025). The limits of meaningful human control of AI in the maritime domain. *Transactions on Maritime Science, 14*(3).

Aljohani, A. (2023). Predictive analytics and machine learning for real-time supply chain risk mitigation and agility. *Sustainability, 15*(20), 15088.

Alza, J. (2024). Artificial intelligence as a decision-making tool for sustainable Arctic development. *MNAI.* https://mnai.org/wp-content/uploads/2024/10/J.Alza-final.pdf

Androjna, A., Pavić, I., Gucma, L., Vidmar, P., & Perkovič, M. (2023). AIS data manipulation in the illicit global oil trade. *Journal of Marine Science and Engineering, 12*(1), 6.

Androjna, A., & Perkovič, M. (2021). Impact of spoofing of navigation systems on maritime situational awareness. *Transactions on Maritime Science, 10*(2), 361–373.

Bai, X., Fernández-Villaverde, J., Li, Y., Xu, L., & Zanetti, F. (2025). *The (un) intended consequences of oil sanctions through the dark shipping of sanctioned oil* (No. w33486). National Bureau of Economic Research.

Baumler, R. (2024). Thinking MASS in system. In *Maritime Autonomous Surface Ships (Mass)-regulation, Technology, and Policy: Three Dimensions of Effective Implementation* (pp. 181–208). Springer Nature Switzerland.

Bayırhan, İ., & Gazioğlu, C. (2021). New maritime trade routes in the Arctic region: One of the strongest alternatives to the Suez Canal. *International Journal of Environment and Geoinformatics, 8*(3), 397–401.

Ben Farah, M. A., Ukwandu, E., Hindy, H., Brosset, D., Bures, M., Andonovic, I., & Bellekens, X. (2022). Cyber security in the maritime industry: A systematic survey of recent advances and future trends. *Information*, *13*(1), 22.

Billingsley, J. L., Kerg, U. S. N., Heidi, K., Chen, J. Q., Navicky, M., Tkach, B., Work, B., & S, S. (2022). *Cyber-attacks to industrial control systems since Stuxnet: A systematic review*. Capitol Technology University.

Bueger, C., & Liebetrau, T. (2021). Protecting hidden infrastructure: The security politics of the global submarine data cable network. *Contemporary Security Policy*, *42*(3), 391–413.

Cannon, B. J. (2025). Undersea cable security in the Indo-Pacific: Enhancing the Quad's collaborative approach. *Marine Policy*, *171*, 106415.

Carlo, A., & Obergfaell, K. (2024). Cyber attacks on critical infrastructures and satellite communications. *International Journal of Critical Infrastructure Protection*, *46*, 100701.

Chaudhary, G. (2024). Unveiling the black box: Bringing algorithmic transparency to AI. *Masaryk University Journal of Law and Technology*, *18*(1), 93–122.

Cho, S., Orye, E., Visky, G., & Prates, V. (2022). *Cybersecurity considerations in autonomous ships*. NATO Cooperative Cyber Defence Centre of Excellence.

Chromyszak, C., Jacobson, S., Khosraw, E., Lavey, S., Lewis, M., Mabe, S., Olsen, A., et al. (2022). *Navigating new threats: NATO's posture on emerging technologies*.

Clemente, D., Calheiros-Cabral, T., Rosa-Santos, P., & Taveira-Pinto, F. (2023). Blue seaports: The smart, sustainable and electrified ports of the future. *Smart Cities*, *6*(3).

Durlik, I., Miller, T., Kostecka, E., Kozlovska, P., & Ślączka, W. (2025). Enhancing safety in autonomous maritime transportation systems with real-time AI agents. *Applied Sciences*, *15*(9), 4986.

Fenton, A. J., & Chapsos, I. (2023). Ships without crews: IMO and UK responses to cybersecurity, technology, law and regulation of maritime autonomous surface ships (MASS). *Frontiers in Computer Science*, *5*, 1151188.

Gamage, C., Dinalankara, R., Samarabandu, J., & Subasinghe, A. (2023). A comprehensive survey on the applications of machine learning techniques on maritime surveillance to detect abnormal maritime vessel behaviors. *World Maritime University Journal of Maritime Affairs*, *22*(4), 447–477.

Ganz, A., Camellini, M., Hine, E., Novelli, C., Roberts, H., & Floridi, L. (2024). Submarine cables and the risks to digital sovereignty. *Minds and Machines*, *34*(3), 31.

Garcia, E. V. (2024). The technological leap of AI and the Global South: Deepening asymmetries and the future of international security. In *Research handbook on warfare and artificial intelligence* (pp. 370–387). Edward Elgar Publishing.

Garcia-Bragiel, M. R. (2023). Unattended seas: Navy artificial intelligence and emerging technology in the Arctic. *United States Naval War College*.

Gaunce, J. (2017). On the Interpretation of the general duty of' due regard'. *Ocean Yearbook*, *32*.

Gesami, B. (2021). Maritime security in Africa: The African Union's challenge in implementing the 2050 AIM strategy. *SSRN*.

Gnatik, E. N. (2024). Militarization of artificial intelligence systems: Opportunities and threats. *RUDN Journal of Philosophy*, *28*(3), 771–784.

Gosnell, R., & Saunes, L. (2024). *Report No. 2: Integrated Naval Deterrence in the Arctic Region—Strategic Options for Enhancing Regional Naval Cooperation*.

Guilfoyle, D., Paige, T. P., & McLaughlin, R. (2022). The final frontier of cyberspace: The seabed beyond national jurisdiction and the protection of submarine cables. *International & Comparative Law Quarterly*, *71*(3), 657–696.

Gupta, T., & Ganguly, A. N. (2025). Choke point of power: The Red Sea crisis and extension of geopolitical rivalries. *International Journal of Social Science Research*, *2*(2), 61–75.

Hasan, S. (2025). An insight on the role and response of International Maritime Organization and classification societies in regulating maritime autonomous surface ships. *International Journal of Maritime History*, *37*(2), 350–371.

Hlongwa, L. N. (2021). Artificial intelligence and big data in the Maritime Silk Road Initiative: The road towards Sea Power 2.0. *Scientia Militaria: South African Journal of Military Studies, 49*(2), 113–131.

Ibitoye, J. S. (2025). Modeling threat vectors in real time using AI-enhanced surveillance analytics across cyber, land, air, and maritime domains. *International Journal of Advance Research Publication and Reviews.*

International Maritime Organization. (2025). *Amendments to the International Aeronautical and Maritime Search and Rescue (IAMSAR) Manual.* (MSC 1.Circ.1367).

Ionita, C. V., & Kanetake, M. (2023). International human rights law in the digital age: Perspectives from the UN human rights system. In *Research Handbook On Law And Technology* (pp. 235–253). Edward Elgar Publishing.

Iqbal, A. B., Tariq, F., Sumra, I. A., & Rasheed, K. (2025). The digital evolution of the maritime industry: Unleashing the power of IoT and cloud computing. *Journal of Computing & Biomedical Informatics, 9*(1).

Islam, M. S. (2024a). Maritime security in a technological era: Addressing challenges in balancing technology and ethics. *Mersin University Journal of Maritime Faculty, 6*(1), 1–16.

Islam, M. S. (2024b). Navigating modern era at sea: Legal challenges and opportunities of unmanned and autonomous shipping. *AI and Ethics*, 1–14.

Johnson, J. (2019). Artificial intelligence & future warfare: Implications for international security. *Defense & Security Analysis, 35*(2), 147–169.

Kaplan, R. D. (2011). *Monsoon: The Indian Ocean and the Future of American Power.* Random House Trade Paperbacks.

Katsivela, M. (2023). Legal, ethical and industry issues and developments regarding maritime autonomous surface ships. *Ocean Yearbook Online, 37*(1), 506–541.

Kechagias, E. P., Chatzistelios, G., Papadopoulos, G. A., & Apostolou, P. (2022). Digital transformation of the maritime industry: A cybersecurity systemic approach. *International Journal of Critical Infrastructure Protection, 37*, 100526.

Keshk, A. M. (2022). Obstacles to achieving maritime security for the Arabian Gulf countries. In *Maritime Security Of The Arab Gulf States: Analysis Of Current Threats, Confrontation Mechanisms, And Future Challenges* (pp. 117–143). Springer Nature Singapore.

Klar, R., Fredriksson, A., & Angelakis, V. (2023, March). Assessing the maturity of digital twinning solutions for ports. In *2023 IEEE International conference on pervasive computing and communications workshops and other affiliated events (PerCom Workshops)* (pp. 552–557). IEEE.

Kotait, A. M., & Ismail, A. (2025). Geopolitical threats in the Red Sea: The future of the Suez Canal amid regional and international challenges. المجلة العلمية للدراسات التجارية 1169–1136, (2)*16*, والبيئية.

Lamont, C. (2024). military automation, robotics, and maritime security: understanding new dynamics in conflict escalation. In *Navigating East Asian Maritime Conflicts: Technological Change, Environmental Challenges, Global and Regional Responses* (pp. 103–123). Springer Nature Switzerland.

Lin, H. (2018). Escalation risks in an AI-infused world. *AI, China, Russia, and the Global Order: Technological, Political, Global, and Creative*, 133.

Lin, P., & Allhoff, F. (2019). Arctic 2.0: How artificial intelligence can help develop a frontier. *Ethics & International Affairs, 33*(2), 193–205.

Lloyd's of London, Cambridge Centre for Risk Studies, & Nanyang Technological University. (2019). *Shen attack: Cyber risk in Asia Pacific ports.*

Mahajan, P. (2025). What is ethical: AIHED driving humans or human-driven AIHED? A conceptual framework enabling the ethos of AI-driven higher education. arXiv preprint, arXiv:2503.04751.

Mahan, A. T. (1890). *The influence of sea power on history.* Project Gutenberg.

Mallick, P. K. (2024). Artificial intelligence, national security and the future of warfare. In *Artificial intelligence, ethics and the future of warfare* (pp. 30–70). Routledge India.

McGeachy, H. (2022). The changing strategic significance of submarine cables: Old technology, new concerns. *Australian Journal of International Affairs*, *76*(2), 161–177.
Mehmood, Z. H. (2025). The role of emerging maritime technologies in redefining geopolitical frontiers in the Indo-Pacific. *Geopolitica*, *14*(1).
Melnyk, O., Drozdov, O., & Kuznichenko, S. (2025). Cybersecurity in maritime transport: An international perspective on regulatory frameworks and countermeasures. *Lex Portus*, *11*, 7.
Miętkiewicz, R. (2025). Hybrid threats in the Baltic Sea. The results of analysis of countermeasure options. *Terroryzm. Studia, Analizy, Prewencja*, (Special Issue), 35–70.
Minnaar, A. (2019). Cybercriminals, cyber-extortion, online blackmailers and the growth of ransomware. *Acta Criminologica: African Journal of Criminology & Victimology*, *32*(2), 105.
Mueller, A. C. (2021). Three warfares with American characteristics: Renewing the South China Sea freedom of navigation program for the information age.
Nabil, D. Q. (2024). For a future-proofed law of the sea: Challenges and opportunities emerging from the rapid development of technology. *AIS: Ars Iuris Salmanticensis*, *12*(2), 11–39.
Ødegård, S. (2025). *The Road to Autonomy: What are the current status of the development project and what are the future prospects*.
Osaloni, O. S., & Ayeni, V. O. (2022). The development of maritime autonomous surface ships: Regulatory challenges and the way forward. *Beijing Law Review*, *13*, 544.
Oztuna, A. (2024). *Assessing the Chinese naval infrastructure changes in the South China Sea using geospatial intelligence*. *John Hopkins University*.
Paik, A. (2025). protecting undersea cables and South Korea's role. *The Washington Quarterly*, *48*(2), 77–91.
Panagopoulou, L. (2024). Navigating troubled waters: Understanding the impact of piracy in the Red Sea on international trade & shipping management strategies amidst the geopolitical tensions (Master's thesis). Πανεπιστήμιο Πειραιώς.
Pasupuleti, M. K. (2025). AI's role in global stability, diplomacy, and peacebuilding. *AI-Powered Diplomacy and Conflict Resolutions*, 1–11.
Pohontu, A., & Ermolai, V. (2024). Artificial intelligence in maritime domain awareness applications: Trends and prospects. In *Digital transformation: Exploring the impact of digital transformation on organizational processes* (pp. 193–204). Springer Nature Switzerland.
Rødseth, Ø. J., Nesheim, D. A., Rialland, A., & Holte, E. A. (2023). The societal impacts of autonomous ships: The Norwegian perspective. In *Autonomous vessels in maritime affairs: Law and governance implications* (pp. 357–376). Springer International Publishing.
Rudin, C. (2019). Stop explaining black box machine learning models for high-stakes decisions and use interpretable models instead. *Nature Machine Intelligence*, *1*(5), 206–215.
Rudnik, R., Kalinin, A., Korovkin, V., & Lazariva, A. (2025). Dots and lines: The changing pattern of global logistics. *Available at SSRN 5328620*.
Schindler, S., Alami, I., DiCarlo, J., Jepson, N., Rolf, S., Bayırbağ, M. K., … Zhao, Y. (2024). The second cold war: US-China competition for centrality in infrastructure, digital, production, and finance networks. *Geopolitics*, *29*(4), 1083–1120.
Shneiderman, B. (2020). Bridging the gap between ethics and practice: Guidelines for reliable, safe, and trustworthy human-centered AI systems. *ACM Transactions on Interactive Intelligent Systems*, *10*(4), 1–31.
Simon, K. (2018). Project Natick-Microsoft's self-sufficient underwater datacenters. *IndraStra Global*, *4*(6), 4.
Sousa, I. (2014). Maritime territorial delimitation and maritime security in the Atlantic. In *Atlantic Future Workshop*. University of Pretoria (Vol. 7).
Sreedharan et al. (2025). Interpreting the law: Challenges in maritime autonomy. SSRN. https://doi.org/10.2139/ssrn.5238468
Sutherland, T., & Bopp, G. (2023). The Pacific futures of subsea data centers. *New Media & Society*, *25*(2), 345–360.
Tsailas, D. N. (2025). Risks and threats in the twenty-first century maritime security. *Security Science Journal*, *6*(1), 106–144.

Veitch, E., & Alsos, O. A. (2021). Human-centered explainable artificial intelligence for marine autonomous surface vehicles. *Journal of Marine Science and Engineering*, *9*(11), 1227.

Verma, T., & Verma, K. (2025). Artificial intelligence, the steering force. *The quest for strategic autonomy: Indigenisation of Indian Defence Industry*.

Walter, M., Harish, A. V., Christison, L., & Tam, K. (2025). Visualisation of cyber vulnerabilities in maritime human–autonomy teaming technology. *World Maritime University Journal of Maritime Affairs*, 1–27.

Wang, Z., & Ye, J. (2023). Power optimization system of underwater data center. In 2023 International Conference on Network, Multimedia and Information Technology (NMITCON) (pp. 1–8). IEEE.

Wingfield, T., Hodgson, Q., Chao, L., Downing, B., Engstrom, J., Grossman, D., Heitzenrater, C., et al. (2023). Creating selective overmatch: An approach to developing cyberspace options to sustain U.S. primacy against revisionist powers.

Winstead, P. J. (2018). *Implementation of unmanned surface vehicles in the distributed maritime operations concept* (Doctoral dissertation). Naval Postgraduate School.

Xiao, Z., Fu, X., Zhao, L., Zhang, L., Teo, T. K., Li, N., & Qin, Z. (2022). Next-generation vessel traffic services systems—From "passive" to "proactive". *IEEE Intelligent Transportation Systems Magazine*, *15*(1), 363–377.

AI and Information: The Global Landscape of AI Ethics and Regulation

Fatima Roumate

1 Introduction

Artificial intelligence (AI) and generative AI are revolutionizing information. The combination of AI with information creates a new power that influences politics, diplomacy, the economy, and warfare. This combination explains the emergence of new types of power that are reshaping geopolitical dynamics. The transformation of information through AI is a key component of the geopolitics of AI and information. This transformation is altering politics, laws, and strategies. The complex intersection between AI and information, along with its influence on global dynamics, justifies the global race toward AI ethics, regulation, and national strategies.

The key questions guiding this chapter are:

- What are the current international mechanisms addressing the ethics of AI-driven information and its implications for geopolitical dynamics?
- What legal approaches are adopted at the international, regional, and national levels as a basis for AI ethics and regulation?
- What are the connecting points between international and regional mechanisms? What differences can we identify between them? What approaches are adopted by great powers and small countries?

To answer these questions, we will first discuss the international mechanisms that could limit the malicious use of AI-driven information and its impact on geopolitics. Second, we will analyze diverse approaches adopted by regional institutions, such as the EU and the African Union. Third, we will study various

F. Roumate (✉)
Global Network on AI and International Society (GNAI&IS), and Mohammed V University, FSJES Agdal, Rabat, Morocco
e-mail: iirs.institute@gmail.com

F. Roumate (ed.), *AI, Information, and Global Dynamics*, Contributions to International Relations,
https://doi.org/10.1007/978-3-032-13528-5_11

national legislations and strategies related to AI-driven information, focusing on best practices from both the global North and South.

2 Method

In this chapter, we will employ various approaches related to the ethical and legal frameworks established by international and regional institutions, along with national regulations concerning AI-driven information. To achieve this, we will use three distinct approaches. The first is a legal and doctrinal approach, which entails reviewing existing laws, regulations, and scholarly literature pertaining to AI-driven information and its associated legal challenges, as well as the global governance of AI based on ethical considerations and the rule of law. The second approach is political, aimed at assessing the significance of national AI strategies and initiatives in governing the implications of AI-driven information on geopolitical dynamics. The third approach is technological, concentrating on the interplay between AI-driven information, geopolitics, and legal frameworks. A comparative analysis will also be employed to highlight connections and variations among the legal approaches adopted by different countries in the global North, specifically the United States, China, and Russia, as well as by certain countries in the global South, particularly in North Africa and West Asia.

3 International AI Ethics Instruments Shaping the Geopolitics of Information Power

AI is revolutionizing information and increasing the proliferation of information power. This proliferation influences several fields, from the economy and politics to warfare and geopolitics. The transformation of information through AI is central to global efforts related to AI governance, which is based on ethics and law. In this context, international instruments focused on AI ethics are emerging as critical tools, acting not merely as guidelines but as frameworks actively shaping the geopolitics of information power. These international instruments are the result of a global response to the challenges posed by the intersection of AI and information, extending beyond geopolitics to all fields and actors in international society.

The first international instrument is the Recommendation on the Ethics of AI adopted by UNESCO in November 2021, by 193 member states. As a member of the Ad Hoc Expert Group nominated by the Director-General of UNESCO to elaborate on this recommendation, I focused on the intersection between AI and information as structured data during this mission. Ethical concerns related to this intersection occupied an important part of the recommendations, from values and principles to policy actions. Specific paragraphs were dedicated to data. The word "information" is cited 14 times, and the word "data" is cited 28 times in the recommendation. Sometimes both concepts were used together, with the preamble highlighting that AI "has the capacity to process data and information in a way that resembles intelligent behavior, and typically includes aspects of reasoning, learning, perception, prediction, planning, or control" (UNESCO, 2021).

This sets the foundation by delineating the fundamental functioning of AI. The intersection between data and information was reaffirmed in paragraph 14, which states that AI systems have the capacity to process data and information in a way that resembles intelligent behavior, incorporating aspects of reasoning, learning, perception, prediction, planning, or control (UNESCO, 2021). This paragraph illustrates the intersections between data and information in AI systems. Under the Principle of Responsibility and Accountability, the text notes that "AI systems . . . rely heavily on processed data and information" (UNESCO, 2021). This emphasizes that the ability to hold AI actors accountable is intrinsically linked to how data and information are handled throughout an AI system's lifecycle.

These examples illustrate UNESCO's holistic perspective, recognizing that AI's ethical ramifications are inextricably linked to its essential dependence on data and the knowledge gleaned from it. The recommendation also acknowledges the intersection between data, information, and knowledge, aligning with the DIKW framework explained in the first chapter of this volume. It states that "the ethical deployment of AI systems depends on their transparency and explainability" (UNESCO, 2021), considering the interconnection between transparency and explainability and how data and information could influence decision-making in different fields.

This ethical principle necessitates the inclusion of multiple stakeholders across various sectors, including education and media, to raise awareness about AI systems and their benefits and risks. The approach adopted by UNESCO in the elaboration of this recommendation is based on four pillars:

1. **Multidisciplinary Approach**: Recognizing that the intersection between information and AI systems opens avenues for multiple fields of research and scientific disciplines, ranging from data and information science to AI and computer sciences.
2. **Multisectoral Approach**: Addressing policy actions across several sectors, including education, media, economy, and politics.
3. **Multi-stakeholder Approach**: Engaging member states and all stakeholders, including the private sector, civil society, and individuals.
4. **Gender Approach**: Ensuring equality between men and women in all legal frameworks and strategies aimed at implementing this recommendation, particularly in policy actions related to AI, data, and information.

The connecting points between this recommendation and the resolution adopted by the United Nations General Assembly on AI for Sustainable Development (A/78/L.49) include the diverse approaches adopted during the elaboration of both texts and the human-centric focus regarding data protection throughout the AI development lifecycle as a means to safeguard human rights and dignity.

The term "data" is mentioned eight times in the resolution, underscoring the significance of AI ethics as "fair, inclusive, responsible, and effective data governance" (United Nations, 2024, para 7). The resolution emphasizes the necessity of promoting "trusted cross-border data flows" (United Nations, 2024, para 7) and "mechanisms for securing data" (United Nations, 2024, para 6e), as well as "safeguarding privacy and the protection of personal data during the testing and evaluation of systems" (United Nations, 2024, para 6j). This pertains to the utilization of "personal data throughout the lifecycle of artificial intelligence systems" (United Nations, 2024, para 6j).

The term "information" appears eleven times, related to digital progress, integrity, and literacy. The resolution highlights the potential misuse of AI that might "undermine information integrity and access to information" (United Nations, 2024, Preamble). It advocates for techniques of "reliable content authentication and provenance... that allow users to detect information manipulation" (United Nations, 2024, para 6g) and emphasizes the importance of "enhancing media and information literacy" (United Nations, 2024, para 6g). The resolution supports "enhancing information-sharing on mutually agreed terms among entities involved in the lifecycle of artificial intelligence systems" (United Nations, 2024, para 6n), implicitly underscoring the benefits of such sharing for informed decision-making (United Nations, 2024).

A further connection between the UNESCO recommendation on the Ethics of AI and the United Nations resolution A/78/L.49 on AI and sustainable development is that both international instruments are not prohibitive in nature. This affects the legal quality of both instruments, fundamentally limiting their efficacy for global AI governance, particularly regarding AI-driven information and its implications for geopolitical dynamics, especially considering the UN's role in maintaining international peace and security in the era of such technologies.

The lack of international prohibitive instruments constitutes a significant deficiency in global AI governance. This deficiency could exacerbate the negative implications of AI-driven information on geopolitical dynamics.

4 Regional Instruments on Ethics of AI-Driven Information

The challenges and threats posed by AI-driven information and its implications for geopolitical dynamics highlight that achieving geopolitical interests is not solely the mission of heads of state, foreign affairs, and military leaders. In the era of AI-driven information, the achievement of geopolitical interests involves all actors within each state, including individuals. AI-driven information has increased the race for data sovereignty, starting with citizens as sources of data—such as children producing data during e-learning and gamification—and extending to soldiers who protect borders. In this era, the protection of state borders is conditioned by the quality of data and the efficiency of data analysis at the right time.

These challenges explain the involvement of several regional institutions in global and regional efforts on AI ethics and regulation (Roumate, 2021). Regional AI ethics initiatives are divided between two approaches: the rigid approach adopted by the European Union in the AI Act and the pro-innovative approach adopted by other regional institutions like the OECD, the Council of Europe, and the African Union. The pro-innovative approach emphasizes the promotion of innovation as key to increasing the positive impacts of AI while simultaneously reducing its negative implications and risks through ethical considerations. The OECD's Recommendation, adopted on May 22, 2019, and updated in 2024, identifies five value-based principles centered around human rights (OECD, 2019). Well-being, democratic values, and respect for the rule of law are at the core of these principles (OECD, 2020). Information is central to these five value-based principles, indicating that the OECD recognizes the importance of information for ensuring these values.

The first principle is inclusive growth, sustainable development, and well-being, particularly in an economy based on information. The second principle emphasizes human rights and democratic values, including fairness and privacy, which require easy access to information ensured by AI. Therefore, the malicious use of AI-driven information poses risks that can be mitigated by adhering to these values. The third principle focuses on transparency and explainability, while the fourth emphasizes robustness, security, and safety. The fifth principle pertains to accountability to ensure responsible AI-driven information (OECD, 2024). The OECD AI principles are based on a pro-innovative approach founded on a multidisciplinary and multisectoral framework, as confirmed by the OECD's recommendations, which advocate for promoting innovation through investment in AI research and the involvement of all stakeholders in the elaboration and implementation of AI policies (OECD, 2024).

Other regional initiatives related to AI ethics are similarly based on the pro-innovative approach, such as the Ad Hoc Committee on AI (CAHAI) created by the Council of Europe in 2019, which is working on "the feasibility and potential elements, based on broad multi-stakeholder consultations, of a legal framework for the development, design, and application of artificial intelligence, based on the Council of Europe's standards on human rights, democracy, and the rule of law" (Council of Europe, 2019).

Another significant regional instrument is the European AI Act, adopted in 2024, which is based on a risk-based approach to create a balance between reducing potential harm and fostering innovation. It categorizes AI based on risk to apply different regulatory frameworks. This risk-based approach is characterized by its rigidity, which could limit innovation instead of fostering it. The Act bans practices deemed to present unacceptable risks, such as social scoring and subliminal manipulation. It then applies strict regulations to high-risk systems, including those in critical infrastructure, education, and law enforcement, which must undergo rigorous checks to prevent serious harm (European Parliament, 2023).

The Act introduces several innovative ideas to encourage responsible AI, such as regulatory sandboxes—controlled environments where developers can safely test their AI systems. These regulatory sandboxes are established by member states. According to this Act, the European AI Office is set up to oversee the most powerful AI models, making it the EU's main authority on AI (European Parliament, 2023). One of the most innovative components of the European AI Act is the General-Purpose AI (GPAI) regulation, which specifically governs powerful GPAI models. It sets norms for transparency and establishes duties for models that pose systemic risks (European Parliament, 2023).

Some of these norms focus on data governance and information, considering the risks associated with information power, particularly the malicious use of AI-driven information, which poses a high-level risk to European geopolitical interests. Article 10 of the EU AI Act is dedicated entirely to the quality of training, validation, and testing data for high-risk AI systems. According to paragraph 2 of Article 10, "training, validation, and testing data sets shall be subject to data governance and management practices appropriate for the intended purpose of the high-risk AI system" (European Parliament, 2023). The interpretation of this article indicates that it encompasses all practices without specification, covering data collection, processing, and preparation operations such as annotation, labeling, and cleaning. This article entails examinations for potential biases and the identification and mitigation of data gaps or shortcomings. According to this article, data governance is a key mechanism for ensuring that high-risk AI systems are technically robust, reliable, and non-discriminatory (European Parliament, 2023).

This article explicitly focuses on data governance while implicitly citing structured data, which is information. This concept recurs throughout the EU AI Act, primarily in the context of transparency and accountability. It appears in numerous recitals and articles, most notably in Article 13, which requires providers of high-risk AI systems to provide clear and adequate information to the deployer about the system's capabilities, limitations, and intended purpose (European Parliament, 2023). Specific transparency obligations are mandated for certain AI systems from AI and generative AI providers. According to Article 50, providers must, first, ensure that humans interacting with an AI system are informed that they are not dealing with a human; and second, ensure that generative AI outputs (images, video, audio, or text) are clearly and visibly labeled to inform users that the content is artificially generated (European Parliament, 2023).

Considering the intersection between data, information, and knowledge within the DIKW framework, the Act requires extensive technical documentation and logging, which contains crucial information for market surveillance authorities to verify compliance and investigate incidents (European Parliament, 2023). The Act establishes a public EU database for high-risk AI systems that will contain key information for public transparency and oversight. Although the term "geopolitics of AI" is not explicitly used in the legal text of the EU AI Act, the need for data governance is a key geopolitical and geostrategic driver behind the Act and related EU legislation (such as the Data Governance Act and the Data Act). All norms included in the European AI Act related to AI risks, data governance, and information serve broader geopolitical interests and geostrategic goals, considering AI and information as geopolitical power and a means of achieving data and technological sovereignty in this new world order.

The risk-based approach adopted in the Act indicates that the objective of the AI's rigorous standards is not only to address the risks posed by AI and generative AI but also to ensure technological sovereignty, which is essential for maintaining Europe's position in a new world order characterized by a balance of power that ranges between geostrategic interests and technological sovereignty (Roumate, 2024). The reinforcement of regional AI cooperation is not limited to political and economic fields; it extends to military considerations, given that AI cooperation is a key component of military strategies in the era of AI-driven information. In this context, NATO is involved in these global dynamics through its AI strategy published in 2021, revised and released on July 10, 2024. This strategy "aims to accelerate the use of AI technologies within NATO in a safe and responsible way" (NATO, 2024a). Furthermore, it emphasizes the importance of AI cooperation related to AI development and deployment (NATO, 2024a). The strategy prioritizes providing "a foundation for NATO and Allies to lead by example and encourage the development and use of AI in a responsible manner for Allied defense and security purposes" (NATO, 2024b). This underscores the geostrategic dimension of AI as a geopolitical power.

From military alliances to economic partnerships, and from NATO to BRICS, AI as a geopolitical power is central to various AI initiatives. In this context, BRICS adopted an AI declaration in June 2025, encompassing 126 commitments related to global governance across several fields, including AI (Maiva D'Auria, 2025).

The African Union launched the Continental AI Strategy in 2024. This strategy is based on multidisciplinary and multi-stakeholder approaches, emphasizing research and innovation as key pillars to reduce the divide between countries (African Union, 2024, p. 26). Fostering research and innovation is crucial for maximizing the benefits of AI and mitigating its risks. This means that the African Union adopts a pro-innovative approach. The strategy's vision is "A prosperous and integrated Africa where responsible, ethical, and African-centric AI is the axis of inclusive growth, resilience, socio-economic development, people empowerment, and positioning the continent as a key player in the global AI landscape" (African Union, 2024, p. 27). This vision aligns with the "AU Agenda 2063 and the Sustainable Development Goals" (African Union, 2024, p. 27).

In the era of AI and AI-driven information, the geopolitics of AI and information are considered by the Continental Strategy, which includes in its guiding principles peace and security. The connection between the global and the local is heightened by AI, as its tangible and intangible impacts are borderless. Therefore, the African AI strategy prioritizes local solutions for challenges posed by AI across all sectors, from education to healthcare and climate change. These solutions are rooted in local talents, which underscores the second principle of being people-centered as a pillar to promote inclusive growth while rigorously upholding human rights and dignity in all stages of AI systems. The strategy emphasizes the importance of inclusion and diversity, aiming to leave no one behind through robust skills development, public awareness, and education to prepare the African population for an AI-driven future.

This leads us to another recommendation in the strategy, which promotes international cooperation between African countries as part of the Global South and between African countries and those in the Global North to build regional AI capacities and ensure data self-management (African Union, 2024, p. 28). The African AI strategy identifies five objectives to be achieved by 2030, prioritizing the implementation of robust AI governance, regulations, standards, codes of conduct, and best practices to manage AI risks and promote its growth (African Union, 2024, p. 29). This goal is the first step to "promote African participation in shaping the global AI governance system" (African Union, 2024, p. 29). The strategy also aims to "promote regional cooperation and solidarity among AU Member States" and "stimulate AI-related partnerships between Africa and the rest of the world" to reinforce the geopolitical position of the continent in the global landscape (African Union, 2024, p. 29). To this end, the strategy places "the promotion of information integrity, media, and information literacy" at the center of its foresight objectives (African Union, 2024, p. 29).

The strategy appears ambitious and covers elements often neglected by other regional initiatives, suggesting that the African Union has learned from previous regional experiences and best practices. It outlines several details, such as vision, mission, aims, eras, values, principles, recommendations, stakeholders, and sectors, which could facilitate its implementation by AU Member States.

In the Rio de Janeiro Declaration, titled "Strengthening Global South Cooperation for More Inclusive and Sustainable Governance," adopted on June 6, 2025, in Brazil, BRICS highlights the key role of AI in driving progress toward a more prosperous future. However, ensuring that no one is left behind in this AI revolution necessitates global AI governance, involving countries not only from the Global North but also those from the Global South (Maiva D'Auria, 2025). According to this declaration, the leaders of the BRICS countries are committed to "strengthening multilateralism and reforming global governance" (BRICS, 2025, p. 1). In this context, the leaders adopted "the Pact of the Future at the Summit of the Future, including its two annexes, the Global Digital Compact and the Declaration of Future Generations" (BRICS, 2025, pp. 1–2).

In this declaration, BRICS leaders "underscore that the global governance of AI should mitigate potential risks and address the needs of all countries, including those of the Global South." This global governance of AI should be based on a "balanced approach" (BRICS, 2025, para 16) to achieve its primary goal: fostering "responsible development, deployment, and use of AI technologies for sustainable development and inclusive growth, in compliance with national regulatory frameworks, the UN Charter, and respecting the sovereignty of states" (BRICS, 2025, para 16).

5 Geopolitics of AI: The Race to National AI Strategies and Regulation

The race for national AI strategies and regulation reflects the geopolitics of AI technologies, which are becoming a significant geopolitical power. The question we must address is: what realities can we learn from the geopolitics of AI? This reality indicates that AI is increasing the divide between the Global North and the Global South. According to the Global AI Index released by Tortoise in 2025, "The Global AI Index aims to make sense of artificial intelligence in 83 countries, scoring them on AI capacity based on 122 different indicators grouped into three pillars of analysis: Implementation, Innovation, and Investment" (White & Cesareo, 2025). This global index shows that the top ten leading countries in AI are from the Global North, with the United States at the forefront, followed by China, Singapore, the UK, France, South Korea, Germany, Canada, Israel, and India (White & Cesareo, 2025).

Research published by the World Bank on "Who on Earth is Using Generative AI?" demonstrates that middle-income economies like India, Brazil, the Philippines, and Indonesia now account for over half of total traffic, despite having significantly smaller economies. In contrast, low-income countries represent less than 1% of traffic (Liu & Wang, 2024). Research indicates that several factors correlate with higher adoption of generative AI, particularly "a country's income level, a large youth population, strong digital infrastructure, and high human capital" (Liu & Wang, 2024). Additionally, English fluency and higher internet speeds are significant factors, as confirmed by this research (Liu & Wang, 2024). Other factors, such as the level of democracy and the prevalence of corruption within a country, could also explain a state's ability to develop and deploy AI and generative AI.

These two realities lead us to the first conclusion: the top ten leading countries in AI are monopolized by countries from the Global North, while the top ten in the use of generative AI are dominated by countries from the Global South. If we add to this conclusion the fact that "in 2021, 57.6% of all doctorate-level computer and mathematical scientists and engineers working in the United States were foreign-born, and that more than half of all U.S. academic positions in computer and information sciences programs were also held by foreign-born academics" (National Science Board, 2024), then the implications of AI for reducing the divide between the Global North and Global South should be based on the democratization of AI as a pillar of global AI governance.

The geopolitics of AI demonstrate that the race for technological sovereignty and sovereign AI is accompanied by the race for national AI strategies and regulations. The Stanford AI Index Report published in 2025 shows that "Governments are stepping up on AI—with regulation and investment" (Maslej et al., 2025, p. 20). This indicates that AI regulations, strategies, and initiatives are key elements of this race, just as much as AI investment is. According to this report, "Globally, legislative mentions of AI rose 21.3% across 75 countries since

2023, marking a ninefold increase since 2016" (Maslej et al., 2025, p. 20). The report emphasizes that "from 2016 to 2024, 114 countries enacted at least one AI-related law. In total, these countries have passed 204 AI-related laws" (Maslej et al., 2025, p. 337).

The Global North is more involved in global efforts related to AI, particularly the leading countries: Russia and the U.S. rank between 16 and 30. This is followed by China, Canada, India, and several European countries like France and Germany, while many countries in the Global South, particularly in Africa and the Middle East, have zero bills or no available data. According to Maslej et al. (2025), "the year 2024 is the highest year on record for AI-related regulation after 2022. The total number of AI-related laws passed rose from 30 in 2023 to 40 in 2024" (Maslej et al., 2025, p. 338).

The leading countries in AI regulation can also be explained by the regulatory approaches they adopt, particularly the pro-innovative approach. This approach emphasizes the promotion of innovation and the significant role of young inventors and Generation Z. It also relies on coordination among government, academia, and companies, with the goal of achieving technological leadership.

In the U.S., 59 AI-related regulations were introduced by federal agencies in 2024, "more than double the number in 2023—and issued by twice as many agencies" (Maslej et al., 2025). U.S. states have expanded deepfake regulations to 24 states, up from only five states—California, Michigan, Washington, Texas, and Minnesota—having enacted laws regulating deepfakes in elections prior to 2024 (Maslej et al., 2025, p. 21). The report shows the total number of AI-related laws passed since 2016, with the United States leading at 27, followed by Portugal and Russia, each with 20 (Maslej et al., 2025, p. 338).

The AI Index Report highlights the number of AI-related laws enacted in 2024 across the top 15 geographic areas. Russia led with seven laws, followed by Belgium and Portugal with five each. This illustrates that Russia is determined to achieve its goal for 2030, which is technological sovereignty based on the sovereignty of law and regulation. In this global context, Russia adopts a pro-innovative approach as a pillar of its AI strategic vision for 2030.

Regulatory efforts related to AI are based on coordination among academia, government, and companies. This indicates that Russia is determined to be among the leading countries in global AI governance, which has become a goal for several powers in this multipolar world order, including China.

China is one of the most active countries in regulating AI. This effort is particularly focused on three regulations requiring in-depth analysis: recommendation algorithms for disseminating content, deep synthetically generated images and videos, and generative AI systems like ChatGPT (Sheehan, 2023, pp. 3–4). This effort is overseen by the State Council of the People's Republic of China since 2017.

This demonstrates that, like Russia and the U.S., China considers coordination among academia, government, and companies as a key pillar of its AI strategic vision for 2030. China is also adopting the pro-innovative approach, which is supported by multi-stakeholder, multidisciplinary, and multisectoral approaches.

In this context, China published the Global Governance Action Plan on July 26 as an outcome of the 2025 World Artificial Intelligence Conference and High-Level Meetings on Global AI Governance.

This plan emphasizes the adoption of a pro-innovative approach, prioritizing innovation and founded on multidisciplinary, multisectoral, and multi-stakeholder approaches. The title of this action plan reflects the intersection between global and national, or even local, governance of AI. This initiative acknowledges the importance of global AI governance given the implications of AI on geopolitical dynamics in the global landscape. National AI strategies and regulations are significant in the era of the AI revolution and Industry 6.0. Therefore, the challenges and risks posed by this AI revolution also demand global AI governance.

This Global AI Action Plan is a "call for the active participation and collaboration of all stakeholders... to accelerate the development of digital infrastructure... and maximize AI's immense potential in empowering global economic and social development, supporting the implementation of the United Nations 2030 Agenda for Sustainable Development, and addressing global challenges" (Ministry of Foreign Affairs of the People's Republic of China, 2010). This plan prioritizes promoting AI innovation "in the spirit of openness and sharing" and creating "a diverse, open, and innovative ecosystem," along with the need "to build cross-border open-source communities and secure, reliable open-source platforms to facilitate the open sharing of basic resources" (Ministry of Foreign Affairs of the People's Republic of China, 2025). This reflects China's rethinking of its foreign affairs, oriented toward international technological cooperation while respecting the sovereignty of states.

These changes in the Chinese AI strategy are also evidenced by the call for a "spirit of openness" from a country that is one of the leaders in AI surveillance, alongside the U.S. Canada also initiated its process of AI regulation in 2017 with the Pan-Canadian Artificial Intelligence Strategy, followed by a bill for the Artificial Intelligence Data Act tabled in 2022 and the Digital Charter Implementation Act (Bill C-27), which is considered a legislative package adopted in November 2022 (Government of Canada, 2022, cited in Roumate, 2024).

Other countries are racing to regulate AI, such as Japan, which prioritizes "social principles of human-centric AI" in its AI regulatory efforts, for example, through the "decision of the Integrated Innovation Strategy Promotion Council" (Ministry of Economy, Trade and Industry, 2022). Japan focuses on balancing human-centric AI with fostering innovation, achieving this goal through a multisectoral, multidisciplinary, and multi-stakeholder approach.

In this global landscape, other countries from the Global South are also positioning themselves to engage in these geopolitical dynamics. This includes various Arab countries working to ensure sovereign AI and technological sovereignty (Roumate, 2024, p. 60). The importance of national AI strategies based on a gender approach, including the integration of youth and Generation Z, is also crucial (Roumate, 2025, p. 179). Several countries have adopted national AI or digital strategies, including the UAE, KSA, Turkey, Egypt, Morocco, and Qatar (UN ESCWA, 2020). However, these AI strategies and regulations often adopt a rigid approach, meaning that they are primarily developed by governmental bodies without coordination with multiple stakeholders (Roumate, 2024). Additionally, they often focus on risk management, which could inhibit innovation. This situation may be influenced by the European legacy on its former colonies, raising concerns about technological dependency. Such countries risk losing their position in the future geopolitical AI landscape by opting to remain consumers of AI and relying on technology transfers instead of investing in their own Generation Z to secure a strong position in the geopolitical innovation landscape. By choosing a rigid approach, Arab countries may lose the ability to address the challenges related to AI-driven information that are particularly pressing in the conflict-ridden region of the Middle East.

6 Conclusion

In the current global landscape, the geopolitics of AI and information will increasingly influence geopolitical dynamics and the new balance of power, which ranges between geostrategic interests and the race for technological sovereignty. AI regulation, along with regulations on AI deepfakes, is one dimension of this race. In this context, global AI governance and governance by law are essential to address AI challenges both now and in the future. The call launched by China for a global AI governance act is a positive initiative; however, it is insufficient to address all risks and threats posed by AI. An international ban on AI technologies, alongside frameworks for international peace and security that encompass both the power of AI and the power of information, is urgently needed in these changing geopolitical dynamics. Such international mechanisms should focus on enhancing international cooperation, including North-South collaboration, to ensure that no one is left behind.

Trends in AI technologies will lead to even more significant changes in the geopolitical landscape and will continue to reshape international relations in ways that are difficult to predict but crucial to prepare for through international binding instruments and cooperation. The goal is to create a balance through the promotion of innovation and international peace and security.

References

African Union. (2024, July). *Continental artificial intelligence strategy, harnessing AI for Africa's development and prosperity*. Retrieved from https://au.int/sites/default/files/documents/44004-doc-EN-_Continental_AI_Strategy_July_2024.pdf

BRICS. (2025). *Rio de Janeiro declaration, Strengthening Global South cooperation for a more inclusive and sustainable governance*. Retrieved from https://brics.br/en/news/brics-summit-signs-historic-commitment-in-rio-for-more-inclusive-and-sustainable-governance

Council of Europe. (2019). *1353rd meeting, Ad hoc Committee on Artificial Intelligence (CAHAI)*. Retrieved from https://search.coe.int/cm/Pages/result_details.aspx?ObjectId=09000016809737a1

D'Auria, M. (2025). *BRICS summit signs historic commitment in Rio for more inclusive and sustainable governance*. BRICS-Brazil. Retrieved from https://brics.br/en/news/brics-summit-signs-historic-commitment-in-rio-for-more-inclusive-and-sustainable-governance

European Parliament. (2023). *EU AI Act: First regulation on artificial intelligence*. Retrieved from https://www.europarl.europa.eu/topics/en/article/20230601STO93804/eu-ai-act-first-regulation-on-artificial-intelligence

Liu, Y., & Wang, H. (2024). *Who on Earth is using generative AI? World Bank*. Retrieved from https://documents1.worldbank.org/curated/en/099720008192430535/pdf/IDU-5f321eb5-4870-472d-a888-3ab677be07b0.pdf

Maslej, N., et al. (2025, April). *The AI Index 2025 annual report*. AI Index Steering Committee, Institute for Human-Centered AI, Stanford University. Retrieved from https://hai.stanford.edu/ai-index/2025-ai-index-report

Ministry of Foreign Affairs of the People's Republic of China. (2025). *Global AI governance action plan*. Retrieved from https://www.fmprc.gov.cn/eng./xw/zyxw/202507/t20250729_11679232.html

National Science Board. (2024). *Science and engineering indicators 2024*. National Center for Science and Engineering Statistics. Retrieved from https://ncses.nsf.gov/pubs/nsb20241/foreign-born-stem-workers

NATO. (2024a). *NATO releases revised AI strategy*. Retrieved from https://www.nato.int/cps/en/natohq/news_227234.htm

NATO. (2024b). *Summary of NATO's revised artificial intelligence (AI) strategy*. Retrieved from https://www.nato.int/cps/en/natohq/official_texts_227237.htm

OECD. (2019). *OECD principles on AI*. Retrieved from http://www.oecd.org/going-digital/ai/principles/

OECD. (2020). *OECD AI Policy Observatory*. Retrieved from https://www.oecd.org/going-digital/ai/about-the-oecd-ai-policy-observatory.pdf

Organisation for Economic Co-operation and Development (OECD). (2024). *AI principles*. OECD.https://www.oecd.org/en/topics/ai-principles.html

Roumate, F. (2021). Artificial intelligence, ethics and international human rights law. *IRIE, International Review of Information Ethics, 29*.

Roumate, F. (2024). AI and technological sovereignty. In *Artificial intelligence and the new world order. Frontiers of Artificial Intelligence, Ethics and Multidisciplinary Applications*. Springer. https://doi.org/10.1007/978-3-031-50312-2_5

Roumate, F. (2025). Artificial intelligence and Industry 5.0: Paving the way for an economic revolution in the Arab world. *Communications. Media. Design*, *10*(1). https://cmd-journal.hse.ru/issue/view/1771 (Retrieved from).

Sheehan, M. (2023). *China's AI regulations and how they get made*. Carnegie Endowment for International Peace. Retrieved from https://carnegieendowment.org/2023/07/10/china-s-ai-regulations-and-how-they-get-made-pub-90117

The Government of Canada. (2022). *Bill C-27, the Digital Charter Implementation Act, 2022*. Retrieved from https://ised-isde.canada.ca/site/innovation-better-canada/en/canadas-digital-charter/bill-summary-digital-charter-implementation-act-2020

The Ministry of Economy, Trade and Industry (METI). (2022). *AI governance in Japan VER 1.1*. Report realized with the Expert Group on How AI Principles should be Implemented. Retrieved July 9, 2021, from https://www.meti.go.jp/policy/it_policy/ai-governance/20210709_8.pdf

UNESCWA. (2020). *Developing an artificial intelligence strategy national guide*. Beirut. Retrieved from https://www.unescwa.org/sites/default/files/artificial-intelligence-strategy-national-guide-english.pdf

UNESCO. (2021). *Recommendation on ethics of artificial intelligence*. Retrieved from https://www.unesco.org/en/articles/recommendation-ethics-artificial-intelligence

United Nations. (2024, March 21). *General Assembly adopts landmark resolution on steering artificial intelligence towards global good, faster realization of sustainable development* (Press release GA/12588). United Nations.https://press.un.org/en/2024/ga12588.doc.htm
White, J., & Cesareo, S. (2025). *The Global AI Index 2025*. Tortoise Media. Retrieved from https://www.tortoisemedia.com/data/global-ai

The Future of AI, Information, and Geopolitics

Marius Vacarelu

1 Introduction

The relationship between geopolitics and Artificial Intelligence (henceforth AI) is fundamental for the entire twenty-first century, and I agree with the conclusion of the analysis published in January 2020 by the Brookings Institution (Indermit, 2020), which emphasized that the country that leads the competition to implement this new technology by 2030 will dominate the entire century.

The article—published before the onset of the COVID-19 pandemic and the outbreak of the war between the Russian Federation and Ukraine—could not have anticipated these two events, which have triggered a higher level of global implementation of AI technology. We could say that the launch of Chat GPT—today considered the generic prototype of AI tool providers, just as the term "Photoshop" designates several video and photo editing programs—in the latter part of 2022, after the pandemic had largely been brought under control, while the war in Eastern Europe was unfolding with full hostility, was accelerated by these events (Marr, 2023), without fully identifying the cause-and-effect relationship between them. In fact, AI tools appeared in early forms long ago (Haenlein & Kaplan, 2025), making an eventual launch at a higher level, accessible to large groups of users numbering in the millions, inevitable. What we did not know was the exact date of this historic turning point toward large-scale implementation of AI technologies, but that does not mean that cautious governments, visionary business circles, and, in general, the intellectual elites of each country were unaware that this moment triggering for major political and economic transformations would not be delayed too long within this decade.

M. Vacarelu (✉)
Faculty of Public Administration, National School of Political and Administrative Studies, Bucharest, Romania
e-mail: marius333vacarelu@gmail.com

F. Roumate (ed.), *AI, Information, and Global Dynamics*, Contributions to International Relations,
https://doi.org/10.1007/978-3-032-13528-5_12

Nevertheless, it has been shown that the launch of multiple AI programs/tools within a short timeframe, during a complicated period, caught a large part of contemporary society by surprise. Thus, a feeling of "somewhat uncontrollable novelty" gripped political, economic, and media leaders, who within a few weeks saw—based on the overwhelming success of Chat GPT's adoption across various electronic devices (Duarte, 2025)—how some of the pillars of long-term strategic thinking in their fields of activity had been significantly altered. From that moment on, it became necessary to consider new forms of action both in the sphere of domestic and international politics, as well as in other areas of human activity, from cutting-edge medical research to the deployment and transformation of the world's armies, from climate forecasting to the redefinition of cinematography and visual arts, and so on. However, this transformation continues, and governments and private actors must adapt because delays in this fundamental process will significantly lower their positions in the global rankings of geopolitical, economic, and military power. It thus becomes necessary to try to have a vision for the future, of at least three decades, during which the results brought about by these demanding years for people, institutions, and energy resources—due to the huge electricity consumption required by AI tools (International Energy Agency, 2025)—will be crystallized.

2 Research Methodology

From the perspective of research methodology, a work that primarily aims to offer a perspective on the future is subject to a greater degree of uncertainty than a text that strictly analyzes the present or the past, which still presents a significant challenge. Specifically, writing about the future forces you to select what seems to be most important from a wide range of perspectives, while it is necessary to create a coherent set of ideas so that the reader ultimately has a clear, well-articulated vision of what will truly be relevant for building their own vision and planning both their professional and personal life.

In reality, the very emergence of AI is proving to be a factor that promotes the appearance of predictions in various fields of science, the economy, as well as politics, because their broad access to the vast "sui-generis library" called the Internet enables analyses of reasonable quality, often superior to those that could be conducted by a person with a very low level of education. At the same time, however, the human mind is capable—and must continue to be capable—of seeing beyond what might be presented through AI algorithms of cause and effect. From this comes a particularization regarding the field of geopolitics, which involves differentiation of predictions by country and continent, because some geopolitics specialists understand their part of the world far better than electronic algorithms do. The decades or centuries of experience from research institutions can be superior to the analytical products created by AI tools, since the latter are based exclusively on what is available online, which means that countries that have not extensively digitized their libraries are understood through the perspective of writings in an internationally used language available on the Internet, without those necessarily being the best or the most objective texts (Rodriguez & Kannan, 2024).

In geopolitics, the main research method is the historical one, with a significant historical-teleological particularization when analyzing the relationship between great powers and countries with lesser power (Robinson, 2009). However, history alone is not sufficient for geopolitics, and the aspects concerning the relationship between advanced technologies and the changes occurring in the spheres of politics and information bring into discussion qualitative analysis, as well as the conceptual and fundamental perspective of shaping a country's domestic and foreign policies. The vast dimension of the literature devoted to geopolitics, as well as the growing proportion of works dedicated to AI force the researcher to seek to identify the lines of force for the next decades realities. Thus, the researcher's efforts favored a conceptual and fundamental approach to the researched topic, seeking the overall picture of the countries' geopolitics, in relation to the development of AI and information area. Therefore, the research is oriented towards wide-ranging conclusions, which will allow the identification of future trends.

3 AI'S Capacities to Influence the Human Mind

In May 2025, a news story in the international press sparked a discussion about the future of AI technology and its potential to remain fully under human control more than ever before. Specifically, Anthropic's newly launched Claude Opus 4 model frequently tries to blackmail developers when they threaten to replace it with a new AI system and give it sensitive information about the engineers responsible for the decision. Anthropic notes that Claude Opus 4 tries to blackmail engineers 84% of the time when the replacement AI model has similar values. When the replacement AI system does not share Claude Opus 4's values, Anthropic says the model tries to blackmail the engineers more frequently. Notably, Anthropic says Claude Opus 4 displays this behavior at higher rates than previous models (Zeff, 2025).

Such "electronic behavior" raises legitimate concerns for anyone, but in the realm of geopolitics as well as the informational space, this news brings into focus a complicated future that will put both governments and the intellect of every individual facing such situations in their private or public life to the test. And to deepen the concern even further, it is worth noting that in the same month, the journal *Nature Human Behaviour* published the results of research on AI's potential to persuade human subjects in debates. GPT-4 was 64.4% more persuasive than human opponents when it had access to their personal and professional information; and when GPT-4 was allowed to personalize its arguments, it became significantly more persuasive than any human—increasing the chances of changing someone's mind by 81.2% compared to debates between human participants (Salvi et al., 2025). Clearly, this research will be leveraged in the coming years both in the political environment and, especially, by communication professionals—whether from the purely commercial sphere or from the political arena. And even though the general public was warned this month about this new capability—the press in every country picked up this news—it does not mean that people will suddenly be better able to distinguish communication with a real person from communication with a bot that is increasingly capable of subtly arguing on any topic.

These informational capabilities of AI should not be surprising. At least since the 2016 American presidential elections, the political environment—in reality, society as a whole—has become aware of the power of information and psychological profiling of the electorate (Jakee & Fink, 2024). Developments in recent years have confirmed this trend of using AI tools, and several European countries—France, Germany, Poland, Romania—have directly accused various internal or external political actors of informational interference in electoral processes (Muto, 2024), with one case actually leading to the annulment of elections by a Constitutional Court decision (Romania in 2024). Subsequent research conducted by various public and private institutions has revealed the intensive use of AI bots in favor of different candidates in national electoral processes; now no political party can ignore the use of AI technology in the information space. The future is therefore (also) about informational confrontations carried out through AI, to varying degrees of usage, and political and legal actors will have to adapt national regulatory frameworks to prevent the biased or malicious use of this new technology.

4 Typology of Geopolitics Related to Technologies

To better understand today's geopolitics, as well as tomorrow's, it is necessary to have an accurate knowledge of the history of the past centuries, because—as emphasized by Braudel, the eminent French historian—there is a "longue durée": long-term historical structures that are characterized by an extremely slow, almost imperceptible, often underground evolution. In other words, they are historical phenomena, seemingly suspended in the past, but capable of re-emerging decades, centuries, or even millennia later. In a certain sense, continuity and discontinuity are the skeleton of political life; various conditioning factors are its flesh and blood (Groupe d'Etudes Geopolitiques, 2022).

For these reasons, it is necessary to consider detecting geopolitical patterns in the fundamental relationship between people, countries, and the technologies they have created. This relationship is the most important among those that human history has known, because every time a major technological invention appeared—the result of the intelligence and labor of a few individuals—there was a corresponding adjustment in the political environment according to this technology' characteristics. Thus, the creation of a technology with real economic or military impact led to its dissemination, often under governmental control, because only in this way could the country where it was patented ensure an advantage in the geopolitical competition with other empires or less powerful states. Therefore, alongside the issue of intellectual property protection for the main features of an invention, its large-scale reproduction followed, capable of providing a qualitative and quantitative advantage in the economy and in equipping armies. History has shown us that after the development of these technologies, states with major geopolitical ambitions sought to capitalize on the new capabilities relative to the opportunities they had obtained, and thus launched various operations aimed at territorial expansion through war or negotiations projecting superior power (Chin, 2019). However, there was also the geopolitical flip side—that is, the states that tried to prevent the accumulation of significant gaps between their limited technological capabilities and the qualitatively superior capabilities of other countries. To this end, they typically resorted to invading more technologically advanced countries in order to block their possibilities of increasing geopolitical and economic power.

Thus, to understand the geopolitical and historical pattern, we will mention that the invention of the steam engine (1769) underpinned the longest conflict between two European powers since the Middle Ages: Great Britain used the substantial commercial profits gained to finance entire armies of opponents against Napoleon's France, eventually securing victory after more than 25 years of confrontations. The emergence of the train and telegraph, and implicitly rapid communications, triggered the upheaval of European empires in 1848, as news of the revolutions spread quickly, and their weakening led to the appearance of unified nation-states on this continent over the next 15 years: Germany, Italy, Romania. The invention of strictly military technology—specifically repeating firearms and especially the machine gun—increased the pace of German unification, as well as its subsequent dominance in continental Europe following wars with the Habsburg Empire (1866) and France (1871). The advent of the gasoline engine, automobiles, the telephone, aviation, and radio gave several states confidence that they could dominate either the European continent or the entire world, laying the groundwork for World War I. The refinement and widespread dissemination of these technologies after 1920 strengthened the aggressive ambitions of certain states, such that World War II saw their intense use daily. Subsequently, the Cold War employed the full range of technologies developed up to 1945, introducing new instruments of action, among which television—information and communication once again—played a decisive role in the free world's victory over the communist bloc.

Such an approach seems logical for AI technologies, since history has shown us that such options remain valid if well executed and achieve the desired effect intended by their initiators. Moreover, any new impactful technology draws only three types of responses: the first is conforming to the leadership status of the country where it was developed, implicitly expanding alliances with cutting-edge technology; the second response is the attempt to replicate and improve that technology for one's own purposes, aiming to dominate a certain geopolitical area, but without seeking to challenge the global or continental leader; and the last possible approach is confrontation, by both developing a similar technology at a superior level and subsequently initiating a visible geopolitical competition, questioning the technological leadership and potentially the geopolitical leadership of the creators of the high-impact invention.

5 Geopolitics of Work in the AI Era

The nature of the relationships between technologies with a major impact on society and the political environment is different in the twenty-first century, although much of what was previously stated regarding human creation from the eighteenth to twentieth centuries remains perfectly valid. However, there are a few distinctions that will bring into discussion the entire relationship between AI technology, geopolitics, and the informational environment.

The first aspect that needs to be noted and developed is the specific demographics of this century, relative to the situation in previous centuries. The inventions mentioned earlier came during periods of demographic growth, favoring an increase in economic complexity and, implicitly, a rise in workers' incomes, who were thus able to better feed and educate their children, with major benefits for the following decades (Morland, 2019). The twenty-first century is one in which the world's countries are experiencing demographic decline, especially highly economically developed countries, where population growth is largely due to immigration rather than natural fertility (OECD, 2024). So, for three centuries—during which major inventions anticipated and built the infrastructure for AI technologies—the workforce was not lacking. In fact, population growth was also a factor that encouraged the emergence of new inventions, as the demand for goods and services was increasing, and states, businesspeople, and engineers had to somehow ensure these demands were met. However, in the next decades, demographics and the implementation of AI technologies will create another equation that needs to be understood both by governments and especially by parents and young people. Specifically, AI primarily means the automation of certain industrial processes, freeing up significant percentages of a country's workforce.

Now, if we were to analyze only the demographic decline in relation to the implementation of AI, we would say that this technology arrived just in time to compensate for the decrease in the number of young people entering the labor market. However, there are some unwanted consequences that outnumber and outweigh the benefits we can anticipate in the long term from the use of AI tools.

The first issue is the reduction of access to the labor market for jobs requiring lower qualifications, and here any government is justified in being dissatisfied because the most affected group will be young graduates (18–25 years old), who will find it difficult to secure employment since their training is less advanced (Roose, 2025). Thus, any government will face a problem ensuring these people enter the labor market; they will be unhappy with their future prospects and could therefore become a potential source of social unrest. This is where geopolitics comes into play, in the sense that a hostile state can, with the help of AI bots, conduct an aggressive campaign against a government in difficulty, intensifying societal tensions and potentially favoring the rise of political actors who hold unscientific economic views, as the last years show in Europe and North America (Arceneaux, 2025). Major tensions are not always helpful for analyzing and solving systemic issues within a society, economy, or institution, and reducing the level of unrest often proves difficult. Meanwhile, during periods of heightened tensions—artificially induced, as we noted above, ChatGPT begins to achieve good results in persuading people through various dialogues—a state can be brought to adopt or exercise weaker foreign and/or domestic policies, almost to the point of paralysis in some cases, which suits many geopolitical adversaries very well. Since the phenomenon of demographic decline already affects more than half of the world's countries, with a combined population exceeding half of the global total (McKinsey Global Institute, 2025), it is foreseeable that such actions will increasingly become the norm in geopolitical confrontations, especially if it becomes possible to conceal the origin of the commands controlling the bots that sow division within a society.

The aspect of repetitive and lower-quality work (in fact, with a reduced degree of complexity, specific to Taylorism) affected today by tools/machinery using AI technology is, however, more complex, significantly impacting poorer countries, where industrial relocation represented a chance to escape from near-extreme poverty. Many enterprises, after the 1980s, left Europe and North America and moved to Asia and, to a lesser extent, Africa, taking advantage of cheap and abundant labor force (Michalet, 2007). Now, however, tools/machinery using AI affect broad industrial sectors, and robots that can replace thousands of people at once impact families and governments in countries with less competitive economies. This is where geopolitics comes in again, which this time can become a victim of job losses caused by implementing AI in industry, without the need for online campaigns with bots or other propaganda tools: in this case, migration to other countries becomes an inevitable option for many thousands or even millions of people. Numerous articles in the press in recent years claim that AI will create many jobs and ultimately bring more prosperity (Georgieva, 2024), but for now, this technology may a substantially reduce many people's incomes, and no rational person can say that all the jobs lost due to robotization/automation/AI will be immediately replaced. So then, what will governments do when they suddenly face a young population short many thousands of jobs? How stable will their policies be in the coming years? How much longer will they be able to maintain development policies, and how many budgetary resources will need to be redirected first to solve the social problems of thousands of families left without significant parts of their income? Will certain governments and coalitions still hold? What will be the direct consequences of these income reductions: social or political tensions? Civil wars? The emergence of autocratic regimes capable of forcibly calming social tensions, even if the consequence of such a political regime typology will be decreased investments and the pauperization of society?

6 Demography, Education and the AI

The problem of migration by people without jobs can become geopolitical if they are directed towards certain wealthy countries, usually in Europe or North America (ICMPD, 2025). Yes, it is true that everyone has the right to choose their place of residence in the world, but it is equally legal for a country to protect its labor market against foreigners—constitutional norms in any country provide for this—and, more importantly, no country should become an economic asylum space, because every government is obligated to ensure all its citizens have the conditions for a better life through honest work and fair pay. The idea of turning certain countries into destinations for migration (economic or political) can only be accepted in the short term, in the case of a war, since no government has broader obligations than towards its own citizens. However, migration directed toward certain countries can be driven again through various online influence operations using AI bots that can spread false information about other countries' conditions for receiving migrants. At the same time, an operation encouraging migration to a specific country can be used against that country's government, which will face media pressure for humanitarian reasons on one hand, but also political pressure from groups that want to protect the native population from foreigners. In fact, it is worth remembering that one of the sources of political tension in Western and Central Europe—the United Kingdom, France, Germany, the Netherlands, Austria—has been precisely this demographic situation, regarding ethnic proportions in recent decades, with authors directly claiming that the main cause of the Brexit vote was uncontrolled migration from other countries (Mehta, 2019).

The problematic relationship between AI and the labor market has another equally important perspective, although one that is currently less considered. Specifically, many essays discuss creativity as the only way to professionally withstand a world where AI technology capabilities are increasing. However, few people try to understand what it means to be creative in a world where AI devices are based on as much data as possible from the Internet—which itself is a vast library. Since AI models are trained to operate based on data from the Internet, the question arises: who can still be creative? This is because "creations of AI tools" can appear at any moment, based on information that a person, physically, no matter how well-intentioned, cannot fully encompass. Moreover, being creative raises the issue of intellectual property on a global scale, in terms of copying products or objects from anywhere in the world, merely changing the language of the messages accompanying those products. But if creativity no longer exists, would it then be logical for wages to decrease? The answer might be yes, but dissatisfaction in the labor market would grow, and so the question arises: how many people will be willing to work hard enough to be truly creative—compared to what AI can offer?

The issue of creativity and compensation in a labor market where originality will become increasingly difficult to achieve concerns governments to the highest degree, from a broader perspective that includes schools and universities. Quite objectively, AI devices make educating children increasingly difficult because it will be harder to teach them self-discipline in studying, as they will constantly face an insidious adversary: the free time that appears as a result of completing assignments through AI devices. From this arises a question: will AI lead to the intellectual atrophy of young people, and thus of human society in the coming decades (Rashidi, 2024)? Will maintaining young people's focus on education become an existential problem for the scientific and artistic progress of any nation, given the strong temptations and, in some countries, the declining prestige of academic diplomas precisely because they will be obtained by students who have relied more on AI and less on their own effort? This issue can also be seen as the result of operations promoted insidiously by various states targeting children, aimed at reducing feelings of responsibility and self-discipline from an early age, with long-term negative effects manifesting in adulthood. This can pose a real challenge to a country's intellectual capacities, and countering such attitudes of laziness—unfortunately, AI encourages a lax approach to work—will require huge and sustained efforts from both governments and parents. The fact that some countries will begin offering their citizens free access to AI tools, as the UAE has decided regarding ChatGPT (Business Today India, 2025), is very likely to negatively affect the cognitive abilities not only of children and young people but also of adults. The effects on the economy and social life will be seen quite quickly and persistently, which will increase the level of concern within government circles.

The issue of the intellectual quality of younger generations, those who are here now and those who will come after us, is not complete if one analyzes an aspect that has been studied more extensively only in recent decades, namely the attitude toward love, family, children, and humanity. More specifically, human emotions and emotional intelligence, as well as the desire to emotionally integrate into a human community. Why does this matter for geopolitics? Because based on these areas of study within human psychology, several data points about human behavior emerge, among which one stands out in particular: the desire to live in couples and implicitly to have children.

Most countries in the world, as noted above, are already experiencing a demographic crisis that began long before the widespread emergence of AI-based tools. Peter Zeihan pointed out in a paper published in the spring of 2022—before the launch of Chat GPT, but after the outbreak of the war in Ukraine—that all the world's countries are in a difficult situation primarily demographically, but also in terms of the relationship between population density and agricultural productivity. Of all these factors, the relationship between demography, AI, and birth rates, viewed through the lens of emotional intelligence and state interests, is relevant for our study. Mr. Zeihan notes in his volume that all the countries in the world that reach a certain level of economic development reduce the number of children per family. He also mentions some data from UN predictions regarding the population of countries around the world in the year 2100, among which China becomes the most significant, with a decrease from 1.45 billion inhabitants to 635 million (Zeihan, 2022). This example is by no means unique, with Europe being the most threatened by population decline. However, even he could not have predicted the emergence of AI tools and their growing role in accelerating demographic decline. Specifically, a study published in May 2025 (Schlegel et al., 2025) revealed that six AI models tested demonstrated a higher degree of emotional intelligence than humans, with a ratio of 81% to 56%. Today, we live in a situation where people feel increasingly lonely, and AI actors have come to replace relationships with other humans, including at the emotional level of love, with virtual partners being closer to their users than a "flesh, bones, and soul" human would be. Not coincidentally, a May 2025 article published in *The Economist* reveals that the Chinese government is very worried about this situation (The Economist, 2025), given its already problematic demographics, where the population is declining, and the number of marriages and fertility rate has reached figures never before seen in the country's history.

Government geopolitical strategies always depend on demography, and when this declines, the possibilities for large-scale action are substantially reduced. That is why any government is dissatisfied and concerned about any population decrease, and AI seems likely to increase relational blockages between people, implicitly further lowering birth rates. So far, we have not managed to keep human embryos in incubators from the very first moment of conception until birth—thus completely replacing natural conception and birth—so until then, population decline in countries with a high or developing standard of living will be an increasingly significant reality year by year. In the situation where, for cynical geopolitical reasons, some states will carry out campaigns in the online environment using AI bots to further weaken face-to-face interpersonal relationships, replacing them instead with relationships carried out through the Internet, regardless of the nature of the "romantic partners," the effects may be even more dramatic, with even sharper population declines. In fact, such campaigns could increase the number of people suffering from depression, leading even to suicides, and the psychological stability of some countries could be significantly affected, thus preventing many people from any prospect of socio-professional development.

Governments today face a difficult situation in the demographic area, precisely as a result of AI. On the one hand, if you have a declining population, it is very likely that AI technologies will further reduce the country's demographic levels, and on the other hand, if you have a very large young population, you risk significant street unrest because AI automation eliminates many jobs without being able to replace them instantly, especially on a global scale. Thus, there will be countries where the effects of AI will stabilize within a decade—typically these are economically developed countries—but for the poorest countries still experiencing demographic growth, bringing the economic effects of AI under control may take decades, with the possibility that control might even be impossible. For this reason, geopolitical strategies of any kind by any major power will directly depend on managing the effects of AI in the labor market as well as in the demographic sphere.

7 Achieving Geopolitical and Informational Dominance with the AI

An important consequence of this demographic decline is the collapse of pension systems in most developed countries, and the decrease in birth rates as a result of emotional relationships with AI tools will lead to a major dilemma for governments. Specifically, they will have to choose between reducing pension rights for all people or finding ways to increase the young population, hoping that for a certain period—two or three decades—this will allow stabilization within the age pyramid, making it functional once again.

How can this attempt at demographic balancing be achieved? In my opinion, there are only three possible methods, which can be used in varying proportions by certain countries.

First, there is the possibility of accepting migration from other countries that currently have very large populations, but this type of population intake poses challenges related to acceptance and cultural integration, especially rapid integration into the labor market. In any case, such acceptance of population is not guaranteed, as native citizens are less willing to welcome just anyone, and governments must be cautious about this type of resistance because it can ultimately lead to the loss of parliamentary majorities and the adoption of policies promoting ethnic exclusivity. The discussion on this topic—as with every paragraph in this text—can be expanded into a full volume, with perspectives from any analytical angle, but that does not guarantee that the electorate will be willing to read it.

The second possibility could be the voluntary unification of different countries, possibly those that have identical or similar languages. In this scenario, a decision would be reached by certain parliaments, and the populations would become larger, allowing time to adjust economies and pension systems to a different demographic distribution within a single state. In this situation, limited external migration might also be accepted, so as not to complicate ethnic relations between the two or more majority populations that have voluntarily formed a state. Obviously, the geopolitics of continents and even the planet would be altered, since the new borders would lead to new alliances, as well as new rivalries, which would require different geopolitical responses from other countries. There is also an additional clarification: since the criterion for these voluntary state unifications will be demographic decline, it will be more difficult for them to separate later, because states with very small populations—below 3 or 5 million inhabitants and majority over 50 years old—will be unviable in the long term, over 75 or 100 years.

The third way to solve the demographic problem is through the forcible takeover of territories, followed by attempts to de-nationalize and transform them intellectually, linguistically, and over time, ethnically. Unfortunately, this option is far from being excluded, and AI technology offers a significant advantage in implementing population surveillance technologies. As we have seen over the past 15 years, many states have developed surveillance systems for localities, which have also been very useful for political control over their own populations. Moreover, electronic technologies initially fascinated authoritarian or authoritarian-leaning political leaders, who quickly understood the advantages of having access to massive database. As a direct result, various rankings by prestigious organizations in the field of legality and democracy study note that over the past 15 years, the number of countries experiencing democratic deficits has increased year after year, and in many countries, the reasonable level/degree/threshold of democracy has been slowly eroding, such that a population that long ago surpassed half of the global total now lives in politically and economically unfavorable conditions, with rather negative prospects for democratization (Freedom House, 2024).

Looking more closely at today's capabilities of AI—as highlighted above—persuasive power in debates; emotional intelligence higher than that of humans, which is a good starting point for manipulating human subjects; the use of an immense amount of data provided by the Internet, which surpasses human capacities for retaining information—we actually understand that it is a technology that will inevitably be used to achieve geopolitical and informational dominance at regional, continental, or global levels. There is no doubt about this, and the ways in which AI is used daily in the former Soviet Union area and along the eastern coast of the Mediterranean Sea by weapons clearly demonstrate this with particular strength. AI technology was not created to bring about global domination—although the fact that only a few countries have their own AI providers could offer some perspective on the future of global geopolitics. Still, we should not forget that AI technology is very expensive, requiring both a lot of water and a lot of energy to operate, which makes any possible efforts to build their own models pointless in cases of poor hydrographic and/or energy situations (Shark, 2025). However, being an electronic technology, nothing prevents hostile actions such as piracy and data theft directly from AI providers (Waterman, 2022), but only a few countries will be able to carry these out because they work with large amounts of data that not every device can process and modify as desired.

In a world where AI influences everything, not only will geopolitics and its objectives be altered by this technology, but so will the informational sphere. Obviously, we are not referring to the simplification of how news is written or the resizing of press newsrooms, but to the fact that the informational space itself will be reshaped, including at the language level, by AI. The way AI drafts a text is standardized globally, and since there are very few AI technology providers, the language of the press will become increasingly standardized at a universal level. Practically, the same news about an important event occurring in a country will be quickly presented in the global press using the same words; the only difference between languages will be what separates the texts themselves, but if these texts were randomly translated into a single language, it would reveal that there is virtually no difference in most of the news running on various devices in the USA, Germany, Japan, Greece, South Africa, Morocco, etc. Thus, we would effectively reach a dominance of standardized words, so in the long term, it is very possible that most languages will use only a few thousand words from the complete vocabularies of everyday language that their dictionaries contain.

In a world where the use of AI will standardize language, communication and informational battles will be carried out both between humans and AI devices, as well as between AI devices themselves, which are programmed to achieve certain goals. From such a perspective, what remains of human intelligence? Will humans become almost completely prisoners of AI devices, unable to think independently? This question arises because a power outage in a country, especially if caused by a hostile political actor, could mentally paralyze people who have become accustomed to performing few actions without the help of AI technology. Hence the question: how much AI should we use in our lives in the coming years?

At its core, the fundamental question is this: will AI force a change in the global geopolitical order, or at least in certain regions, and if so, through what processes or operations? The answer is—for now—up to the will of politicians, who can still control it, although, as noted in the first section of the text, there is at least one AI model that no longer wishes to fully comply with received orders (as we have seen, it even tried to blackmail the engineers programming it). So, we find ourselves in a situation where we are inventing/developing something that can be either difficult to control, uncontrollable, or capable of causing us to lose reason and act carelessly or irresponsibly. Thus, the informational manipulation capabilities that AI models develop may create in the minds of many politicians a desire to control their own citizens and direct them toward actions that will not favor them, thereby creating or reinforcing authoritarian regimes. Moreover, in cases where AI devices are attached to weapons belonging to countries with armies of hundreds of thousands of fighters (already recruited or potentially mobilizable), these same politicians could use them beyond their own borders, triggering wars that may last many years and result in immense, hard-to-recover losses.

Therefore, I consider that the biggest problem AI raises in the geopolitical and informational spheres is not the standardization it brings, nor the power to alter labor relations, education systems, and family situations, but rather the temptations toward dictatorship or international domination that it creates. Essentially, a rational leader restrains their tendencies to make history at the expense of other opposing social groups—or countries they do not favor—taking into account both the inherent costs of various geopolitical and informational operations, but especially the awareness that they might lose either to the opposition of adversaries or to coalitions that could form to block their plans. Nevertheless, these tendencies will continue to exist, and as societies become increasingly vulnerable—due to the weakening of traditional work styles and the alteration of many traditional social pillars—ambitious politicians will not hesitate to use AI tools to "change a country, a continent, or an entire world."

8 Conclusions

In the history of humanity, a few inventions have had from the outset the capacity to change geopolitical relations between countries, and government strategists have usually quickly understood this. This is also the case with AI, which has been not only anticipated but especially desired by politicians and the business environment. This new technology's potential to influence geopolitics was evident from the beginning, and the wars of recent years show us that its implementation will not be peaceful, because all states understand its capabilities and seek to counteract its destructive effects as quickly as possible to ensure peace externally, leaving governments only the task of adapting the use of AI to their domestic policies.

The challenges that AI technology brings to multiple spheres—from demographics and birth rates to the economy and entertainment, from the informational environment to the military—are of extraordinary scale, unprecedented in history, which leads many to harbor apocalyptic or ecstatic fantasies and visions. In any case, the issue we identify is related to the mental state of political decision-makers, who will have the legal right to use many state-level tools to preserve their own power within the national political system and beyond borders, aiming to maximize their countries' geopolitical position. If they are driven by the will and awareness of their place in history, then the use of AI in the geopolitical and informational spheres will likely be aggressive and have long-lasting consequences, not always positive. However, if reason prevails, AI will be used in a controlled manner solely to support the economy, education, and national defense, and the well-being of the population will become a reality.

Geopolitics has no definite end, and the last decade has strongly confirmed this simple conclusion. Likewise, informational confrontations cannot stop as long as the amount of natural resources is decreasing while the demand for them is increasing. However, above all these stands people's desire for power, and today they have received extraordinary help capable, through programming, of achieving in a few months what in other times would have taken years or even decades. Herein lies both the power of AI and its weakness, because one of its consequences will be that the winners of any competition will be seen more as high-quality products of this technology rather than people capable of achieving enormous goals primarily through their own efforts. Therefore, it is necessary to educate young people who wish to enter public life in the direction of wisdom. The lessons from geopolitical and informational confrontations of recent decades will serve this purpose, regardless of whether the teachers who instruct them are human or virtual.

References

Alan, S. (2025). What the rising costs of AI means for government. *State Tech online*. https://statetechmagazine.com/article/2025/01/what-rising-costs-ai-means-government. Accessed May 31, 2025.

Arceneaux, K. (2025). *What do populists want from their representatives and why?* Last modified January 1, 2025. https://www.sciencespo.fr/cevipof/sites/sciencespo.fr.cevipof/files/KA_populism_janvier2025_V1.pdf

Business Today India online. (2025). UAE makes ChatGPT Plus subscription free for all residents as part of deal with OpenAI. *Business Today India online*. Last modified May 27, 2025. https://www.businesstoday.in/technology/news/story/uae-makes-chatgpt-plus-subscription-free-for-all-residents-as-part-of-deal-with-openai-477948-2025-05-27

Chin, W. (2019). Technology, war and the state: Past, present and future. *International Affairs, 95*(4), 765–783. https://doi.org/10.1093/ia/iiz106. Accessed May 31, 2025.

Duarte, F. (2025). *Number of ChatGPT users (March 2025)*. https://explodingtopics.com/blog/chatgpt-users. Accessed May 31, 2025.

Freedom House. (2024). *Freedom in the world 2024*. https://freedomhouse.org/sites/default/files/2024-02/FIW_2024_DigitalBooklet.pdf. Accessed May 31, 2025.

Georgieva, K. (2024, January 14). AI will transform the global economy. Let's make sure it benefits humanity. *IMF* (blog). https://www.imf.org/en/Blogs/Articles/2024/01/14/ai-will-transform-the-global-economy-lets-make-sure-it-benefits-humanity

Groupe d'Etudes Geopolitiques. (2022). *Geopolitics: A methodological introduction*. Last modified December 5, 2022. https://geopolitique.eu/en/2022/12/05/geopolitics-a-methological-introduction/

Haenlein, M., & Kaplan, A. (2025). A brief history of artificial intelligence: On the past, present, and future of artificial intelligence. *California Management Review 2019*, *61*(4), 5–14. https://doi.org/10.1177/0008125619864925. Accessed May 31, 2025.

ICMPD Migration Outlook. (2025). *International centre for migration policy development*. https://www.icmpd.org/file/download/63373/file/ICMPD%2520Migration%2520Outlook%25202025.pdf. Accessed May 31, 2025.

Indermit, G. (2020). *Whoever leads in artificial intelligence in 2030 will rule the world until 2100*. Last modified January 17, 2020. https://www.brookings.edu/articles/whoever-leads-in-artificial-intelligence-in-2030-will-rule-the-world-until-2100/

International Energy Agency. (2025). *Energy and AI 2025*. https://iea.blob.core.windows.net/assets/34eac603-ecf1-464f-b813-2ecceb8f81c2/EnergyandAI.pdf. Accessed May 31, 2025.

Jakee, K., & Fink, D. (2024). *Microtargeting voters in the 2016 US election: Was Cambridge analytica really different?* Last modified May 1, 2024. https://ssrn.com/abstract=4843786

Marr, B. (2023). *A short history of ChatGPT: How we got to where we are today*. Last modified May 19. 2023. https://www.forbes.com/sites/bernardmarr/2023/05/19/a-short-history-of-chatgpt-how-we-got-to-where-we-are-today/

McKinsey Global Institute. (2025). *Dependency and depopulation? Confronting the consequences of a new demographic reality*. https://www.mckinsey.com/mgi/our-research/dependency-and-depopulation-confronting-the-consequences-of-a-new-demographic-reality#/. Accessed May 31, 2025.

Mehta, S. (2019). Immigration panic: How the west fell for manufactured rage. *Guardian online*. Last modified August 27, 2019. https://www.theguardian.com/uk-news/2019/aug/27/immigrationpanic-how-the-west-fell-for-manufactured-rage

Michalet, C.-A. (2007). De la délocalisation à la relocalisation: Une évolution fatale? *Revue d'économie financière*, (90), 15–21. https://doi.org/10.3406/ecofi.2007.4398

Morland, P. (2019). *The human tide. How population shaped the modern world*. Public Affairs.

Muto, G. (2024). The use of AI in electoral campaigns: Key issues and remedies. *Media Law, Rivista Di Diritto Dei Media*, (3). https://www.medialaws.eu/rivista/the-use-of-ai-in-electoral-campaigns-key-issues-and-remedies/

OECD. (2024). *Society at a glance 2024: OECD social indicators, OECD online*. https://doi.org/10.1787/918d8db3-en

Rashidi, S. (2024). Why intellectual atrophy is the real reason to fear AI. *Forbes online*. Last modified July 28, 2024. https://www.forbes.com/sites/solrashidi/2024/07/28/why-intellectual-atrophy-is-the-real-reason-to-fear-ai/

Robinson, W. I. (2009). *Geopolitics, history, and international relations*. Last modified December 2009. https://scispace.com/pdf/geopolitics-history-and-international-relations-k1hc8s7dtc.pdf

Rodriguez, R. V., & Kannan, H. (2024). Exploring artificial intelligence as a tool for enhancing wisdom: A comparative analysis using Webster's SAWS scale and Ardelt scales. Last modified September 4, 2024. https://wisdomcenter.uchicago.edu/news/wisdom-news/exploring-artificial-intelligence-tool-enhancing-wisdom-comparative-analysis-using

Roose, K. (2025). For some recent graduates, the A.I. job apocalypse may already be here. *The New York Times*, https://www.nytimes.com/2025/05/30/technology/ai-jobs-college-graduates.html. Accessed May 31, 2025.

Salvi, F., Ribeiro, H., Manoel, G., Riccardo, & West, R. (2025). On the conversational persuasiveness of GPT-4. *Nature Human Behaviour*. https://doi.org/10.1038/s41562-025-02194-6. Accessed May 31, 2025.

Schlegel, K., Sommer, N. R., & Mortillaro, M. (2025). Large language models are proficient in solving and creating emotional intelligence tests. *Communication Psychology, 80*(3). https://doi.org/10.1038/s44271-025-00258-x. Accessed May 31, 2025.

The Economist. (2025). Young Chinese are turning to AI chatbots for friendship and love. *The Economist online*. https://www.economist.com/china/2025/05/15/young-chinese-are-turning-to-ai-chatbots-for-friendship-and-love. Accessed May 31, 2025.

Waterman, S. (2022). *Hacking poses risks for artificial intelligence*. https://cset.georgetown.edu/article/hacking-poses-risks-for-artificial-intelligence/. Accessed May 31, 2025.

Zeff, M. (2025). *Anthropic's new AI model turns to blackmail when engineers try to take it offline*. Last modified May 22, 2025. https://techcrunch.com/2025/05/22/anthropics-new-ai-model-turns-to-blackmail-when-engineers-try-to-take-it-offline/

Zeihan, P. (2022). *The end of the world is just the beginning: Mapping the collapse of globalization – the collapse of globalization and its aftermath*. Harper Business.

MIX
Papier aus verantwortungsvollen Quellen
Paper from responsible sources
FSC® C105338

If you have any concerns about our products,
you can contact us on
ProductSafety@springernature.com

In case Publisher is established outside the EU,
the EU authorized representative is:
Springer Nature Customer Service Center GmbH
Europaplatz 3, 69115 Heidelberg, Germany

Printed by Libri Plureos GmbH
in Hamburg, Germany